About the au

Phyllis McDuff was born in the outback in Hillston, western New South Wales. After travelling extensively through Europe, Africa and Asia with her family in her childhood and teenage years, she was educated at Brigidine College, Randwick, in Sydney, and then the University of Sydney, the University of New England and the University of Queensland. Her early career of training horses was based on instruction she received at the Spanish Riding School of Vienna.

Phyllis's lifework has been an exploration of the communication process and she now works as a professional storyteller and teacher of the art. She lives on the outskirts of Brisbane.

A Story Dreamt Long Ago

a memoir

Phyllis McDuff

BANTAM
SYDNEY • AUCKLAND • TORONTO • NEW YORK • LONDON

A STORY DREAMT LONG AGO
A BANTAM BOOK

First published in Australia and New Zealand in 2003
by Bantam

Copyright © Phyllis McDuff, 2003

All rights reserved. No part of this publication may be reproduced, stored in a retrieval system, transmitted in any form or by any means, electronic, mechanical, photocopying, recording or otherwise without the prior written permission of the publisher.

National Library of Australia
Cataloguing-in-Publication Entry

McDuff, Phyllis.
A story dreamt long ago.

ISBN 1 86325 400 5.

1. McDuff, Bettina. 2. McDuff, Phyllis. 3. Women refugees - Austria - Biography. 4. Austria - Social life and customs - 1955- . 5. Austrian Australians - Biography. 6. Country life - Australia - Social life and customs - 1945- . 7. World War, 1939-1945 - Refugees - Austria - Biography. I. Title.

325.21094360994

Transworld Publishers,
a division of Random House Australia Pty Ltd
20 Alfred Street, Milsons Point, NSW 2061
http://www.randomhouse.com.au

Random House New Zealand Limited
18 Poland Road, Glenfield, Auckland

Transworld Publishers,
a division of The Random House Group Ltd
61-63 Uxbridge Road, London W5 5SA

Random House Inc
1745 Broadway, New York, New York 10036

Cover design by Darian Causby/Highway 51
Cover photo courtesy of Getty Images
Typeset by Midland Typesetters, Maryborough, Victoria
Printed and bound by Griffin Press, Netley, South Australia

10 9 8 7 6 5 4 3

To Bettina and to Otto,
To Fritz, Lucie and Marianne,
To their forebears and their families – in whatever country of the world their spirits roam

Contents

Author's Note　　xi
Prelude　　xiii

1　Days of Desperation　　1
2　First Memories　　25
3　Separation　　57
4　We Go to Fairyland Together　　77
5　Living in Villa Mendl　　95
6　Getting a Good Education　　120
7　Caught in a Whirlwind　　132
8　The Brief Reign of the Ugly Duckling　　142
9　The Years Go By　　168
10　Connecting with the Past　　186
11　Meeting Sara Murphy　　206
12　Collecting Fragments of the Past　　215
13　Searching for Solutions　　243
14　The Curtain Closes　　262
15　Adieu　　267

Family tree

Fritz Mendl (1865?–1930) – Emily (1875?–1929)
I

Bettina	Otto	Fritz	Lucie	Marianne
1909–1999	1907–1944?	1904–1931	1899–1963	1895–1966
married	married		married	married
Joe	Mimi		Lou	Gustav
I	I		I	I
Phyllis 1942	Hans 1930–2000 – married Evamarie		Erika 1928–1965	Elizabeth (Lizzie) 1930
Dawn 1944	Eva 1940 I		Richard 1930–1970	Cornelia 1932
	Stephan 1966		Lou 1932	Sybille 1934
	Thomas 1967		Fritz 1934	

Author's note

Those who go in search of 'truth' are destined to suffer many disappointments. The truth is often painful, playful or elusive. The search teaches us how narrow are our references, how fragile the knowledge we have cherished. We look for evidence and confirmation and are offered interpretations, perceptions, and helpful points of view leading in directions we never dreamt existed. We enter the maze.

My search involved my family, the facts obscured by layers of emotion. Scar tissue deformed the answers I was given. The search led across cultural boundaries where confusion and misunderstanding distorted evidence. The passage of time clouded memories, hid clues. I struggled to reach back and grasp 'the truth'. I do not claim success.

I pieced together threads and stitched the fabric to create a patchwork cloak to warm myself. Many threads are broken and many joins are ragged, fragile at the edges, inclined to pull apart and admit a chilly draught. At any moment I might hear a ghostly whisper: 'No, go back, you've erred, you missed a foothold leading off another way.'

I began the search for Bettina convinced there were firm edges to her shape, determined to extract the one authentic version and to understand her inconsistencies.

My mother's Picasso drawings were symbolic – too unlikely to believe in, too apparent to deny. What was their history? How could they be authenticated? How much evidence was needed to earn the label 'proof'?

As for the stories Bettina told throughout my childhood, in what way were they true? Was this truth coloured like a rainbow, changing and disappearing as the light fell from a different angle?

It is time now to cease my stitching. Many questions veil the evasive 'truth'. I can only share my journey, offering the fragile threads that lead towards Bettina.

Prelude

The old screen door flapped shut, almost, then gave a grating sigh and sagged. The hinge that had gasped and wheezed its disapproval through twenty-five years of family exits and arrivals had finally surrendered its responsibility, as though it sensed we were leaving and was protesting the abandonment.

I glanced about for a lump of wood to keep it open while we surged back and forth with boxes, bags and armloads of childhood treasure salvaged from oblivion. Awkward mementoes denying us a clean-cut goodbye to the old farmhouse.

Bettina, my mother, was taking her belongings and leaving the farm where she had lived for almost twenty-five years. At nearly seventy, she had resigned herself to living somewhere less challenging. With wisdom and grace, she was submitting to the limits imposed by the gathering years and was moving to be near my younger sister, Dawn.

This Bettina was a mellower version of the Bettina of my childhood, but she remained invincible. She was small, wiry and busy. Dressed in faded jeans and a red checked shirt she hurried back and forth. Her thick, curly, grey hair was closely cropped. The sun had worn deep creases in her olive skin – lines of authority. She radiated an aura of determination. Her black eyes flashed as she issued instructions. It was my role to impose some structure on our activities. I trod carefully. I knew that structure was resented. I knew to keep my distance. Inevitably she surprised me once again.

We were helping her to strip the cupboards and walls bare, taking down photographs, out-of-date calendars, paintings – the few remaining treasures of my mother's European life. There on the wall, where they'd always hung, were two framed Picasso drawings – two sketches of a man holding a sheep. Because of my farm background I always thought of the man as a shearer. Bettina had told us that they were by Picasso and had indicated that they held some personal, mysterious significance for her, quite apart from their value as artworks. Yet now she seemed to have overlooked them.

'What about these?' I asked her. 'If they really are by Picasso, they must be worth something. Perhaps they ought to be insured. What would you like done with them?'

She turned away and said casually, 'You can have them if you like.'

'But they're yours. You love them. You'll miss them.'

'No,' Bettina answered, 'I'm not so attached to them any more. Remember, I gave two to Dawn years ago when she married, so you take these and do whatever you think.'

A Story Dreamt Long Ago

I took the drawings down and peered through the smeared glass at the signature – Picasso – and handwritten dates: 23/Mars/43 and 26/Sept/43. I reflected that in 1943 I was barely one year old. I was growing teeth, learning to walk, stealing eggs from under the chooks and playing with our pups.

The next day I rang Mother's solicitor and asked him to make a file note that I had taken the two drawings at her insistence and would store them until I had traced their origin and value. In the days that followed, my sister and I helped to finish clearing the farmhouse and settled our mother into her new home, close to Dawn at Tarpoly where we had all lived during my childhood. I gave no further thought to the Picassos until I tackled the long drive back home to Brisbane.

Behind me on the back seat were the drawings, posing questions in my mind. As I drove I had time to wonder how my mother had acquired the drawings, which I saw as an incongruous 'treasure'. There had been no other major works of art in our simple home. I reflected on the little we knew of their significance to her. Just as an Oscar is more than a brass statue, these drawings seemed to be attached to some distinct achievement – about which she had avoided all discussion. I thought these questions would have simple answers. I trusted a logical sequence of events linking Bettina to the drawings. Life was black and white, wasn't it? You could rely on facts and the history of the drawings would be simply and easily established.

As I drove on, however, the questions became more complex. Clouds formed around the 'facts' and the notion of a simple history melted from my grasp. I searched my memory to define exactly when I had first seen those two drawings. Was it before or after I had married? Was it in the 1950s when I came home from school? Was it one of the many times when Mother returned from her trips overseas?

I had asked my mother when I first saw them where they had come from but I received no satisfactory answer. I was used to that when asking questions that concerned her past. She hated my questions and refused to answer them.

'What are they?' I'd inquired.

'Picassos,' she'd replied.

'Where did they come from?'

'Otto.'

'When did he give them to you?' I was aware that there were two 'Ottos' in my mother's life, one a brother, the other a close friend. As usual, I was trying to make sense of an alien European world far from our Australian farm, a habit that caused considerable conflict between my mother and myself. She hated the questions, refusing to answer them, accusing me of stupidity because I was never satisfied. In those days I thought my questions merely bored and irritated her.

As an adult I had given up the questions. I accepted the confusing information and the gaps. I accepted that Bettina and I had different ways of making sense of our experiences. On those few occasions when I could not accept her explanations I questioned her and I faced her ridicule or her rage. There was no dividend in either and I lacked the courage to persist. Much later I would realise that her evasions were a defence and a façade.

I was still labelled 'difficult' as I struggled to establish the truth about my strange family. So many branches of our tree had been 'lopped off'. Bettina would suddenly declare that a familiar connection was 'impossible'. We were discouraged from contact with such 'lunatics'. After months and years the rift would widen to a chasm. I wondered at the pattern. The one constant was that whenever Bettina decided to impart some 'official information', it was likely to be biased, vague and unreliable; details of the reported character lapses changed from time to time. I had long since learnt to treat such information cautiously.

As an adult and a mother myself, supposedly mature and approaching wisdom, those memories of my abrasive relationship with my mother nagged at me. Why did she so dislike my questions and turn them to ridicule? If she answered truthfully, what would be revealed?

Could the silent drawings on the back seat of the car expose some of her secrets at last? They were solid and dependable – there would be a provenance.

1

Days of desperation

To understand my earliest beginnings I had to stitch together many different fabrics. The stories I heard changed as the light fell from divergent points of view. My mother and father each told me their own versions. Bettina's sister Marianne offered some missing pieces. Her children were my cousins and shared what they had witnessed from their adolescent perspectives. Lucie, Bettina's other sister, gave me snippets and threads to add to my construction. After her death her children continued to pass on her stories. They were delivered with love, with regret, idly, with passion. Whispered lovingly, shrieked in rage. Told through fits of laughter and through sobs.

The stories came from friends and forebears on different continents. Some were written down on fragile slips of paper or existed as parchment documents. They were inserts to my childhood and into my middle years and they will continue to unravel around me. No one piece fits neatly into place. Each has to be adapted, trimmed, turned to be understood in context.

I was born in the outback, on the edge of a bitter winter. In fact it was in Hillston, west of Bourke. I was premature, weak and ugly. A drunken midwife at the nearest nursing station advised my mother not to feed me. I would surely die and she could save herself the trouble.

On that same day, in the same room, a frightened Aboriginal girl struggled to give birth to a robust, honey-coloured son. Afterwards she slipped into exhaustion, too weak to hold him and with meagre milk to feed him.

As the long night settled, the midwife passed into an alcoholic stupor. My mother knew she had to stay awake and feed me every two hours if there was to be any hope at all. As she urged me to suck she listened to that angry, hungry Aboriginal boy scream his frustration to the world and she prayed steadily for his young mother to stir. Every hour she herself grew weaker, with exhaustion, with fear and with the growing pain and fever of having too much milk.

Edging toward delirium, Bettina was afraid that if she could not recover from this difficult birth quickly she would be removed to an official hospital. This might trigger an inquiry into her origins and her status would become apparent; she would be recognised as an enemy alien and interned. Many stories circulated about the well-established German and Italian farmers who had been taken off to camps, leaving grieving families abandoned and farms unworkable without their precious labour.

My mother gazed with longing at that sturdy little Aboriginal boy. She loved his warrior rage. She loved his chubby limbs. She loved his silken lashes, wet with tears. She picked him up and fed him till he slept, full and contented. He had cheered her up and given her strength to battle on with me.

The next day passed. The midwife revived sufficiently to provide some basic food but no real medical attention. The Aboriginal girl stirred, but not enough to nurse her babe. Perhaps she liked the look of me; I was so small and quiet in comparison to her robust, newborn son. In the absence of the nurse my mother tucked me in beside the girl while once again she fed the sturdy little boy.

The Aboriginal mother picked me up and with infinite patience began to feed me. She seemed to understand that I needed feeding constantly, drop by drop. To keep herself awake she softly sang her tribal songs, the corroboree songs, the old, old, spirit songs. Through the blur of days and nights she sang me into life and gave my mother sleep. Every four hours Honey Boy's siren scream shattered our Dreamtime and he was fed generously by my mother.

So the days passed until my father came to take us home. Honey Boy and his young mother left, melting into the dark shadows on the back veranda. Recovered from her stupor, the nurse weighed me in at a little over two pounds (one kilogram), put me in a shoebox with some cotton wool and sent me home to take my chances.

Home for me was a rough log cabin, a boundary rider's hut, a dirt floor and an open fireplace. The drought was bad, and my father, at that time manager of Bimbil Station, was keeping the sheep and cattle alive on the last rough scrub, two days' ride from the main homestead.

All of this was a far cry from the elegant life my mother had led before Hitler's troops rolled into Austria. She was the daughter of Fritz Mendl, a wealthy businessman who ran a renowned Viennese bakery firm and owned numerous rural estates, a valuable collection of artwork, and champion thoroughbred horses. He had designed a grand home and gardens for the family in Vienna, which went by the name Villa Mendl. My mother was educated at Cheltenham Ladies College, an exclusive boarding school in England, and holidayed in the great cities of Europe. Back home in Vienna she enjoyed an endless round of concerts, dances, parties and tennis matches. Most of all she adored riding horses and was on the way to becoming a renowned horsewoman. She had two elder sisters, Marianne and Lucie, and two elder brothers, Otto and Fritz.

When she was only a teenager, this idyllic family life began to disintegrate. First, at the age of eighteen, she lost her mother, Emily, to cancer. And after years of hard work her father's health was failing too; his heart was weak. Only two years later he died. Next, her elder brother Fritz was killed in a skiing accident. In 1931, at only twenty-two years of age, it fell to her to run her father's bakery firm and manage the considerable Mendl wealth.

Meanwhile, Hitler began his rise to power. Bettina was a passionate and outspoken supporter of the Austrian Chancellor Schuschnigg and his anti-Nazi policies. She was a renowned rider and her horses were well known. In 1936 she had been chosen to ride in the Berlin Olympics. She refused, giving as her reason that she 'did not like the politics' of Hitler's Third Reich. Her chief tournament horse, Bubunut, bred in Hungary, was the only foal of Kinchem, winner of ninety-two races. Highly strung and unreliable, she proved unfit for racing but such bloodlines were irreplaceable. When Bettina fell in love with Bubunut she had to seek state permission to take Kinchem's offspring across the Hungarian national border into Austria. The young mare lived in luxury in a specially built stable in the garden of Villa Mendl. Bubunut's groom slept beside her and a pet white rabbit sat on her feed trough to encourage her to eat. In November 1938, during the brutality of Kristallnacht, when the Austrian Nazis went on the rampage smashing and destroying Jewish property, Bubunut and her groom disappeared forever. I remember my mother telling us how worried she had been about the pet rabbit – the one anxiety she permitted herself to mention.

Bettina described what had happened at the stables at Veich, one of the other Mendl country estates. She seemed to cringe from the words as she spoke. The German commandant arrived with trucks to remove the horses. He instructed the fourteen-year-old stable boy to bring the horses into the courtyard. The boy replied that he could not vary his routine without an express directive from Fräulein Bettina. The commandant withdrew his pistol and shot him on the spot. Was all this in retribution for Bettina's boldness when she refused to ride in the 1936 Berlin Olympics – or were there deeper issues at stake?

Immediately after the Anschluss – Nazi Germany's annexation of Austria – Nazi thugs rounded up everyone known to have opposed them and commenced the implementation of Hitler's 'Final Solution'. My mother got out of Vienna just hours before Hitler's storm troopers entered the city on 12 March 1938. The Anschluss was a death sentence from which she narrowly escaped. Immediately, all of the Mendl assets were taken over by the Nazis.

According to my mother's telling of the story, she travelled first to Switzerland, then in 1939 she arrived in Sydney via New Zealand, her sole asset a crumpled English five-pound note that she'd discovered in the pocket of her overcoat. This was well short of the forty pounds 'landing money' required for the entry of non-British migrants. Her only option was to present a written guarantee concerning her character from a sponsor, within twenty-four hours of her disembarking the ship. By this time both Australia and New Zealand were at war with Nazi Germany and, since the Anschluss, this included Austria. Bettina was now considered an enemy alien. She was vulnerable to internment, even at risk of being shipped back to Austria – and whatever else that might have meant for her. Although her sister Marianne had already been settled in Sydney for some time, my mother was reluctant to identify her, fearing that she too might come under threat of internment. Lacking any other inspiration she went to confession at St Mary's Cathedral. At the end of her confession she pushed the sponsorship document through the grille and asked the priest to sign it. Initially he refused, declaring that he did not know her – she was not a regular parishioner. She suggested that he exercise faith. After some discussion on the nature of God, the issue of faith and the obligation of the church to protect with compassion, the young priest signed, and Bettina was able to return the document to the authorities in time to prolong her temporary stay legitimately, in time to avoid immediate internment.

Marianne and her husband had managed to bring some money with them to Australia and had bought a house in Mosman. It was small and renovations were desperately needed, but Bettina moved in. Once past the crisis of her arrival, Bettina knew she must make her own way. She could not bear to be dependent and sought work as a domestic, which approached absurdity; she did not have domestic skills and had rarely been without her own servants. On one occasion, arriving for an interview, she was recognised by her would-be employers, fellow Austrians who had made a more timely exit from their homeland. They were horrified at her situation, offered her tea, and spoke with fond memories of Austria and her family. Bettina left feeling disgusted. Hungry and broke she wanted a job, not sentimental social interludes. She headed to western New South Wales, answering advertisements for work on country stations, relying on her expert skills with horses to survive in the rough conditions she was offered. She dared not stay in any place for long. The fragile threads to family might easily betray her. The name 'Bettina Mendl' on letters at post offices and distant station outposts could arouse suspicion. Her accented English put her at grave risk. She moved on, trying to learn bushcraft, trying to be independent, trying to disappear into the landscape.

In the hilarious stories she later knitted from these experiences, only once did she admit how hard it had been. Briefly, in mid-sentence, she hesitated to say: 'I couldn't do the work, it was too hard, I wasn't strong enough . . .' She used her humour as a shield, describing with delicious ridicule situations that must have been quite painful.

Working as a domestic on an isolated property she was once asked to help prepare the children for a visit from Santa Claus. My mother washed the little girls' hair and carefully set it in rag curlers to fall to their shoulders in ringlets. Trying to entertain them during this tedious process, which took place on the veranda beneath an iron roof in the furnace heat of December, her mind turned to the rituals of candlelight and Christianity from the white Christmases of her childhood. She asked the children what they knew about the celebration. 'Oh,' the seven-year-old gushed, 'we get heaps of presents!' 'But why?' Bettina asked. 'What are we celebrating?' No response. At last she asked, 'What about the story of Jesus Christ?' Two mouths gaped, two pairs of eyes glared disapproval. The elder of the two hissed warningly, 'Betty! Mum only says that when she is *very* cross!'

Initially my mother stayed well clear of the small back porch of that farmhouse: each time she drew near she would be greeted by a raucous, gravelly voice telling her to 'Go to buggery!' For weeks she imagined an aged, cantankerous family member. Curiosity got the better of her; safely settled into the job, she decided to spy on this mysterious character. No matter how carefully she sneaked around the corner, she was spotted and a vicious 'Go to buggery!' would greet her. Her unusual behaviour was noticed by the boss's wife, who decided to follow her. One pitch-black night on one such sortie, they bumped into one another. Shocked, both women screamed into the dark, waking the old white cockatoo who instantly screamed back: 'Go to buggery, go to buggery!' Bettina took some convincing that it was the bird who had been issuing the order all along. Dawn and I loved to hear that story. It turned into a game. On the darkest nights we used to creep about in the dark looking for each other, finally leaping out screaming, 'Go to buggery!' Ultimately the game was vetoed by our parents – not because of the unsuitable language, but because I lost my nerve. At the end of each episode I would be white-lipped and tearful, couldn't go to sleep for hours and was frightened of the dark for the next twenty years.

For a time, Bettina worked on a property near Hillston, in far western New South Wales. Joe McDuff was a bachelor of mature years and manager of a sheep station nearby. He admired my mother's horsemanship, which was one of the few useful skills she had brought with her from her exotic pre-war life. He watched her struggle in the harsh conditions and tried to help her. He taught her how to trap rabbits, even making her a gift of fifty rabbit traps. The traps gave her a source of food and income from the rabbit skins she sold. Wartime restrictions meant that the heavy metal traps were hard to obtain. They gave my mother freedom and conveyed my father's message that he cared for her and trusted her with those fifty irreplaceable traps. They were a truly loving gift.

Eventually Bettina left the property where she was working and camped out alone. My father checked the sky for the smoke of her campfire and the waterholes for her fresh tracks. One day, during the vicious western winter of that year, both the camp smoke and her tracks vanished. He went to look for her and found her suffering from exposure to the piercing cold. She had been bitten by a poisonous spider and was in a coma. He took her to his cabin, fed her and thawed her out.

As an Australian with a British name, he suggested that he should arrange their marriage to protect her. He was well liked locally. There were neighbours he could trust.

Despite her situation Bettina was not easily courted; she made a careful and deliberate decision to marry Joe. From time to time Joe killed fresh meat and took a portion, together with fresh vegetables, to an elderly 'widow woman' living alone, distant from any neighbours. Sometimes Bettina accompanied him in his smart sulky with his beloved mare Jinny trotting briskly, and the sunrise showing off the bush in all its charm. They would arrive mid-morning, have a bite to eat, and in the afternoon Joe would take out his axe and chop enough wood to leave a generous stack. He also made whatever desperate repairs were necessary to the house and yards. They would return home slowly in the evening cool, enjoying the stars.

On one such visit, the last of the cold roast served up was full of maggots. Bettina, filled with disgust, avoided eating it and that night, as soon as they were out of earshot of the house, she turned to Joe. 'Didn't you know the meat was full of maggots?' she asked him. 'It was terrible. I watched you eating it and couldn't tell you.'

'I never knew a maggot to do a man much harm,' he replied.

'But Joe – the meat was rotten!' Bettina protested.

'Betty, she shared the last that she had. That is all a person can do. I couldn't hurt her feelings for a maggot. She makes a lovely pickle; I enjoyed that and told her so.'

Bettina considered his response and, as they journeyed on beneath the stars, she decided to become his wife.

Joe McDuff was the eldest son in a large family left in difficult circumstances by his father's untimely death. He had left school prematurely to support his younger siblings; he boasted proudly that one had become a High Court judge. With his easy-going nature it seemed surprising that he had never married – jokingly he said that he had so many sweethearts he could not decide between them. Underlying the humour was a deep ongoing commitment to his brothers and sisters, a desire to 'see them right'. McDuff was a Scottish name, but the stronger influence came from his mother's Irish family. My father sang the traditional Irish ballads, his speech had the Irish swing and lilt, he talked familiarly about the Blarney Stone and the Great Famine as though they were part of his own experience, when in fact even his mother had been colonial-born.

Bettina and Joe were married in September 1941, a week after her thirty-second birthday. Although my mother did not know his age, Joe was now sixty. The wedding documents say fifty-five (based on his misleading information).

Of course, Joe McDuff was not the first man to have shown an interest in my mother. Anton Chlumecky was a familiar name to me long before I learnt to speak. Bettina told me stories of sailing trips with the affluent Chlumecky family around the islands of the Adriatic. In Vienna in 1937 and 1938, Anton and Bettina had a romantic understanding. They had planned to marry when the European political circumstances became more settled and Anton completed his studies. However, Bettina started a whole new life in Australia and Anton began working for the Allied war effort as part of British intelligence. He was stationed in an isolated village in the north of England where he worked on decoding devices. As 'cover' he worked as the village watchmaker. After the war he moved to Canada. Anton and my mother remained friends throughout their lives, and when I began researching my mother's past he sent me the letter my mother had written to him just after she had married my father.

Phyllis McDuff

March 28th 1942

Dear Anton,

I got your letter today and felt like writing straight away although the next mail won't go before Tuesday.

Well you want to know what kind of mate I took and it is only right that you should know. He is half Scotch and half Irish. Six feet high, very well built and extremely strong. He can work with the ax all day or pick and shovel or do any sort of work. He is just as much a horse krank as I am and we have a beautiful pair of trotters. They take us into town 14 miles in 40 minutes. Nearly as good as a car.

How it all came about. I left my job in Queensland for I could not stand up to the hard work there any longer, and went to Sydney to see the Royal Show. I earned my living there going washing and scrubbing for the day and earned enough to live and buy a few things I needed badly.

My sister Marianne gave me a small flat containing a bedroom and little front room and bathroom which I furnished with fruitcases and there I batched and was quite happy. I took fiddle lessons again and that was the only thing I actually enjoy while I stayed there.

Of course I spent my last penny at the show and had to take the first job offered the day after the show was over. I had advertised in a Farmers paper and got plenty of replys. One telegram amongst them 'Position yours £2 and tucker. Awaiting you on next train. Urgent.' Well I was on the next train.

I met Joe the first week I was there and I liked him, and he, although known for never taking any notice of females and living in the bush on his own, seemed to like me too. He came down to Andersons frequently, came in his best rigout to the paddock where I was working, for rides on the horse-drawn seed planter and invited me for Sundays to come hunting with him in the hills out the back.

We were generally lucky and often caught not only a Kangarooh but a fox or Emue and had a great time. As rabbit skins started to rise up in price and the lifting of three bushel wheat bags did not agree with me too well I started to dream about going out into the bush on my own. Joe, whom I consulted encouraged this idea and promised me the lend of horse and cart and harness and a few traps he possessed.

Well I never explained Joe is the Manager of an 80 000 acre station back from Andersons on the hills and lives in a real log cabin. When I came here first there were only just doors made of bags, no windows, a few skins on an old bed, an open fire to cook on and a few boxes to sit on.

A few jam tins with handels acted as pots and there was a washing basin with a big hole one side which only held water in a certain position. Five dogs lived in this log cabin with Joe besides all the harnis and skins were kept there and traps and poison and rags and bags.

In spite of all that this log cabin fascinated me somehow. I saw in it not what it actually was but what it could be. Well one day Joe invited me to come to town to go to the pictures with me. It was the 13th of June and a Fryday on the top of that and pitch dark and icy cold night. When we came to town a woman and child crossed the road in front of us. The child asked 'Do you love me Mummy?' 'Yes, come along' said the mother, 'so will you buy me lollies' said the child. Joe, who had never said a word to that effect suddenly asked 'Would you buy me lollies?'

We laughed and that was all.

The next morning I had a row with Anderson and walked off. Joe had just come down with his cart. I said 'I am coming up trapping today.' He said 'All right, I will come down this evening and fetch all of the luggage.' I camped in my cart with one sheepskin to lie on and a few Kangarooh skins to cover me up.

By degrees I cleaned the house up and as Joe taught me trapping I started to cook a bit, although he had to show me how to cook on the open fire. When he saw my attempts to make that log cabin look respectable he stopped home one day and helped and it took us a full day to just see daylight. Joe made a few shelves and things.

We found a few bits of table on the rubbish heap and a few good tins and stuck a bit of paint on and from that day on we spent the long winter evenings with straitening up the place. We lined the inside with bags and stuck some newspaper on to keep the wind out. I painted old tins and Joe mudded-in the fireplace. I helped Joe with every work he had to do, we built yards and went fencing, mustering and even trapping together.

As we had no books or wireless and no lantern every night one had to tell the other a story. It was Joe's turn and he told me the story how his grandfather, a brewer, came out from Scotland, and got married and had a son called Joe, who got married and had a son called Joe who also got married. 'And who was she?'

A Story Dreamt Long Ago

I asked. 'A land girl,' he replied, 'and I think we had better go to Weethalle next Saturday to see the priest about it.'

I had been thoroughly happy until this moment. Now I felt as though a noose had suddenly tightened round my neck. The next week passed as if nothing had happened but Fryday Joe greased the cart and very carefully fixed the harnis, brushed the horse and on Saturday at daybreak, he called me to get ready to be off as soon as possible.

We travelled 40 miles to Weethalle through the hills on a rocky bush track, meeting mobs of Kangaroohs – The priest was not there that day – on the way back I told Joe I wanted to return to Sydney and see my sister.

He did not object but he never talked much. He just said 'If you could have only stayed, I could have got you a nice hack and we could have gone to all the shows together and then there would be harvest and shearing time and you would get any amount of jobs here and you would not be so far away.'

'Well,' I said, 'I might come back, and then we will see.' And I went on the next train. I came to Sydney and although my sister gave me a glorious time I felt out of place. I felt so strange amongst them and got so homesick for Joe and the bush that I could not stand it any longer. I told Marianne and she said I should go back but wait another few weeks to really know him properly and not rush it. As I had a bit of a cheque I bought a couple of matrazzes and blankets and had some sheets and towels and plates and pots, bought 4 dozen traps to add to the ones Joe had already given me and a stretcher and a lantern and returned home. Joe was not in town that day. He had been in waiting at every train since I left, said one of his friends.

I got a lift out as far as Andersons that evening and walked across the paddocks home. It was the first time ever since my father had died that everything seemed beautiful and better than before. We both were relieved and we both knew then. I think that we will never part again.

I never thought that life could be so good and I am terribly happy. Our log cabin is quite a respectable little house now. It is still rough but our home. Every bit on it has a story. I have 100 chicks, 3 cows, 2 lovely horses, one sulky, 11 sheep I reared and a very good dog I broke in myself.

I have been going out working and trapping and saved up every penny and have a copper and washtubs and a real table and two beds and a lot of things that make life a bit easier. We have to cart water 3 miles to the hut, clear it with ashes to use for washing and slopping. There is plenty of wood about.

We are starting to burn charcoal now to have a bit of a cheque. Joe is on the pick and crowbar, I am on the shovel. By the time you get this letter I will have a baby and we will need some extra money then.

Well I do think you should marry, Anton. Don't be ambitious in picking your wife and don't look at anything but her heart and her health. Her heart for your own sake, her health for your children's.

I reckon all ambition is wrong. I think we live to be happy and to appreciate the world God made for us to live happily in. Joe per example does not often write, he never went to school much, he worked ever since he was 8 years old and battled along giving every penny to his mother to help her rear the little ones. There are tons of things he understands and can do that no one *else can. His brain is not spoilt, he enjoys good things, loves good pictures, can jump with joy at seeing a beautiful sky or sunset, loves the stars and trees and is not ambitious at all.*

I caught a fox mother in a trap and Joe was very upset about it. 'The poor little ones' he said all day. The next morning I saw him travel down a mile to the burrow with a tin in his had, and from that day on he fed them every day. That's Joe.

I do wish you would come out here, that is if we really will be able to defend this land of freedom, because I don't think there can be real happiness anywhere than here in the wide bush where you can find yourself.

Well it is late now, terribly late, I do wish you all the luck and happiness in this world, Anton, and send you a lot of love.

Bettina.

I was born early in May, as the dry, cold wind blew hard across the pebbled plain. At my parent's log cabin where my mother brought me after she left the nursing station, the tank was long since dry, the grass was long since gone. By the end of June the horses were too weak to ride each day from the hut to the ever-searching mob.

With fewer and fewer waterholes and only sparse patches of feed, the stock needed constant management to survive. Access to the water could be treacherous; the retreating water left deep mud that held the weaker animals fast. The weakest had to be shot before the water became polluted and to save what feed there was for those that might pull through. His constant scouting for patches of better feed enabled him to push the mob through dusty plains on to better grass. The mob staggered over the barren ground, relying on him to cut edible scrub to get them one more feed. It was hard, despairing work. Success depended on conserving every drop of water, every ounce of feed. The quality of the herd in five years' time would depend on his judgment in saving the best breeders. My father made the decision to take the cattle further afield.

Before he left the hut he cut wood and carted water from the last deep river hole, three miles away. When he said goodbye he walked with my mother past the dam. Squinting at a cloudless sky he said, 'Surely to God we'll get a little shower to put a drop of water in the tank . . . but if it doesn't rain you'll have to use *this* water, Betty. It will keep you going till I get back.'

I can only imagine my mother's thoughts as he rode away, and in the days that followed. I can only imagine how she felt as she measured the precious drops of river water in the row of kerosene tin buckets my father had filled. Pannikin by pannikin, each day her supply diminished, until at last she took her empty buckets to the dam.

She stood and looked at the clinging muddy access, at the soupy, stagnant water. She then took the empty buckets back to the hut. To get to the river would take two hours. She could not leave me alone in the cold hut without a fire, and it was too dangerous to build up the fire and leave me with it. She would have to wrap me carefully and take just one bucket, heavy enough on the three-mile trek from the river after it was filled.

That first day she managed to drag one half-filled bucket halfway back before she staggered home with me. The next day she went back and picked it up. So she toiled to bring back four gallons of safe water every second day. Sometimes she saw bare footprints

A Story Dreamt Long Ago

in the dust and glimpsed shadows on the track. She knew the Aborigines were close but had no idea how to contact them. They came to the hut only when 'the Boss', Joe, was home, a restraint that echoed the cycle of fear that had existed between isolated white settlers and 'wild blacks' since Australia's earliest days.

One day her most precious buckets vanished, the ones with the best handles that did not cut her hands. She cursed and wept and went to bed to keep me warm. Next morning she woke to a faint sound, not really a sound but a sense of someone breathing, someone moving, someone close. Through the cracks in the door she saw her favourite buckets in a row. Buckets filled with fresh, clear river water. Buckets that were miraculously refilled, day after day, for two more long, dry months. Water mysteriously provided.

September came, winter had passed, and soon it would be her birthday. Her early life had conditioned her to look forward to her birthday which she shared with her father. She was his treasured birthday gift. The blessed timing had defined their relationship. This year of 1942 she considered her strange Australian–September–spring birthday a special symbol of survival: according to bush lore, stock that survived drought through winter to the end of August would not perish.

Joe rode back to the hut. In the last daylight he passed the dam and stopped to water his horse. He read the signs as bushmen do, and his heart filled with fear. There were no tracks to show that my mother had been there and no drag marks from the bucket. He knew the water he had left would be gone – he knew that we must both be dead. Too afraid to go inside, in dread of the scene he knew he would find, he went to the back of the hut, took down the pick and a shovel, and chose a place to dig a grave in the moonlight. As the pick struck stone in the silent dusk my mother appeared at his side. She had come to ask would he not come in – and what was he digging that great hole for? My father stepped back from the edge of the grave and wiped his face on his shirt. He wiped away his sweat, his tears and the dust and with instinctive irony said, 'To be sure, I'm digging a hole for your birthday, Betty.'

•◆•

Even after a few storms had come and put some precious drops of water in the tank, my mother was reluctant to stay alone again. She could not go over to the homestead; although she liked and trusted their boss's kindly wife she thought their boss 'a bastard' and did not trust him to keep her safe from internment if the authorities made inquiries. Her opinion of him was one of her instant passionate judgments, which may have been right or wrong but my mother knew no middle ground. My father was far too wise to contest her views. At the conclusion of one of Bettina's long tirades, he would reflect, 'You could be right'. It also meant 'You could be wrong' but it was spoken in a language my mother could accept and was the only way she was likely to review her conclusions.

My father had left his mob of cattle on decent feed but had to go out again to move them on or to cut scrub 'to keep them going'. While he was home he made contact with the local Aborigines and they officially met 'the Missus'. My mother, remembering the young mother at the nursing station with her lusty son, was delighted to have their company. The women were fascinated with my mother's tiny pink baby and had helpful suggestions about caring for me, which my father encouraged her to follow. As the days grew warmer I was taken outside and smeared with an 'ointment' mixture of goanna fat and ashes to protect me from the sun.

My mother's skin was olive and under the cruel sun she was soon very dark. Gradually, the solution to the problem of my mother's reluctance to stay alone while Joe was away dawned on them. If my mother went with the Aborigines while my father was away she would not have to stay by herself. The few storms that had come encouraged the spring growth of light herbage and the native animals were close at hand. My father could be confident that she would be well cared for; if necessary, someone from the tribe could go to him with a message. All things considered, the circumstances of tribal life were no more primitive than those within his hut. So my parents spent the balance of the spring, summer and autumn until my first birthday living separately, meeting occasionally, visiting the hut from time to time. At last my mother felt safe. With the tribe my mother learnt to track and hunt in the bush. In the garden schoolhouse of Villa Mendl she had studied art under the tuition of Cizek, a revered Austrian painter and teacher; now she used these strategies to paint with the tribe while learning their techniques. This was one of the happiest times of her life but there was just one area where Joe felt she had failed him. My mother told the story of how a passing missionary priest had approached the tribe, preaching fire and brimstone to their wide-eyed wonder. He totally accepted my mother as one of their number. Disgusted at his inappropriate tirade of criticism of the Aboriginal lifestyle, she could not help engaging him in a defensive theological discussion. This was expressed in the beautiful English she had learnt at her English boarding school, Cheltenham Ladies College, flavoured with her charming Austrian accent. The visiting missionary was astonished. Unable to defend his narrow views, he stumbled to his car and drove away. Bettina, elated with her victory, relayed the details to Joe. He was furious. 'How dare you put them all at risk! He'll talk all over town. They'll come out looking for the smart-aleck black gin. All sorts of harm could come of this. Just stay out of the way of anyone who comes near – hide, go bush, don't talk to anyone.' Whenever my mother related this story, Joe would shut his mouth in a hard straight line and shake his head.

Now, with the encroaching winter, my mother and father had to make decisions about how to carry on. My father owned many horses. There were three in particular he would not be separated from, the trotting mares that constituted the foundation of his stud. Finally they decided that Joe should give up his job as station manager and we would live in a canvas-covered wagonette pulled by the three mares, moving from place to place, together but itinerant – and, they hoped, safe.

We travelled the stock routes and back tracks, my parents working as casual station hands: mustering, fencing, bag-sewing for the wheat harvest. We travelled east into a better rainfall. Years earlier, my father had spent some time as a timber cutter around Dorrigo. He loved the mountains and the forests. Our horses pulled the wagonette across the Moonbi Range as my parents explored the possibility of making a life there.

A Story Dreamt Long Ago

•◆•

In 1944, with growing savings from their work and now that my mother was pregnant again, my parents dreamt of a place of their own. Neither of them wanted to relive the experience of my birth. This time Mother took me to Sydney to stay with Marianne for the last two months of her pregnancy. My father's favourite sister, Tess, also lived in Sydney, and they went on occasional shopping trips and enjoyed race meetings with her. Five years after her arrival my mother felt much safer. She had my father, her own money and a large network of family and friends. The internment policies had lost momentum and any risk of being discovered in Sydney paled against the memory of giving birth in an isolated settlement without proper medical care and the thought of bringing the new baby home to our itinerant campsite.

Dawn was born in the red-brick hospital not far from Marianne's house. I was delighted with my baby sister. I remember the exquisite softness of her body and my immediate determination to protect her, which put her in grave danger. I was used to being helpful, feeding pups, locking up the chooks. Later Mother told us stories about my efforts. Dawn was left between two pillows on the bed while our mother had a bath. When Dawn started to grizzle I pulled her off the bed and dragged her by the legs into the bathroom. She survived undamaged. I was told I must never, ever, do that again. Did I understand? The next time I heard her grizzle I carefully put her in a partly opened drawer and pushed it closed. Dawn was happy and robust; once again she survived.

Phyllis McDuff

The *Agricultural Gazette* advertised a tiny property for sale at Tarpoly, near Barraba, on the western foothills of the Great Dividing Range, which Joe and Bettina bought. It was called Mostyn Vale. The land was 512 acres, some of which could be farmed with a horse and single furrow plough. On the fertile flats beside the creek we grew lucerne for hay, melons, tomatoes, lettuce and other small crops. Any surplus produce was sent by train to be sold at Barraba. The hills provided shelter and good grazing country. It had a permanent spring-fed creek and a tiny two-roomed wooden shack with verandas front and back. There was a single, sacred tank to collect rainwater from the roof guttering. A waist-high wooden tank-stand accommodated an enamel washing dish and a pannikin for drinking water. Our very own water supply!

The kitchen, built of corrugated iron with an open fireplace, was separate from the house. Beside the fireplace long flat stones provided comfortable seating. There were also two wooden kitchen chairs, one held together with twists of fencing wire. Other seating consisted of empty kerosene tins topped off with folded corn sacks.

This was where we settled in May 1945, once the war was over, when it was safe, when names on documents could not condemn.

2

First memories

My legs stuck out straight. I couldn't bend my knees. Jinny had her head down eating grass. Of course, the horse was much too fat. In fact, she was pregnantly lopsided and misshapen. Little kids have little legs, especially when you are a very small and skinny three-year-old. I knew enough to let her have the whole length of the reins or I would be pulled down along her neck.

I glanced ahead to see my father, mounted on his horse, patiently looking back at me.

'I need a stick to make her go – my legs won't bend,' I told him. I squirmed in preparation for the long slide down Jinny's side to get the stick, and then to somehow manoeuvre her to a rock or stump that would allow me to climb back on again in stages, gripping my precious stick between my teeth. It didn't occur to me that any adult might assist me. I knew I had to work it out for myself.

'I wouldn't get a stick if I were you,' Dad said. 'She may not take too kindly to a stick. She knows about the trotting whip – not that I'd ever flog her – but she might get a bit unsettled with a stick.'

He rode ahead and called, 'Come on, ol' girl.' Jinny lifted her head and waddled off, following him along the stony track down to the creek. Until now I had ridden behind Dad's saddle or earlier inside his split-bag, my small weight balanced on the other side by rabbit traps and tucker-bags. You don't have to hang on inside a split-bag, but it can get squashy. Now, at last, I was riding independently. Jinny was not a kid's pony, Jinny was a trotter, Jinny won races. I had seen her streaking to the front at Barraba showgrounds; I'd stood balanced on the railing, shrieking, clapping, laughing. I'd watched Mum and Dad open the envelope with the prize money inside and I knew how important that was. Jinny had a pedigree written down on paper. Her registered name was Jean Lou Lou; her father was a famous trotter called Lou Lou Boy. I could read that, and I knew that to be champions, horses, dogs and cattle had to have pedigrees. Bloodlines were important. Jinny had good bloodlines; Dad said she was 'worth her weight in gold'. Dad loved Jinny and I was allowed to ride her.

My mother, of course, was an excellent rider, fearless and competent. She told us stories about a place where she used to ride horses over jumps, where she had galloped through the forest and trotted along soft, sandy pathways in a park. The horses lived in stables and had grooms to care for them. That place was very far away.

My mother told me that her riding teacher used to make her sit up very straight. She had to wear hot, scratchy, tailored jodhpurs, gloves and a hat. I was allowed to ride in anything, in trousers made from soft cotton moleskin cut from the worn legs of Dad's strides. No one made me wear gloves or boots. I was a very lucky kid.

Dad and I were riding down to Mum and Dawn, who were at the vegie garden near the creek. In the afternoon the vegetables had to be hand-watered with a bucket, a square kerosene tin with homemade wire handles. Mum scooped the water from the creek and carried it across to the garden, which was fenced to protect it from the rabbits and wallabies. I helped with the watering. I had a billy can with the same sort of handle, and my own row of plants to water.

The best things in the garden were the watermelons. Dad knew when they were ripe by tapping them. When we finished the watering we sat on the bank of the little trickling creek. Dad sliced up one of the melons with his axe. It was hot, and Dawn was naked and dusty. She pushed her face into her melon slice and the juice ran down her belly, leaving dribble tracks. When she took her face out of the melon she giggled and I tickled the juice tracks on her belly. She was round and happy and beautiful and I loved her. I remember her as always happy, quietly smiling or giggling. She was a contented, gentle child, though she could be determined on occasion, and prove effective in a crisis. She and I were a good foil for each other. Our differences meant that we were not competitors. We were close companions in the things we shared, but easily able to go our separate ways. One of my first memories of Dawn is of her learning to walk. She pushed an empty oil drum along, wobbling and staggering as she went. I was enormously proud of her achievements.

After the melon we had to wash, and if we washed in the creek it saved the rainwater. We all had to get cool and clean before we went back to the house. We let the horses go beside the creek and Dad filled a big tin bucket to carry up to the house. 'A bit of extra water for the dogs and chooks,' he said as he set down the bucket and shrugged off the saddle he had carried on his shoulder. I cleaned the water tins in the chookhouse and the kennels, using the remaining water to wash each one. Dad refilled them from the bucket.

'If you lock up animals you have to feed and water them before yourself,' he told us. 'They depend on you. You don't fill your own belly first. When your own belly is full you can get a bit forgetful.'

⁕

My father's hair was snowy white. I remember the spring in his step and his hands: big, straight-fingered, strong and strangely elegant. His forearms, brick-red, were covered with wiry black hairs, useful for testing the razor-sharp edge of his axe. In silence, Dawn and I would squat beside him to watch the sharpening ritual as he worked with the oilstone. The finale was the shaving of a little patch of hair on his left forearm. Then he would take the leather cover and clip it firmly over the axe head. He would break the awestruck silence with his firm pronouncement: 'You must never lay a finger on that axe. Do you understand?' We nodded solemnly. We never dreamt of disobedience.

My father had a playful side, too. Amongst our meagre furniture was a large wooden table with folding legs that Dad had bought from an army disposals store. One day when he was looking after us, he collapsed one set of legs to make a slippery slide, and contributed to the atmosphere by sprinkling around a handful of flour to create a snowy landscape. My mother was furious when she discovered this bizarre and wasteful behaviour and, despite our pleading, it never happened again.

When I was a child it did not occur to me how tiny my mother was, but in her most determined, square-shouldered stance she measured just five foot two. She herself attributed her small stature to her deprivation of food following World War I. In 1919, at the age of ten, she contracted tuberculosis: she had horrific memories of the clinic where she was sent to recover.

Mum was wiry and noisy. Her energy preceded her and trailed in her aftermath. She was passionate, intolerant, even ferocious. She was beautiful and fearsome. Her black eyes danced with the emotion of the moment. She was never, ever wrong – except on rare occasions when the sheer lunacy of a project suddenly struck home. Then, collapsed with laughter, she was able to concede her error. It was only after her death that I was able to understand the impact of her experiences. Every project was driven by total commitment and a fierce determination that drove her on. Before, I had not always seen the courage that lay behind her lurching decisions.

•◆•

The one-room, one-teacher bush school at Tarpoly was supposed to have a minimum of ten pupils. In fact, the numbers had dwindled to eight. If there were not ten pupils then the school would have to close and the teacher would be withdrawn, or else the parents would have to contribute to his pay. In 1946, shortly before my fourth birthday, I became the next possible enrolment. A deputation was sent proposing that I should start school the coming summer. By fudging birthdates, and in the expectation that by the time a check was made I would be many months closer to the legitimate school age, it was hoped that both the teacher and the school could be retained. Would my parents cooperate?

It was a short walk to school, a little over a mile. If the school closed, there was Dawn to think of, as well as other little ones, younger than I was, round about the neighbourhood. They all deserved to have a school. Another strategy was to make a deal with an older boy who had recently left school to go shearing with his father. Unlike those who went away to boarding school, he did not appear on any other roll, so his name could still be included, and he might appear in the classroom from time to time.

My parents did cooperate and I went to school with great enthusiasm. I could already read the words on pedigrees and jam tins. I knew the popular Banjo Paterson poems by heart. I knew the map of the world. In the middle of Europe I could find 'little tiny Austria' and I knew that the Alps were very high mountains with snow all over them. Yes, I was ready for school.

My mother stitched a uniform for me made from blue serge, cut down from her own school uniform. It had arrived all the way from little tiny Austria as part of the 'rescued treasure' packages my mother had received over the last few months. These were sent with loving determination by someone my mother called 'Baby' and were greeted by her with delight, although I often sensed her sadness and frustration as she examined the contents after unpacking them. The diaries and mementoes they contained were the sentimental residue of her former life, of which I knew so little.

The war in Europe had ended last year. My mother realised that all over Europe people were starving, and worried that Baby could not afford to send these parcels. However, she went to work on her old uniform with glee; this treasure could be put to good use. With no sewing machine and limited dressmaking skills she adapted it to fit me, and as she stitched she told me stories about Cheltenham Ladies College.

She told me about the boarding school – the dormitories, the rules, the lacrosse and hockey pitches. She told me how she had missed her doona – this, she explained, was a soft, warm cloud she slept beneath at home in Austria. The British slept under tightly tucked-in blankets. Young ladies were not supposed to curl up in bed or flop on their bellies; they were supposed to sleep on their backs to maintain a good posture. Someone very important called Miss Wraith supervised all these rules, which my mother had found very difficult to obey. At school she was often punished for her misdemeanours. Her brother Otto visited from time to time but her treasured outings with him were forfeited when her 'black marks' accumulated. Years later, in the autobiography she left the family, she wrote: 'Cheltenham was very interesting for me. Not always happy because I didn't always understand the English people. I revolted against their attitude. For example, once we had to illustrate *The Tempest*, and every girl did the same thing, a ship in a storm at sea. I painted a long picture of what I saw in my imagination. Hell was below the round earth and in the air above were all the ghosts.

God was sitting in the middle and around him were saints and angels praising Him. Hell, of course, was red and yellow.

'I was sent to the Headmistress who asked me why I painted such a different picture. I was so cross; all the other girls boasted that their mothers and their grandmothers had attended Cheltenham. So I said, "Because my mother, my grandmother, my great grandmother (and so on) did NOT go to Cheltenham. That's why I painted a different picture." The headmistress looked horrified but simply said, "Very well, you may go."'

At the completion of her studies she returned to Villa Mendl. She had not been home for six months. When she arrived she rushed to find her mother. She loved Bach and Bettina had been painstakingly practising a Bach fugue to play for her. She wandered through the big house with her violin in her hand, looking for her mother.

'Where is Mama?' she asked the servants, but they avoided answering her question.

'You must see your father,' she was told.

When evening came and Fritz Mendl returned home, my mother, still carrying her violin, knocked on his office door. 'Where is Mama?' she asked once more. He told her that in her absence her mother had died of cancer. She was outraged that she had not been told. She accused her father of betrayal and demanded an explanation.

'No one ever spoke to my father in that way,' she told me. 'No one would have dared.'

Her father simply said, 'You were not informed because you had your studies to complete. Duty comes first. Above all else you must learn discipline. Remember that.' Despite the harshness of his words my mother forgave him and from that time on they were very close. He admired her courage and she had glimpsed his sadness through the tough façade.

•◆•

My bush school was very different from Cheltenham Ladies College. I must have been taken up and introduced to the teacher beforehand, because when I set off alone on my first day I went with the utmost confidence. I was aware that my mother was delighted with the teacher. Eddie Rascall was young; perhaps Tarpoly School was his first appointment. His family was of Swedish origin, which held some significance and reassurance for my European mother. 'It will be all right, he's Swedish,' I heard her say, and: 'He'll understand, he's Swedish,' in a calm, relaxed way.

Shoes were part of my new uniform. They had arrived from Sydney, handed down by my cousins. They were black with a wide strap across the arch and a fat buckle like the ones on saddlebags. I could already do up buckles. They were lovely to look at but I didn't like wearing them. The only shoes I'd ever worn were the soft rabbit-skin slippers my mother made for us, which were much more comfortable than these new ones. My father tried to help by polishing them until they gleamed. His own boots were rough and oiled with mutton fat, but a new tin of black polish had appeared along with the school shoes. Ceremonial polishing took place to accustom me to the idea of wearing them.

On my first independent trip to school I set out in the tunic my mother had made, carrying my shoes and socks and lunch in a cut-down sugarbag. I explained to my parents that the distance was too far to walk in shoes. I promised that when I reached the farm gate I would sit down and put on my shoes and socks. I intended to arrive complete and civilised, a proper citizen of the British realm.

At the gate I took out my shoes and socks, bent down to put my foot inside the sock – and froze. Impossible to put that dusty foot inside the snowy sock! Just before foot touched sock I had to stop. So I gave up on my promise to my parents and decided to take the problem to the all-knowing Swedish teacher. In the short distance between the farm gate and the schoolyard I thought hard about this shoe dilemma, and arrived at school with a clear solution.

I placed my sugarbag on the veranda, took out my shoes and socks and left them on display. I'd arrived just in time to join the line of pupils standing at attention, one arm's length apart from each other, before the march into the school.

'Good morning', Mr Rascall greeted each one of us. He glanced down at my bare feet. 'Where are your shoes, Phyllis?'

'I've got shoes and socks. They're on the veranda. I just don't want to wear them because it isn't fair.'

He looked at me gravely. 'The other children are all wearing shoes.'

'Yes,' I agreed, 'but they are all bigger, they can run with shoes, but I'm the smallest, I can't run in shoes, and that means I won't get picked for cricket.'

The row of evenly spaced children stood still in silent attention.

'There are bindis everywhere,' the teacher said.

'I've got tough feet,' I declared.

'There are catheads, too.'

A Story Dreamt Long Ago

'If I get one I can get it out myself – and I don't cry!' was my response.

The all-knowing teacher needed his tenth pupil. It was time to sing 'God Save the King'. From his elevation on the steps of the veranda, Eddie Rascall declared for all to hear: 'Phyllis McDuff is allowed to leave her shoes on the veranda and run barefoot at playtime.' The row of children sighed in unison and immediately burst into the national anthem.

For the most part I liked school. I sat at the back of the room and was given coloured pencils. There was a Sunshine Milk tin full of smooth cowrie shells. I loved the feel of them and pleaded for more. I was only allowed to have as many as I could count. Counting became a passion. I wanted a hundred shells, a thousand, a million. I could easily say 'one million' but had to work hard at all the numbers in between, and Eddie Rascall was no soft touch. I had to count and group shells into tens and take some away from others before he gave me more.

Sometimes I daydreamed, peering out of the windows at the soft blue hills beyond. There were two faded prints on the back wall. I knew that painter understood the hills – the light, the forms of trees. He owned the special magic of making the hills come inside the house. It would be twenty years before I knew his name. It was Albert Namatjira.

I loved to listen to stories of history and literature and to poetry. Whatever the bigger kids were doing overflowed to me. I learnt the Australian poem 'My Country' by Dorothea Mackellar and another about English daffodils, by William Wordsworth. I had to repeat the lines over and over to keep them in my head. I wasn't yet able to write them down.

One history lesson terrified me. Eddie Rascall told the story of the arrival of 'the Whites'. They came in ships, they had long magic tubes to see things at a distance, they had guns and poison and soon they invaded the land and hurt the black people. After a while they took away some children and locked them away. They took little kids like me from their families and kept them away for years, even forever. Sometimes they took the fathers and put chains around their necks. Horrified, I saw the pictures in the book in Eddie Rascall's hands. I analysed each skin tone in the room, from the dark brick-red on the older farm boys' arms, to cream, pink and tan. There were many colours, but none were black or white. Who were these strange and violent people? How could I hide from them?

I was forced to put up my hand to ask the pressing question: 'Will the Whites come here? Will they get us too?'

The answer I was given was too awful to accept.

'They are here already,' said the all-knowing teacher. I carried this truth home with a heavy heart. Nightmares stole my sleep. I woke screaming with visions of white-faced ghosts coming to get me through the dark. They came singly and in groups, they came on horseback and on trains. They hissed and spat and woke me up. I crept into my parents' bed, but I couldn't voice my terror. I grew hollow-eyed and gaunt. 'She needs a tonic; cod-liver oil might do her good,' Dad said. Obediently I swallowed down the oil and even grew to like its flavour, but the terror did not pass.

Finally, as I cringed by the fire one night, afraid to go to bed, I asked my father, 'Dad, what will we do if the Whites come?'

'Who's coming? What Whites?' he asked, puzzled. Then, at last, I broke down and told him the terrible stories I had heard.

A Story Dreamt Long Ago

I wanted him to say they were not true. He stared into the fire for a long time then he took me on his lap and held me tight, and whispered into my hair, 'It happens.' He was very gentle, and I was almost calm when he set me down and said, 'You don't need to worry, you *are* white. They don't take white kids away.'

I thought he had gone mad. 'Where?' I hissed. 'Where am I white?' I held out my brown arm. 'I'm brown,' I said. 'I'm never going to be white. We're all brown, everyone, Mum, Dawn, all the kids at school, all different sorts of browns. I've looked and looked; nobody's white and nobody's black!'

He tried to joke, saying: 'You might be white on your belly.' He lifted up my shirt, exposing my brown belly. He was wrong. He didn't understand the danger we were in. He didn't seem to understand anything about our situation. He couldn't even see what colour his own skin was. I thought he had gone mad.

•◆•

The school was the cultural centre of the community. A little knot of about ten families, many related to each other, met at Parent and Citizen meetings and arranged school sports days, Christmas parties and tennis afternoons. They built a tennis court on the red clay flat beside the school. The talcum-powder dust rose up all afternoon, setting the scene in sepia. The ladies wore large hats, and gracefully lobbed balls across the net. Mixed doubles were played with gallantry. There were frequent tea breaks with discussions about rainfall and crops. There was no air of competition until an episode that changed this tennis court into my mother's battleground; even its sepia hue could not subdue the passion of her play.

Listening to her stories I had been unaware of the intonation of her English, I could detect no accent; only now did I realise that she sounded different from the other mothers who came to school. I had been at school for two years. The war was over. The men were home. One day at lunchtime, uncles who had fought the 'dirty Hun' were mentioned. Someone swung around to me and said accusingly, 'Your mother's German. She's a Hun!'

'No she's not, she's Austrian,' I protested weakly, wanting to defend her. But I knew no one had ever heard of Austria.

'She talks funny! She talks German! She's a Hun!'

I leapt to my feet in protest, screaming, 'She's not a Hun! She's *Austrian!*' There was pushing and shoving. The words 'Nazi bitch!' rang out. I felt a thump on my mouth, then sickening pain. I could taste blood and feel gravel. I spat into my hand: there, swimming in pink blood and spit, were my four front baby teeth. My head swirled and my mouth felt huge and numb. I knew I was going to cry, and worse, I would break my promise to Mr Rascall that I never cried!

Eddie Rascall gathered the children together and marched them into the school; he handed the worn brass key of the water tank to the biggest boy and told him to help me wash my face.

Bruce was large and gentle. He had a clean handkerchief folded in his pocket. He ran the water into the enamel basin and holding me by the back of the neck systematically washed my face. The blood kept flowing from my mouth, making his job difficult. I spat and wept, clutching my four teeth in a clenched fist. Bruce took a pannikin of water and I dropped the teeth into it one by one. Each one made a sad little *ping* as it hit the bottom. Bruce washed my hand in the dish, swabbing with his saturated hankie. Finally he took out the teeth and laid them carefully on the wet hankie. I'd stopped crying by now and quietly watched this solemn ceremony. He brought a round matchbox out of his pocket, emptied the wax matches into another pocket and carefully placed each tooth in this small container. He fixed the lid firmly. Looking up, we discovered Eddie Rascall observing us.

Quietly, almost coaxingly, he asked, 'Would you like to tell me what happened?'

'Nothing,' Bruce and I replied in unison.

We went inside, where the all-knowing teacher read a story.

That afternoon I walked home very slowly. My top lip felt huge and tight. I didn't know whether I'd done something wrong. I wasn't sure exactly what had happened.

Dad was outside when I got home. He had seen me coming and had walked a little way towards me. 'That's a bit of a mess,' he said. 'Put your head back; let me have a look.' My fat lip hid the missing teeth until I tipped back my head and Dad gently looked inside my mouth. 'Did you get in a fight?' he asked. I drew out the wax matchbox and handed him the teeth, which he shook into his palm. 'Who gave you the matchbox?'

'Bruce Bowman,' I told him. I was sure that Dad could see Bruce's clumsy, determined kindness as he wiped the tears, the snot and the blood from my face. I felt better then. Nothing seemed to be my fault, so I asked quite confidently, 'Dad, what's a Nazi bitch?'

The colour left his face, his mouth went thin and tight, he seemed to be in pain. He didn't answer my question. He stood up very straight and walked towards the house, where smoke was curling from the chimney and Mum was cooking bread. By the time we reached the door the stiffness had gone out of Dad. He pushed me on ahead and said half-jokingly, 'Don't you panic, Mum. Phyllis got in a bit of a fight – see her fat lip?'

Mum looked across; her eyes went wide. She reached over to tip back my head to get a better look. I smiled at her, revealing the huge gap behind my purple lip. 'Oh, Joe!' was all she said. Dad flicked his eyes at me to indicate to get myself outside. I was glad to go. The difficult explanation of the evil thing that happened was now up to him.

Eventually I returned. I stood leaning against the doorpost, absorbing the tension in the silent room. Dad was sitting by the fire, cradling a mug of tea in his big hands. Mum was kneading dough on the kitchen table. Both seemed too deep in thought to notice me, till Mum glanced up. She continued kneading as tears ran down her face. She rubbed them away with the back of one floury hand while she whispered, 'Bastards! They are bastards.' She looked across at Dad and banged the table with her fist. 'They are bloody stinking bastards!' The old table trembled with the force of her blow, then she spun around and walked outside, sobbing wretchedly, her whole body shaking. I could feel her desperation and I was afraid.

Dad held out one arm for me to come to him. I stood encircled. 'She'll be all right,' he said. 'She'll need a bit of time.' We stared into the fire, waiting for Mum's recovery.

The tennis parties changed about that time. To the surprise of everyone in the tennis set, Bettina's game revealed brilliance. She was vicious in her victories; she played with fierce absorption. She was tiny, fit and determined – she didn't win, she slayed. She hit every shot as though it was a punch in the teeth. Nobody suspected that she'd once been the darling of the Vienna-International tennis set.

•◆•

As students of Tarpoly school we were encouraged to participate in the local eisteddfods in the nearest town, Barraba. Dawn and I both entered in the 'creative presentation' sections. I chose 'The Bushman's Song' by Banjo Paterson and practised hard with my father till the day I swaggered across the stage, dressed in a cut-down, checked work-shirt with my father's greasiest old felt hat jammed tightly over my tucked-in plaits.

> *I'm travellin' down the Castlereagh, and I'm a station hand,*
> *I'm handy with the ropin' pole, I'm handy with the brand,*
> *And I can ride a rowdy colt, or swing an axe all day . . .*

True to her nature, Dawn chose a much gentler style. Dressed in an antique lace gown, with her hair in ringlets, face aglow, Dawn recited from an unknown author:

> *The bush was grey a week today, with olive green and brown and grey,*
> *But now the spring has come this way, with blossoms for the wattle.*
> *It seems to be a fairy-tree, and hums a little song to me*
> *And dances to the melody, the graceful, swaying, wattle.*

She had been carefully tutored by Aunt Marianne, supported by our cousins, using the best of Viennese and Grete Wiesenthal theatre methodology. In the event, neither stage technique was successful. We were not among the place-getters. The winner of the competition, the grand champion of histrionics, was a ballerina clad in a brief tutu and wearing a skin-toned leotard.

Bettina was furious. She promptly dubbed the winning act 'The Bum Dancer' and declared that if you had to be a bum dancer to get anywhere in Australian theatre she wanted no part of it *and* she didn't want her daughters on the stage. Typically, she did not abandon the arena before she had followed up by nominating us in the eisteddford in the larger township of Manilla and finally in Sydney. The results were the same – although the identity of the ballerina changed. Mum fumed for months, Dad and I continued to recite Paterson to each other, and Dawn danced about like a bush fairy.

•◆•

The entire family was fascinated by racing in its various forms. In the cool of the late afternoon Dawn and I would 'line up' to race on the stretch of dry red earth in front of the house. Dad sat on the veranda and rolled a cigarette, then he would nonchalantly stroll across to 'set the handicap', which required him to solemnly measure out several paces and then draw a line in the dust with the heel of his boot. The winning post was a tree or a rock in the distance. We then circled around pretending to be horses in the saddling paddock while Dad provided a commentary on our ownership, training methods, breeding and the expectations of our performance. To give the event greater impetus he included phantom competitors in this commentary. These were based on human, equine or other acquaintances; our school companions, saddle horses or milking cows might become temporary stars of the turf. Our favourite commentary included the line: 'She must be fast, she can't be slow – she's out of Black Betty by Hungry Joe.' We thought this hilarious and ran inside to tell my mother, who emerged to tell my father he was 'impossible!'. But this became our favourite commendation – we fought over it, each declaring it was 'my turn' to be the one who was fast because she was 'out of Black Betty by Hungry Joe'. In later years it became a catchcry in times of challenge.

After a long prelude Dawn and I 'took our mark' and at the 'go' command sprang forward towards the distant winning post. My father's handicapping was so well done that the result was inevitably a dead heat with passionate protests from us both. 'But I won, Daddy, I really did, I got there first, I was looking over my shoulder, she was miles behind.' To which he would reply, 'You'll fall arse over head if you run around looking over your shoulder.' (Of course, *we* were never allowed to use this favourite expression!) He could never be budged from his 'dead heat' decision but would often concede that he 'couldn't see too well at that great distance' and the whole thing would have to be done again, and again . . .

•◆•

In due course news via the grapevine reached us that Eddie Rascall would not return to teach us after the holiday break. My mother was upset at this totally unexpected news. There had been no goodbyes, no chance for gradual adjustment to the idea of someone new.

'I thought he was quite happy,' she muttered to herself. 'Perhaps he was offered a bigger school – but the kids were learning so much. He was a very good teacher.' She cast about for explanations.

Dad said, 'I'm not surprised. He sailed a bit close to the wind at times. His version of white settlement is different from any school book I've seen. There will be those who didn't like his thinking.'

'Did they deliberately get rid of him?' my mother asked.

'Quite possibly; I'd say so. They'd be thinking he's a communist.'

My mother, feeling helpless, getting angry, said with emphasis, 'He's not a bloody communist; he's just had a decent education.'

'That could be his trouble,' said my father. 'You can't afford to think too much if you can't keep your mouth shut.'

I was baffled by the conversation and wondered what a 'communist' might be. I could not imagine school without Eddie Rascall's gentle wisdom.

This was about the time of my fifth birthday, which I have always remembered for its single gift. Since babyhood I had gone fencing with my father. On hot days I remember wearing a huge hat and sitting in the cool earth inside the shallow, half-dug postholes where I could observe the differing layers and construction of the soil. I could see how roots went down, how shale broke up, ants' tunnels, spiders, worms, and, from that perspective, my father's giant feet.

I loved postholes. And they were safe. I knew that normally you should not go into holes if you didn't know what lived inside, but you could see right into a posthole. It was new, Dad had made it with the crowbar. How I longed to have a crowbar! But a crowbar was a sacred and dangerous thing. It could not be left lying in the sun because it got too hot to touch; it would burn Dad's hands. To stay cool it had to be stuck upright in the soil and I knew that I must never touch it. I must never try to wobble it or lift it up because it was very heavy and could fall and injure me. I understood all that and from a safe distance I circled around the crowbar admiring its symmetry, its surface with its soft, rich glow from years of handling. I liked the flattened shape of the knob on the top and the bluntly pointed end. I was unaware of how closely Joe was watching me.

One day, a neighbour gave him a lift to town in his car. In the late afternoon he came over the hill, and as we hurried towards him Mum asked, 'Did you get it, Joe?' Dad closed his face and mumbled, 'It's all right, I'll get it later.' That night while I was asleep he walked back to the gate to recover the mysterious item. In the morning, stuck in the ground beside Dad's crowbar stood a miniature version of it. Just my size. My very own crowbar for digging holes and levering things. Rocks and logs and heavy objects of all kinds could now be dangerously rearranged. The kids at school didn't seem to understand its value. When I announced that I'd got a crowbar for my birthday their faces remained blank. There was no sign of the eager envy I had expected, but it didn't really matter. For the first time since I started school I couldn't wait to get back home to try a new experiment. By inserting the tip of my crowbar underneath a boulder and chocking it with a lump of wood I could apply enough leverage to gradually roll large rocks some distance. From time to time the neighbouring children visited. They were all boys, older than I was. They were bigger and could be coerced into assisting with my building plans. I selected the best rocks and built my own Stonehenge, a circle within a circle. This was my fortress and my castle. If the rocks were lifted onto a bed of stout sticks they could be rolled more easily. Thus I had magic doors which could be rolled at my command. Dad watched with some concern and curtailed my attempts to lift the rocks to balance on each other. He said he didn't want to see me squashed.

Well into my adulthood the little crowbar was kept with the farm implements and was an infinitely adaptable and useful tool. From time to time someone would hold it up and say: 'This will do – just perfect – but what is it, actually? It looks like a sort of kid's crowbar.'

•◆•

At this time we had no car. 'Town' for us was the small settlement of Barraba, some twelve miles away. Occasionally Dad went to town alone. He took the train that went through our little farm – the railway line passed a few hundred metres from our house. He would walk along the line to the siding, a simple structure built of railway sleepers. Here the train stopped to enable the loading of heavy goods and for the guard to collect mailbags, passengers and verbal messages.

Sometimes we walked there with Dad, waited for the train, bade him fond farewells, and wondered what adventures he was up to throughout our lonely day without him. Dawn and I made extra sure our jobs were done well before dark. We filled the chip-box beside the fireplace to overflowing, checked the calves were all locked up, scrounged around the chook-house one more time to find an extra egg . . . Then, as darkness fell we listened for the hiss and thrum of the locomotive far down the track.

'I can hear it! I can hear it!' we would squeal, grabbing my

Bettina, dressed for a formal occasion in 1911. From a very early age, and through all the vicissitudes of her life, my mother always had the capacity to charm.

Bettina's two sisters, my aunts Lucie and Marianne, as children in Austria. They offered me some of the missing pieces, snippets and threads of stories that helped me understand my earliest beginnings.

Bettina, aged 3, in the garden of Villa Mendl, whispering secrets and delivering kisses to her brother Otto, aged 5. He was the one sibling she was close to in her childhood.

Bettina, aged 3, hatching a plot.

Bettina's father (my grandfather), Fritz Mendl, a debonair young army officer who sang dangerously witty songs and caused his parents great concern with his outrageous business proposals.

The family circle. Bettina's siblings, back, left to right: Fritz, Marianne, Otto and Lucie; front: Mama – Emily Mendl – with a barefoot Bettina.

Bettina's first adventure on horseback, on a summer beach holiday in 1914, protected by her brother Fritz.

Bettina with her brother Otto against the backdrop of the Manor House at Velm, not far from Vienna.

Bettina and Otto with their beloved nanny, Abby. Glorious summer days at the Velm estate.

Bettina and 'Gluck' on the pathway from the orchard. Bettina loved her dogs but was not aware they had a serious role. Each one was trained to protect her. Bettina discovered this when her dog attacked the butcher. He'd entered the room wearing an apron over his knife pouch.

Tante Maria von Kozaryn-Oculez (Baby), the companion of Bettina's youth who, in lieu of her mother, became Bettina's beloved associate. Tante Maria was the closest Dawn and I came to having a grandmother – from either side of our family.

The back view of Villa Mendl seen from the Master's Garden. Emily reads to her younger children, Otto and Bettina, while their nanny looks on from the veranda.

Bettina on the kitchen steps at Villa Mendl. She loved to be barefoot and unrestrained, surrounded by animals.

Bettina's first passport photo, probably taken for her trip to England with her mother to be interviewed at Cheltenham Ladies College.

My grandfather Fritz in the Master's Garden of Villa Mendl towards the end of his life.

Bettina was a crack shot, familiar with many styles of firearms. She loved the stag stalking that culled the deer herds on her mountain estates and provided venison for the dining table.

A Story Dreamt Long Ago

mother's hands and rushing her from the house in time to see the long bright light slide around the bend as the train burst through the cutting.

The two-wheel track leading from our farm gate to the house crossed the railway line. Heavy wooden sleepers had been laid parallel to the lines and dirt pushed up against them. This made a 'level crossing' and this was where we stood three times a week to catch the mailbag the guard pitched into the darkness. The screaming dragon approached, hooting and hissing clouds of steam. At the very end of it there was a square of light: the door of the guard's van, wide open. A black stick figure stood within the frame. With a mighty swing of his arm he aimed the mailbag at the feeble lantern that we held to guide him. It landed close by with a swoosh and a plop. As the train drew away the moonlight outlined the mailbag and it was '*my* turn – *my* turn – *my* turn!' to pick it up and take it to the house.

This was also where my father alighted from the moving train. The train would emerge from the cutting, sparks flying from its wheels as the driver slowed to assist his exit. For a moment he stood silhouetted in the doorway of the guard's van, poised with one hand on the brass rail, the other clutching parcels, some of which he tossed out in advance of his great leap into the darkness. Then he would disappear from our sight. The train rushed by and vanished into the distance. In the darkness and silence Mum, Dawn and I stood barely breathing. At last, after a terrifying pause, familiar words emerged. 'Are you there, Betty?' he would ask. Of course we were there. We always were. It was him we worried about. Which part of the darkness hid him from us? 'Over here, Joe,' Mum would call. After the glare of the train our eyes took seconds to adjust. At last we recognised each other's outlines and rushed forward groping for parcels to carry, denying ourselves hugs. No one had vacant arms to hug with.

One night the ritual changed. We saw Dad outlined against the open door, stooped over, hunched, unclear. Sparks showered more than ever, the train slowed to walking pace, then stopped. He descended slowly from the van and something large was handed down to him. The guard waved, flashing his lamp to signal to the driver and the train rolled on.

The familiar voice from the darkness said, 'I could do with a bit of a hand here, Betty.' We wondered what that could mean. Gradually the moonlight revealed something leaning against him. It fitted under his arm and clung to him. It had no real shape but flopped about awkwardly.

'Just get a good hold on him, Betty, while I pick up a few things I missed,' my father said. Now the floppy thing clung to Mum. Although the air was full of questions no one spoke as we shuffled towards the house, where my father put the parcels on the veranda, relieved my mother of her burden and went with it towards the shed.

We gathered in the kitchen where my father joined us. 'I've made him up a swag; he'll be all right.'

Mum could not help herself. 'Who *is* it, Joe?'

'A mate. I brought him home to help you.'

'Is he sick?'

'He'll be all right. He's on the booze. He'll sober up with a bit of tucker – be a new man in a few days.'

The air seemed chillier; my father realised that Bettina did not share his enthusiasm. He looked straight at her with pleading eyes. 'I couldn't leave him in town, Betty – he'd die in town, no one to feed him. He's been on a bender for weeks. No one will give him a job in that condition. He'll be a great help to you; he'll do some of the heavy work. I'll fix him up a bit and if you're still not happy he'll have to go. He won't get in your way.' Then, with emphasis: 'Hilly is a gentleman, you have my word on that.'

The next morning we met Hilly, a tiny, frail, grey man with wrinkled skin and a staggering gait. The liveliest part of him was his eyes, twinkling with energy and mischief that belied his fragile state. He sat beside the fire and my father pushed a pannikin firmly towards him. It contained a warm brew of hot milk and egg with a good dash of spicy 'Pick-Me-Up' sauce. Hilly looked as though he might resist. 'Drink it; it'll do you good,' Joe told him. Obediently Hilly sipped.

Gradually Hilly recovered. He helped with the watering, went out fencing with Joe, proved himself competent with dogs and horses, and sat around the fire at night spinning stories of the 'racing game' in the days when he rode winners every week in Melbourne. He treated my mother with gracious old-world charm. Before long she was in full agreement that 'Hilly was a gentleman'.

About this time, Dawn had begun to toddle off to school with me (once again to keep the numbers up), and Bettina, Joe and Hilly were an effective team against the workload of the farm.

Over the months, Hilly would disappear from time to time. Sometimes he arrived home a bit worse for wear, sometimes my father went to town to bring him home, but he never reappeared in the terrible condition of his first arrival. Anxious not to inconvenience us, he always stated his intentions, advising my mother that he would be away for a while, and asking if he could do any messages in town for her. He took care to attend to these before he hit the bottle. He was unfailingly dependable.

One evening, as I skipped out onto the veranda, I saw an astonishing sight. Standing under the single kurrajong tree at the front of the house was a small round lady. As I stood gaping at her she silently stared back at me. Eventually I pulled myself together sufficiently to retreat into the kitchen and stammer, 'Mummy – there's a lady.'

'A what?' she said.

'A really truly lady.'

'Where?'

'Under the kurrajong tree.'

'You must be seeing things.'

'Mummy, she is so there! Look, see?' I pointed at the tree.

My mother glanced into the sun glare. 'There's nothing there; I can't see anything.'

I gathered up my courage and sneaked out to the veranda again. She was still there, standing silently in the shadow of the kurrajong tree.

I took my mother's hand and dragged her to the veranda, where together we gaped at the apparition, which suddenly spoke.

'Good evening, missus. I'm wonderin' if you could help me know the whereabouts of a Mr Halbert Hill.'

My mother had a good idea. 'Go and ask Daddy to come,' she told me.

I rushed to get my father, leaving the two women staring at each other, my mother unable to fathom the question she'd been asked, the lady patiently waiting for a response.

I arrived around the side of the house towing a reluctant and

A Story Dreamt Long Ago

disbelieving father. With a glance he summed up the scene, pushed his old hat back and scratched his head. The lady repeated her request to this new audience. 'I'm wonderin' if you could help me know the whereabouts of Mr Halbert Hill.'

'Hilly? Are you looking for Hilly?'

The lady nodded. 'That'll be him.'

'Will he be expecting you?' asked my father.

'It might come as a bit of a surprise,' the lady said.

Dad resettled his hat and retreated, murmuring, 'I'll let him know you're here.'

By now, Mum had grasped the situation. She asked the lady to come in for a cup of tea. I used the opportunity to get a closer look at her. She had the softest, kindest face I'd ever seen. It was the face of all the gentle grannies in every children's story-book. Despite her very round shape she had a sprightly step as she entered the kitchen. She was about to drink her tea when Hilly arrived, twisting his hat in his hands.

'I wasn't rightly expectin' you,' he said. His words sounded honest rather than dismayed. Then he turned to us. 'This is Hannie,' he told us with a strange little smile. After drinking her tea she admitted she'd 'Left me few things at the gate'. When it got cooler I went up with my father to get them: two cornsacks, each half full, clothes, a blanket and cooking utensils, all left at the gate in case she was not welcome. Even then, with my meagre knowledge of the world, I knew that this was very light luggage.

Hilly's wife was a wonderful cook. She settled in immediately, making cakes and pies and scones. Her speciality was pumpkin tart; in all my life I have never tasted better. She loved the house and the kitchen. She rarely ventured outside except on brief kitchen-related business to the woodheap or the fowl run. She did not 'fancy' vegetables and could see no point in watering them. She did not want anything to do with the dogs or horses. Hannie was a perfect foil for my mother, who now had some freedom to do the things she liked.

Yet Hilly's wife became the cause of the first row I witnessed between my parents. Working in the vegetable garden my father said, 'Betty, you mustn't call the woman *Hannie* all the time.'

'What should I call her?'

'Annie.'

'*What?*'

'Annie.'

'But I thought her name was Hannie.'

'Her name is *Annie*,' my father said deliberately. 'That is what you should call her. Otherwise she'll think you're making fun of her. You might hurt her feelings.'

'Is Hilly's name *Albert*?'

'Could be.'

'Don't you know?'

'I just know him as Hilly.'

'How long have you known him?'

Dad was getting tense, speaking slowly and clearly, gritting his teeth. 'I've known the man thirty or forty years; his name is Hilly. You don't have to concern yourself with *Halbert*; just call him Hilly and call her Annie. That way they don't get their feelings hurt. There, I've said my piece.'

It was Mum's unwitting 'making fun' of a common speech pattern, particularly among the less educated working class, that so infuriated Dad. Both Hilly and his wife unconsciously added 'h' before many vowels and dropped the 'h' when it actually should have been part of the word. Mum did not understand this. She started to giggle. 'I quite thought their names were Hannie and Halbert.'

'Well, now you know different!' Dad pulled his hat down hard, got up and walked away. As I ran along beside him he said, 'You must never hurt anyone's feelings. Not if you can help it. Your mother doesn't understand that.' I was never in any doubt what names I should use. To me they were always Mr and Mrs Hill.

•◆•

One afternoon I arrived home from school to find the kitchen full of people: Hilly and Annie and Mum and Dad and a strange lady with long fair hair with a little girl, taller than I was, who also had long fair hair. The grown-ups seemed to be at the end of a discussion in which they had reached agreement. The lady with the long hair was leaving and my father was reassuring her. 'It will be all right,' he said. She waved to everyone assembled on the veranda and walked up the hill alone to wait by the road for someone who was coming to pick her up.

Later I asked my father why the lady had gone and left her little girl behind. 'Too many mouths,' he said sadly, 'too many mouths.' I had no idea what he meant but I never forgot the straight back and the firm steps and the fact that after that one wave the lady did not glance back again.

The child with the long fair hair was Annie and Hilly's grandchild, Colleen. For mysterious reasons that only grown-ups understood, she stayed with us and became my first friend. She was a welcome extra pupil at the local school. Colleen was seven; she was a good reader and could write in even copperplate loops without ink blobs. This mystified me. Colleen could even spell. She learnt her words over and over and got them all right the next day. I tried to copy this technique, rarely with the same success.

Hilly and Annie and Colleen were all accommodated in the harness shed where my father had made up a swag for Hilly when he had first arrived. From these primitive conditions Colleen emerged each morning as tidy as a princess, her hair brushed and plaited, wearing one of two carefully mended and ironed frocks. As Annie had taken over kitchen duties, identical lunches were supplied to all three of us children, neatly packed in starched pieces of sheeting wrapped over the greaseproof paper that contained our sandwiches. At lunchtime we would spread the cloth napkins across our knees and unwrap our sandwiches. We always smoothed and folded up the greaseproof paper, enclosing it in the starched napkin to use again. You couldn't waste it. You couldn't throw it away.

When the school day was over, Colleen, Dawn and I walked home together. Annie was always ready with fresh bread and treacle and instructions to change out of our good clothes. We had a long list of jobs, which we thoroughly enjoyed and rarely needed a reminder. We gathered chips and kindling for the fire. We collected eggs and locked up the chooks, luring them into their pen with a single handful of grain. We had our favourites and were more generous with these pets. We collected feathers to make calligraphy pens for the brief time after tea when we sat at the kitchen table to practise writing. We walked across the paddocks to bring the milking cows home and carefully locked away the calves so there would be good milk in the morning. We helped with watering the garden and we washed out the dog dishes and checked they each had a full tin of clean water. We gouged moist clay from the creek banks and modelled figurines and tea sets, which we left on the flat rocks to dry. While we did all this we drifted and dawdled. We stopped to pick the occasional flower; the resilient bluebells were taken home to press in books. We jumped over fallen logs and followed lizards to their lair. We had a constant stream of 'good ideas': let's climb – let's find – let's pretend – let's see if . . . We were never bored.

These domestic arrangements went on for perhaps a year or so. One evening, after Hilly and Annie and Colleen had gone to bed, Dad said quietly, 'George Raffan has offered Hilly a job. I think he ought to take it. It will mean regular wages and a proper house.' He continued to explain, as though trying to convince himself: 'It's a decent little cottage and will be more suitable for Annie and the child. Winter's coming on; it's a Spartan camp out there in the shed, not even a fireplace. They'll do better in the cottage. He'll come over and give me a hand from time to time when I need it.'

'What about Phyllis? She gets on so well with Colleen,' my mother said.

'Well, they'll see each other at school,' Dad answered, 'and there'll be times Colleen will visit here.'

Our friendship did continue until it was eroded by the changing patterns of our lives. Through all my years at school I was never able to replace the easy, generous sharing of her nature nor find someone I admired so much for her courtesy and her personal elegance.

Years later, when Colleen married a tall, shy man, the reception was held in the house we lived in at Tamworth. By then Colleen and I were strangers but I was very glad that Mum had somehow found out about the wedding and made the arrangements.

Mum never forgot Hilly. Forty years later she reported with delight, 'I've found Hilly! He's in a nursing home. I visited him and we went to the races in Tamworth.' Her eyes shone with pleasure at the memory of those simple, happy times at Tarpoly.

3

Separation

Soon everything was changed forever by the blue airmail letters that came fluttering from the mailbags. They were addressed to my mother from an old friend in Austria, Otto Schönthal, who wrote that it was now possible to reclaim property and to re-establish oneself in society. Bettina should leave Australia and come home.

Otto Schönthal had become a close friend of Bettina in the years between 1931, when she inherited her father's estate, and 1938, when she was forced to flee after Germany annexed Austria. Notwithstanding his youth and inexperience in business, Otto had steered Bettina through these difficult years, helping her develop strategies to keep her properties intact despite taxes, civil war, personal betrayals and the outbreak and duration of World War II.

Given the great differences in personality between Bettina

and Otto Schönthal, I once asked her how their bond was formed.

'He saved my life,' she stated simply. 'After the deaths of my father and elder brother, when I had to deal with everything alone, he came to a tennis party. In conversation he remarked how lucky I was to own Villa Mendl with its lovely gardens, the family estates, and to control Ankerbrot. I looked at him in amazement and confessed that I was considering suicide because I just could not cope with all the conflicting responsibilities. He calmly told me that I need not feel like that – we would discuss the problems together and make a plan. Well, there was nothing to lose. I followed his suggestions and from that time on we planned our way through everything.'

In 1948 Otto returned to Vienna from Sweden, determined to grasp the opportunity to reclaim Bettina's assets. She described him to us as a genius, charming and ruthless. At the time, my sister and I barely knew what these words meant. I tried to understand when Bettina told me that some people had taken her 'treasure' and she had to fight to get it back. In turn, I told her, with a seven-year-old's certainty, that this wasn't fair. Why couldn't she just tell someone (perhaps like Eddie Rascall) who would tell the bully to restore her treasure?

Ultimately the letters were successful in luring her back to Vienna for nine long months. In 1950, when I was eight years old, we watched her take off in a flying boat from Rose Bay in Sydney, waving until the tiny speck in the sky disappeared. The terror of her absence haunts me still.

With hindsight I realise that my parents had thought carefully about my mother's return to Vienna. Chiefly, they

A Story Dreamt Long Ago

considered Dawn and me. The farm was small and stony. My father was significantly older than my mother. Now that the war was over there had to be some thought for the future. My mother had known the bitter struggle of attempting to survive without any accredited work training. Dawn and I would need a proper education one day. It was necessary for Bettina to reclaim whatever family property she could.

For our father, it must have been an axeblow to the heart to have his little family torn apart, to relinquish his Betty to her mysterious war-torn homeland – to him an utterly foreign place. Given the complexity of the negotiations she was involved in and Europe's post-war chaos, no one knew how long Bettina's trip would take.

My mother's sister Lucie, recently widowed, came from New Zealand to our farm to care for Dawn and me and to help my father. By way of introduction we were offered a simple story of her life. Lucie had been educated as a teacher and had worked in England while my mother was at school in Cheltenham. She had endeavoured to develop successful strategies for dealing with the wandering bands of homeless orphans created by World War I. She had progressive ideas about education and one day at a meeting when those ideas were rejected she stormed out into the street and narrowly missed being run over by a passing motorbike. The rider, Lou, stopped to check there was no damage and offered to drive her home. They fell in love and married. Both families firmly opposed the union. Lou's English family, with memories of World War I, were aghast that he had married an Austrian 'enemy alien'. After the birth of their daughter Erika, Lucie and her husband, who were now in their early thirties, decided to emigrate to New Zealand; there, they felt sure, they would be free from family and national politics.

Aunt Lucie was fun and kindly but we missed our mother, longed for her unreliable presence and unthinkingly rejected Aunt Lucie's kindness.

After some time, Lucie returned to New Zealand, accompanied by Dawn. I was taken to Sydney to stay with Aunt Marianne and her family while my father remained alone on the farm.

Marianne had been a dear and generous aunt throughout our lives. She would say, 'Now come here Honeysuckle' and she would hug Dawn and me, or offer us something to eat or make us mugs of hot strong cocoa. Marianne was the family beauty, with long copper-coloured hair tied in a knot and green eyes that beamed affection. We loved her husband, Gustav, known as 'Google', who taught us simple piano pieces. We were awestruck by our three beautiful cousins, Elizabeth, Cornelia and Sybille, who were almost grown up. They had long hair and ballgowns and went to university. They were not dabbling in tertiary education; they studied Agricultural Science, Medicine and Dentistry.

Their departure from Austria in 1938 was very different from Lucie's. Marianne had taken her three daughters to St Anton, a village in the mountains, to hasten my cousin Lizzie's recovery from persistent bronchitis. An unseasonal, late snowfall meant they could enjoy some unexpected skiing. Gustav had stayed working in his business in Vienna. Day by day he listened to the radio with increasing concern. Finally he withdrew all the cash, took the family jewellery from the safe and caught a train to St Anton. He asked his wife to pack and leave. She was happily settled in; Lizzie was recovering well and they were enjoying skiing lessons. Marianne did not want to leave. Gustav insisted. Marianne questioned him further. 'Give me one good reason!' she demanded.

'I don't like the political situation,' he replied.

'I'm not interested in politics,' was her retort.

Gustav went into the nursery and gave instructions to the nanny.

'Rosie, ignore Madame. Pack everything.'

He then asked the stationmaster when the next train 'out' (to Switzerland) was due. He was told that an express came through just before midnight. 'Can you stop it so that my family can board?' Gustav asked. 'Impossible, I'll lose my job,' was the reply. The stationmaster's wife was standing close by. Her parents owned the guesthouse where Marianne and the girls had stayed year after year, and she had grown to know and like the family. 'Stop the express,' she told her husband. '*You* may lose your job, but if you don't stop it these people will lose their lives.'

My cousin Lizzie remembers running through the snow, climbing on board, struggling with the last bundles hastily pushed toward her. In a split-second decision, Rosie, the nursemaid, boarded with them. As they crossed the border from Austria into Switzerland they were expected to forfeit all valuables to the Third Reich. Rosie seized the large ceramic potty, emptied the jewellery and cash into it, and sat her youngest charge on top of the loot. Briefly, the three-year-old protested, 'I don't have to – I don't want to.' Rosie told her bluntly to 'Shut up and sit!'. The family fortune survived the search and Rosie spent the rest of her long life in Australia. They had caught the last train out. At midnight the Austrian borders were closed and strict documentation was imposed on any exit.

I will always remember the tender kindness of Aunt Marianne and Uncle Gustav. When I reflect on the demands they faced to nurture their own family I am in awe of their sensitivity and patience with me during my stay with them. I was in despair. Angry, violent, I slept with some of my mother's clothes around me, lovingly provided by Marianne so that I could smell my mother's presence and know that she was coming back.

In my vivid imagination my mother was in danger, among bullies, fighting for her treasure. I knew I should be helping. I knew I was tough and strong and that she could rely on me. At least I could have looked after Dawn but that too was denied me. I was suddenly impotent to share my mother's peril. There was nothing that we could not fix together – barbed-wire fences, mad cows, measles. What had I done that she did not trust me enough to take me with her? It was *wrong* for her to be alone and nobody could understand my rage. I missed her lunacy, her laughter, her dancing and swearing. I missed being embarrassed by her strange outbursts. As the months passed I was losing faith in her return. What if they had told us a lie? What if Austria did not even exist?

Like many new arrivals of that era, Uncle Gustav had been obliged to use whatever skills he could muster to earn a living in Australia. He had been an engineer with his own business in Vienna, but here his qualifications were not recognised; he lacked the necessary contacts and technically skilled staff. With the capital he'd brought out of Austria he had invested in a clothing factory that proved very successful.

I was allowed to go to the factory, which was at Surry Hills near the dental hospital. Despite the grey buildings, the colourless streets, the grime that settled on every surface, I loved that place. I loved the trip there and the trip home. On Saturdays we took the ferry across to the city, then went by tram from Circular Quay along Elizabeth Street. Usually I went with Lizzie, who went there to cut the fabrics for the following week's sewing. There was a large wooden bin with cut-off pieces and this was my treasure trove. Thick wads of scrap fabric were thrown into the bin and close at hand was a small sewing machine which I was allowed to use. I selected, patched and stitched fantasy garments for hours while Lizzie worked on the real products. The long banks of industrial machines were silent. The composite smells of oil, cloth stiffening, new buttons and wrapping paper filled the room: heavenly incense. I loved the feel and colour and variety of the textiles. I matched buttons from the bin where the odd ones were kept and plaited strands of cottons into cords. There was infinite variety for play. Afterwards we went home to Mosman across the harbour, watching the green water churn in our wake. No doubt the weekday ritual was different, the ferry trip crowded, the working factory noisy, business problems insistent.

But often, on weekdays, Uncle Gustav returned home from work to find me limp from sobbing, beyond consolation. He would sit me on his lap, pressing my face into his jacket with his long, soft hands. I can still feel the violence slowly leaking out of me in that safe embrace. Patiently he held me until the sobbing ceased and I regained some measure of comfort.

I woke each day praying that this would be the day of Bettina's return. I was unable to reason or to calculate. For me she was either there or gone. *Gone* was desolation.

The school I attended was a short walk from the house. The concrete playground was vast and noisy. I had no understanding of how to participate; I had no friends there. The sort of things that interested me, such as levering stones into place to build a castle, were beyond the comprehension of my classmates. When I dared to talk about them I was considered either mad or a liar. It was safer to be silent. But my silence irritated and I was approached with probing questions that I mismanaged. When asked what my father 'did' I said he rode a big black horse, galloped over the hills, could crack a whip, chop down giant trees and split the trunks for posts. I declared that I knew how to split the timber, exactly where to put the wedges. That I could lever the split posts apart with my own crowbar. This was all considered fantasy. Lies! They yelled at me. I spat at them – I was frightened. I hid in the only quiet place I knew, the toilet. I latched the door shut. I was found by a teacher who told me kindly, but in front of the whole class, that the toilet was not a nice place for a little girl to spend the day. Why would I want to do *that*? The answer hanging in the chalky air above the room was that I was mad and not very nice. But this time I kept my promise; this time I didn't cry *and* I didn't tell.

Like all the Mendl children Marianne had received a generous education in all of the arts. She studied music, dance and art under well-known teachers and later taught art herself in Vienna. Now she gave painting classes at Sydney Technical College and other venues.

At the back of the house was a lean-to shed converted into a studio, and here Marianne encouraged me to paint. She set up easels with large sheets of creamy paper and explained the use of paints and brushes. She mixed colours, explained techniques. In a sweet cloud of gum arabic fumes I painted often. Perhaps as therapy she encouraged me to paint the farm. She provided a very large piece of paper – from memory it was about a metre high by two metres wide. It was firmly positioned on an easel and adjusted to the perfect height. I worked here steadily depicting all of the animals, buildings and activities that I had left behind. Marianne watched and encouraged. She popped little squares of dark chocolate into my mouth to keep up my energy and insisted that I stop each day before I tired and ruined the work. In time, the masterpiece was entered in a competition and duly won a major children's art award.

There was also a drum of modelling clay from which I was allowed to take scoops to work with. I loved the squishy feel and damp smell of the clay. It was familiar from the creek banks where I used to claw out handfuls to pat into lumpy tea-sets that cracked and fell to pieces after I left them to dry on warm rocks in the sun.

The house was filled with music, art books and discussion. My three cousins danced and sang. I was taken to the beach and offered ice-cream; I wasn't spoiled but always generously included. Yet I remained withdrawn, thin, prickly, waiting for my mother to come home.

In her attempts to help me in my distress, Marianne took me to the local library on Military Road in Mosman. I remember crossing the big, busy road clutching her hand tightly. She was as frightened as I was; we would not have taken such a risk for anything less satisfying than a visit to the library. We waited patiently until there was a traffic gap, then scuttled to the other side.

'Hold on, hold on, they are not allowed to kill us all together,' my aunt gasped encouragingly.

At the time I thought these words a sacred incantation that would save us. Later I rocked with laughter at the memory and the loony logic of the statement. Now I wonder if it was an echo of some genetic memory. *'They are not allowed to kill us all together'* – but they did.

At the time, I could not have understood the significance of her comment.

•❧•

Meanwhile, my father worked the farm alone, which was not strange to him. He'd been alone most of his life. Letters came from time to time, sometimes a phone call from Tess, his sister. She lived in Crows Nest, which was so far away I needed an adult to take me in the tram. She always rang to share any news of my father and the farm, where his life continued in its steady pattern.

One day a different call came from Tess, to let us know that she was going to Mostyn Vale. 'There's something wrong,' she said. She had no information but her gut – her bones – urged her to go. Her brother needed her. She was leaving in the morning on the train. She would let us know about Dad after she arrived.

Tess got there to find that he had been hospitalised after a mishap with a horse. While he was lying flat on the ground to retrieve a rabbit trap the reins tangled through the horse's legs. It was a young horse – Jinny's foal – and it panicked, reared, then

A Story Dreamt Long Ago

came down again and again, crushing him beneath its hooves, crushing his skull and ribs.

Once it had overcome its panic, the horse stood still, outlined against the sky. A passing neighbour saw it as he drove to town, noting that my father was working on the ridge. Returning late that night, the same neighbour saw in the clear moonlight the saddled horse in silhouette – on guard. He went to check the cause and found Joe unconscious but still breathing. It took some hours to go for help, to carry the big man now awakening into agony down the steep, rocky hillside, to brace and balance the improvised stretcher and its burden on the flat bed of his truck and get my father to hospital.

The injuries were complicated by sunstroke. He had lain all day without protection in the glaring summer sun. His eyesight and his sense of balance were damaged. Now it was time to go back to the farm – alone, as he thought. Throughout his recovery he had forbidden the hospital to notify anyone. He withheld contact addresses, refused to cause concern. But now Tess was there. She took him back to Mostyn Vale. A week later, after making arrangements for the dogs and turning the horses out, it was decided that my father should return with her to Sydney.

I was delighted to have Dad in Sydney again. Although he stayed with Tess I saw him often. I barely noticed that the spring had left his step, that his face was thin and pale or that his hugs were more carefully delivered. I didn't sense him flinch when I leapt onto his lap or when I rushed to meet him. Sometimes a watching adult would gasp, 'Phyllis, be careful!'. It was beyond my understanding that my father could be fragile.

Someone had sent a telegram to Bettina to let her know about the accident and at last she was on her way home.

I have no clear memory of the family reunion. I just recall standing beside my father to watch the tiny flying boat splash down at Rose Bay. I can't remember who was there, where Dawn was or what my mother looked like. My dread that at this last moment something would go wrong completely blanks my mind, until suddenly it is Christmas and we are all back home on the farm.

•—•—•

In Austria my mother had made headway with her claims for restitution of family property. She must have already been able to sell something for cash, because she brought back a little money to make improvements to our run-down farmhouse. We gained another water tank, the open back veranda was enclosed with glass windows, and the fireplace was fitted with a slow-combustion stove. Now we had a bathroom with a cement floor and a tub that drained. Unimagined luxury! Eventually more goods arrived in crates, including linen sheets and soft damask pillowcases with matching covers for the goose-down doonas. Until now we had known only grey army blankets, supplemented by canvas horse rugs in frosty weather. I couldn't believe the luxury of those goose-down doonas, with butter-yellow covers for me, rose-pink covers for Dawn, and, in one corner, monograms of our initials. I have mine still.

The improved homestead was wired for electricity. Most of this work was done by Bettina. She followed diagrams supplied with the equipment offloaded from the train. The guard, helped by the engine driver and some passengers, worked for an hour to settle the heavy generator into position. Watching, I recognised my father as suddenly aged and fragile. I saw the men gently slap him on the back as they were leaving. I sensed what was happening but did not know the words: they were helping out a mate.

I was eight years old.

•◆•

The letters from Europe, USA and New Zealand resumed, fluttering from the mailbag regularly. The envelopes bore rows of coloured stamps which we ceremoniously saved.

Dawn and I learnt to recognise the names of the senders. As part of her 'official information' Bettina told us stories and made connections. 'Baby' was Countess Maria von Kozaryn-Oculez, daughter of an aristocratic family who had been left impoverished by war, spinsterhood and the injustices to women of the old laws of inheritance. She had been reared in the French Sacred Heart Convent and spoke fluent, elegant French. Initially she came to the Mendl home as a highly recommended French tutor to my mother. After my grandmother died, Maria von Kozaryn was engaged by my grandfather Fritz Mendl as a chaperone and companion for my mother. Baby had survived the war, as had her brother and her niece Mucki. The other niece had not. Mucki's sister, Olga, had been engaged to a young army officer. Towards the end of the war, during a time of desperation and starvation, while awaiting liberation, a message came that he'd been killed. That night Olga went to the top floor of the house and leapt to the street below. Her father found her body in the morning. The following night, under cover of darkness, Mucki and her father took the body in a wheelbarrow to the cemetery. There they dug a shallow trench close beside her mother's grave and gently tucked Olga in.

Some months later the young officer returned, briefly, desperately, in retreat. He was killed in the last weeks of the war. *Er ging in den Tod* – he went to his death. I sensed that he went voluntarily. At first I pieced this 'Romeo and Juliet' tragedy together from conversations I overheard between Joe and Bettina. The details came fragment by fragment from Vienna in 1952. After that, whenever I saw Mucki, I glimpsed her shadow sister. I wanted to ask about Olga, wanted to grieve with Mucki, but never dared to open the wound.

•◆•

Many letters came from someone called Agathe. Over the years, her distinctive writing covered pages that fluttered through the farmhouse, lay on benchtops and under beds – gossip for Bettina, and for me secrets that no one else had the courage to reveal. Agathe's family had owned the most beautiful house in the street, a few doors away from Villa Mendl and her friendship with my mother began in babyhood. Agathe was quiet and pretty. The antithesis of my mother. Perhaps this perfect balance explains their lifelong affection. Agathe's athletic talent lay in skiing. A passion she had shared with my mother's elder brother Fritz. They enjoyed the mountains, the solitude, and the precision of the sport. In time, Agathe fell in love with the quiet, artistic Fritz, and he returned the affection. There was an understanding they would marry. The official engagement was delayed by Grandfather Fritz's illness and then by his death. No one could have foreseen that young Fritz would be killed so soon after his father, leaving Agathe 'not quite' a member of the family. When Agathe's family fell on hard times my mother honoured the connection. Among other gestures, she paid for Agathe's brother's education and later for the trip that enabled him to settle in America.

Letters on fine white paper continued to arrive from Otto. Not my mother's other brother Otto – she told us he was 'lost'. We never thought of him as dead. We felt he would turn up, recovered, an adventurous and romantic hero. The letters were from Otto Schönthal. When mother had met him back in 1931 she was twenty-two years old. Then, Otto had been a young architecture student. Baby had considered him an 'inappropriate companion' for my mother at tennis parties and other social functions at the pre-war Villa Mendl. It seems that he had presumed to make an afternoon visit *wearing a leather jacket!* Despite Baby's anguished disapproval, my mother and Otto had become firm friends.

In deep grief from the recent loss of her mother, father and brother Fritz, my mother had been obliged to take the helm of a vast commercial enterprise, to steer through volatile political times, to pay crippling death taxes, and to navigate the conflicting advice of her executives, none of whom she trusted. She was totally unprepared for her role. In notes for her memoir, she wrote: '*My father never had business people to the house. Business was never discussed. When I was young I didn't know what my father did. When I was asked I said he was a gamekeeper. I had no idea ... At dinner my father would ask what we did at school, what Kant said to so and so, what Nietzsche replied to Kant, what Mozart wrote, what Beethoven said, what relationship Haydn had to Mozart, the importance of Bach in music . . . we didn't learn anything about money. Not a thing!'*

Increasingly, my mother drew closer to Otto, relying on his advice and testing his tactics for conducting meetings and negotiations. She recovered her spirits and they carried on the game with strategies they planned together. It was he who had encouraged my mother to return to Austria.

The fight to reclaim all of her family's property seized by the Germans during the war was not yet over. Hearings were to be held to decide on the full restitution of my mother's property. Having cut her trip to Austria short to hurry home to my father, she had not completed her preparation for those hearings, so she occasionally had to go to town to make phone calls or send telegrams. Sometimes telegrams were sent to her in German. This could prove difficult. Our neighbour, who was rich enough to have his own telephone, would come across to let us know he'd received a phone call from the post office. A telegram had arrived. The message was often a jumble created from unfamiliar sounds phoned through on unreliable equipment. Bettina always worked it out. But the telegrams caused tension. They were in German. German was the language of the recent enemy. So my mother spoke German. She had said that she was Austrian. Where was Austria, anyway? Weren't Austria and Germany the same? All bloody Krauts! Why all these telegrams suddenly? These days, whispers followed us as we walked down Barraba's dusty main street.

A Story Dreamt Long Ago

The stories, the letters, the telegrams all threaded through the daily ritual of our lives. I had no way of knowing that they were any different from the stories woven into the lives of other children. They took place in distant lands, much like the myths of ancient Greece that I was reading with rapture. The whispers in the street were more unsettling. There was a sense of threat. I pushed the memory of the 'Nazi bitch' episode aside but I clenched my fist as I walked.

Because from the earliest days of their friendship my father knew all my mother's secrets, now she could share all her concerns. He was wiser in his grasp of international matters than his isolated life might imply. He had a profound understanding of human nature. He was able to console and advise appropriately and provide a calm sounding board as she wrote her careful letters in reply.

•◆•

I was nine years old and growing quickly. My joints ached. Night after night my father rubbed my knees when I woke sobbing from 'growing pains'. Even during the day my legs ached. I stopped running, I walked carefully, I sat around, I had mysterious fevers and my mother felt my swollen neck glands with concern. There were whispers of rheumatic fever and of polio – there was an epidemic at that time – but the symptoms did not seem to fit. When the pain could no longer be ignored I was put in hospital for observation. Tests showed no clear results. I stopped eating, lost weight and grew weak. My thick hair grew lank and brittle then fell out in chunks, leaving bald patches; I must have been a frightful sight. The only treatment offered was bed rest and observation. I was given tonics, iron supplements and cod-liver oil. Once again I was separated from my mother but this time my desperation was overshadowed by the pain. I felt too weak to worry, too weak to fear, too weak to care and I knew my mother was safely at home; on the farm with my father and Dawn.

As soon as it was evident that I would be in hospital for some time, boxes arrived from Sydney. My cousins had collected books and dolls and Lizzie made me a beautiful pink satin nightie, the neck edged with a wide band of lace. I was too tired to hold the heavy books and I did not have the energy to construct games for the dolls, but the nightie was a joy. When I wasn't wearing it I would take it from my bedside locker and rest my hand on its cool, slippery surface.

For three long months my mother visited each day. By now we had a car, but even so the twelve-mile drive must have meant the fragmentation of her busy day, with my father not well and Dawn barely past babyhood. She sat beside my bed and told me stories, peeled oranges and fed me sections, coaxing: 'One for Daddy, one for Dawn, one for Jinny, one for Lizzie . . .' but by then I had pushed her hand away. Four segments of an orange was a huge amount to eat. I could just manage it to please her.

My mother's usual impatience vanished during these visits. I never had the sense that she was in a hurry or that she wanted to get away. I counted the hours till she came back again. After three months of unchanged illness and no diagnosis, one afternoon I begged my mother not to leave, or else to take me with her. She went to see the matron and announced that she was taking me home. There was a conversation in the corridor; two determined, intelligent women in debate. The matron argued that it would be life-threatening to take me away. My mother stated that there had been no diagnosis, that I was terribly unhappy and would have more stimulus at home. The matron demanded that an indemnity be signed and that the doctor be informed before I leave.

Bettina hurriedly complied. She threw my things into the car and didn't stop to dress me, just picked me up and left before her courage failed.

I was happier at home, ate a little more, read books to Dawn and slowly gathered strength. Dawn did most of my jobs now. She had become my father's helper and he offered encouragement by heaping praise on all her efforts. I did not feel jealous, just diminished, and when my legs ached badly I didn't really care.

My condition did not improve. Pus-filled wounds appeared on my swollen joints. Finally we all went to Sydney to see a specialist. He felt sure I had osteomyelitis, an infection of the bones causing abscesses and degeneration. It does not appear to have been a rare condition amongst children at the time. My knee joints and right elbow were affected. Open seeping abscesses throbbed and drained and showed no sign of spontaneous healing. Ultimately an operation was performed to clean and sterilise these wounds. The specialist who performed this at a small private hospital was elderly and extremely gentle. I was conscious of his soft voice, explanations, cool hands and repeated eye contact throughout the operation. I was completely reassured. My father was beside my bed and held me steady. I felt we were working together on a project to 'fix me up' and I knew that it would work.

Dad and the doctor separated on the veranda outside my room. I watched the way they shook hands and read into their relationship a deep affinity and trust. This confirmed my safety.

Years later the diagnosis was confirmed and doctors were astounded at the resilience I'd shown before the days of sophisticated antibiotics. In the new year I went back to school and gradually resumed some of my chores, although never again with the same assurance. I had become thin, fragile, inept. My sense of purpose had been shattered. I was no longer the invincible helper and supporter of my parents, protector of Dawn. I was not the competent builder of castles, splitter of logs, cunning catcher of horses. I had become a vulnerable little girl in a very big, strange world.

4

We go to Fairyland together

Within six weeks of the operation the abscesses had healed and I was eating voluntarily. I was still walking carefully as the damaged bone needed time to heal. There were days of pain but my body was mending.

Towards the end of the year a new plot was hatched. Bettina was excited. She had refused to return to Austria again alone; now the plan was for all of us to go together, to go with her to Fairyland. She made applications for our passports. There was a problem with my father's documentation; there seemed to be no record of his birth. He said that often happened in the bush. Statutory declarations were signed but this did not suffice. Time was slipping by and my mother canvassed my father's family for information. Aunty Tess was always calm and logical. She asked my mother exactly what searches had been made, covering what years? When my mother gave her answers Tess responded,

'You'll not find anything after the 1890s – try about the time I was born – the 1880s.'

Mother was astonished, 'He couldn't be that old! That would make him seventy! Are you sure?'

Tess smiled. 'I always thought he'd had you on a bit. I ought to know – he's my twin – he was born on 31 July 1881. I was born on 1 August. We didn't share a birthday.' Eventually the documents confirmed this truth.

We were to travel by boat. A huge ship with real beds. Painted white, with funnels. It was called the *Oceania* and belonged to the elegant Italian cruise line, Lloyd Triestino. We were to sail from Sydney to Genoa. Mother told us stories of her adventures aboard ships, about the world trip she made in 1937. She had left Vienna by train for London. Otto Schönthal saw her off. He pressed a St Christopher medal into her hand to ensure a safe journey. She and Baby embarked at Southampton and sailed on a cargo boat through the Mediterranean, the Suez Canal and along the coast of Africa, heading south. She explained that on a passenger boat the passengers were cargo – on a cargo boat the passengers were . . . *passengers*! She and Baby were nurtured with loving care by a specialist crew used to serving travellers with exotic tastes. Meals were varied and fresh, based on the purchases from local markets as the ship slid down the coast from Aden to Mombasa to Durban and other ports between. They offloaded manufactured goods: clothing, books, whisky. The ship reloaded bales of sisal, copper ignots, coffee and ivory. My mother sat on deck sketching the workers in the holds, the markets, the wharfside traders. When the cargo exchange was scheduled for several days the passengers hired cars and went on overnight sorties exploring Africa. Some of these outings were safari style with crew members going along to ensure that all went smoothly. My mother was a keen and talented painter, and a small collection of watercolours commemorates the journey.

However, my mother remained silent about the second trip she made in 1938 when she crossed the ocean to reach New Zealand and then, precariously, Australia.

•—•

Now that we were about to embark on our own journey Bettina gave us details of the big house we were to stay at, Villa Mendl, with its enormous garden, forty-five acres of lawns, orchards, vegetables, stables and outhouses, quite close to the heart of Vienna. We learnt about the wineries and the forestry estates in the mountains. We were told about snow and music concerts in palaces with crystal chandeliers.

My father was stronger now and happy. I could sense his relief that we would not be separated once again. My parents had lived under the constant threat that Bettina would have to return to Vienna to press her claims to her property personally or forfeit them. Now the threat of separation was replaced by eager anticipation of this new adventure. Enthusiasm suffuses the scenes that flash across my memory. My father made arrangements for the care of the farm and animals. Some stock was sold, the mares were put in foal. Fences were secured. Dawn and I, now aged seven and nine, were sent to Sydney to be outfitted for the voyage.

As though a spell was cast, two shy children were turned into fairy princesses. We were equipped with frocks, strangely unfamiliar and clinging around our legs. We had been used to overalls and cut-down dungarees, much more suitable for farmyard occupations. Now there were red gingham sundresses, floral frocks with frilly sleeves, soft velvet pinafores in bottle-green with lacy blouses, and outfits of grey woollen slacks with cosy silk-lined jackets. All of these were designed, assembled and stitched in Marianne's household. Our vocabulary grew. We learnt new words: organdie, Vyella, brocade, hailspot, taffeta, chantilly . . .

The *pièces de resistance* of our Fairyland wardrobe were our formal dinner dresses. Two each. I remember every detail as though I had hand-stitched it. They were lovingly designed by Lizzie, a genius with fabric and colour. The organdie dresses were identical, white with huge puff sleeves, narrow bodices and wide ankle-length skirts. Around the hem mine had giant blue water lilies, handpainted, and there was a blue taffeta sash, tied in a bow at the back, its tails hanging to the hem. It was to be worn with blue ballet slippers.

Dawn's organdie was identical except that the handpainted flowers were pink roses and she had pink ballet slippers. The ballerina length had been chosen so that we could walk more naturally as we negotiated stairs, and would not step backwards onto our skirts.

As well as organdies, we each had a 'brocade', a more elegant full-length frock, high-waisted, with a 'Josephine' neckline. Mine was a glimmering blue and silver; Dawn's a sunrise-pink threaded through with gold. Matching ballet slippers completed the outfits again. These were to be worn on the most formal occasions, including dining at the captain's table on board the *Oceania* en route to Genoa.

Our inexperience in wearing formal clothes was carefully monitored. Under the rigorous tuition of our cousins, Dawn and I were shown how to walk in slippery patent-leather shoes. The waxed floor demanded grace and balance. The unfamiliar skirts brushed against our legs, shortening our steps. Our bodies were adapted from rock climbing, chasing after calves, jumping over logs and stinging nettles to the more stately requirements of indoor occupations. We were taught to hold our heads as though wearing coronets, to keep our shoulders square, our rounded tummies in. We clutched imaginary posies in our left hands and lifted our long skirts with our right hands as we climbed the stairs. 'Left hand, right foot, do not look down, eyes up, smile.' All this was carefully practised and critiqued.

We also learnt to curtsy, dropping to the appropriate depth according to the age and title of the person we were meeting. We practised ardently. We could not afford a gaffe. To become tangled up and flattened to the floor in the midst of a curtsy was our greatest dread.

This training in etiquette and deportment was carried out under the title 'Learning to be a Princess'. It's not surprising that the tuition had effect; later I discovered that my Aunt Marianne had once been creative assistant to the famous Austrian dancer Grete Wiesenthal. Grandfather Fritz Mendl had built a dance studio in the garden of Villa Mendl. There, the great Wiesenthal coached Marianne and, in turn, Marianne coached the lesser acolytes and, eventually, her nieces.

Dawn and I were gleeful students and embroidered lessons

with our own embellishments. We created silver paper 'jewellery' at every opportunity, we invented complicated titles, we gave grand speeches designed for every possible occasion. We were quickly developing our lifelong aptitude for accepting any situation. 'Normal' did not seem to apply to us. We didn't understand its meaning. We had no way of weighing our experiences against the more usual lives of our peers. As long as the family was going to be together we felt happy and safe. We were always treated kindly and we clearly understood what was expected of us in the diverse situations we found ourselves in. After all, carrying a posy was only slightly different from carrying the eggs up to the house – you did it carefully.

Could the adults have really been so desperately committed to 'making a good impression'? It seems they were. Even now one of the 'Old Vienna Network' will remind me of some small faux pas that occurred during that family visit, tenderly forgiven because they knew about my strange childhood.

When the transformation of Dawn and me was well under way my parents joined us from the farm. The shopping began all over again. We had only ever seen Joe in dungarees and his one good pair of flannel strides. Now he strutted about showing off smart suits, cream tuxedos, silk cravats, a smoking jacket in turquoise-blue velvet, and, to our delight, he waddled and flapped the penguin tails of his dinner suit. He turned out to have a flair for fashion and was totally at home in every outfit. The formal black bow ties were a challenge; I was deputised to handle them while my mother dried her nail varnish. Bettina, Marianne and sometimes even my gentle Uncle Gustav, Google, tutored me. I stood on a chair to fix

A Story Dreamt Long Ago

the bow tie in place with an infallible series of wrist flicks. This became a skill considered more important than knowing where the speckled hen was laying her eggs back on the farm. Values changed.

Marianne provided a large black leather trunk fitted with gleaming brass handles and lined with silk. One side housed a series of small drawers. The trunk was slowly filling with Mother's clothes. Sparkling evening clouds of cream and silver. Sunset-patterned silks and a deadly number in black crêpe; on the back, embroidered with sequins, was a mobile but discreet black dragon. I have it still among my treasures, crumpled and dull, yet I cannot pass it on: it has too much of my mother woven through its threads.

During these last weeks of preparation Joe and Bettina took the opportunity to go out. They both loved the 'flicks' but were highly selective about what they went to see. They analysed the themes, the stars, the director's previous history. When all of this passed muster they set off with an air of excited anticipation.

Bettina's interest in flicks was a little more than casual. Years later I learnt of her involvement.

In 1931, Otto Schönthal had befriended a very beautiful young Jewish model and film hopeful named Hedwig Kiesler. With the increasing anti-Semitic influence from Germany, Hedgwig, or Hedy as she was called, was anxious to establish a film career in America. According to the stories that Bettina told, Hedy discussed this dilemma with Otto. He was already a very clever and creative operator in the Viennese business environment. Following the death of Fritz Mendl junior, he'd become Bettina's key support in her struggles with the directors and board of Ankerbrot. She was now the chief custodian of the Ankerbrot empire. Like Otto, Bettina was increasingly despairing of European politics and willing to assist anyone of Jewish background who was trying to exit Europe for a more hopeful future.

Hedy was not willing to leave Europe without sound contacts in America. She had made some minor films and felt she had a toehold on an acting career that would be very difficult to re-establish as an unknown outsider in America. She needed a strategy for instant recognition. Schönthal came up with the solution. 'Do something shocking!' But what to do? 'Take your clothes off – on screen,' was his suggestion. After much deliberation, Hedy agreed that this might produce the attention she needed to make her escape.

Then it came down to practicalities. If such a film was to be made, who would make it and how would it be financed? Inquiries led the little group, which now included Bettina, to the Czechoslovakian director Gustav Machaty who had recently released the daring film *Erotikon* with impressive success. Now Machaty was commissioned to write and direct the vehicle of Hedy's escape. The film was to be bankrolled by a loan from the Ankerbrot advertising budget, on Bettina's authority. It was hoped that the film would be successful so that the earnings would repay the loan and no questions would be asked. In case the scheme misfired there was to be no publicity about the financing and production.

This careful plot was completely successful. The film *Ecstasy* was made and released in 1933 and went down in history as the first to present nudity on screen. It is recognised, even today, for its artistic merit and is often shown at film festivals. At the time, the response was mixed, varying from outrage to admiration, but there was universal recognition that a milestone in film-making had been reached.

Although the film was banned in America and severe censorship limited viewers and earnings, the debt was repaid. More importantly, the notoriety gave Hedy the fame she needed to attract Hollywood attention. When Louis B. Meyer visited London in the months following the film's release in 1933, he welcomed an opportunity (orchestrated by Schönthal) to meet the actress. Before Meyer left Europe, Hedy had secured a contract to go to Hollywood; there, as Hedy Lamarr, she became one of the best-known stars of her era.

•◆•

At last the preparation for our great adventure was complete. My father's relatives were visited, farewells made. We surged through milling crowds and looked up at the huge white ship. We walked the inappropriately fragile gangplank and stood along the rail, holding coloured streamers connected to our cousins on the wharf. Among the cousins now visiting Sydney was a New Zealander – Richard, Lucie's eldest son.

During my visits to Sydney in the last two years, in my mother's absence and for my operation, I had got to know Richard, or Dick as we called him, well. He had come from New Zealand to work on the Snowy River Scheme and often stayed with Uncle Gustav and Aunt Marianne when he was on brief breaks from work. At twenty-three, he was of a similar age to our three cousins there. On his visits he took time to encourage me. He admired my painting. He told me about his work as an engineer, which to me seemed very similar to building a castle or a fortress. He included me in outings. As well as the streamers in my sweaty hands I clutched my birthday presents from this beloved cousin: a seventy-two-piece Lakeland coloured pencil set and a book about the adventures of the legendary cowboy Tom Mix. I loved both gifts with a passion.

Then the ship moved away, the streamers broke, our cousins waved, grew smaller, disappeared.

•◆•

Life on board the *Oceania* settled into a blissful routine. There were very few children, but Dawn and I were used to that. There were two fair-haired American boys of roughly our age who responded gleefully to our initial approaches only to be called away again and again by their parents. Finally Bettina explained that they were not allowed to play with us as we had dark hair. It seems the parents suspected that we were Aboriginal, but after making discreet inquiries they decided my mother must be of Gypsy ancestry. In any event, they did not want to risk contamination from these unsavoury sources. In response to this my father said in his broadest brogue, 'Aye, I'll not tell them of my mother from the Auld Country fer fear they might jump overboard.' We all hooted with laughter. The boys were further handicapped by having a person called a 'nanny' who got in the way of every enterprise. We thought this most peculiar and felt sorry for the boys who missed out on our adventures.

My parents quickly formed a bond with a couple of fellow passengers, Irene and John Vincent, who conveniently had three daughters of similar ages to Dawn and me. They were blonde too but had a very different outlook. Irene and John travelled and lived in many parts of the world working with native people, researching, writing, lecturing. Our education on board ship took on a new direction as we learnt about their experiences and beliefs. There was a loosely formal arrangement that the five children gathered on deck at ten each morning. At least one of the parents would be present for two hours. What I now recognise as a lesson was presented. Bettina contributed the history of the Hapsburg Empire, which had not been touched on in any of my history classes at school. She gave descriptions of Viennese social life and details of the personalities of artists, musicians and philosophers. We wrote, painted, looked at photographs, told stories and discussed the current-affairs topics of the day.

We learnt about different world currencies, trade agreements, and the adults related their travel experiences. My father discussed bush lore, imparted his knowledge of Aboriginal lifestyle and its essential connection with sustainable land use. He was well aware of the deterioration of grazing lands due to overstocking in the low rainfall areas where he'd lived, and was concerned about the misuse of precious water when the old sacred watering places were opened out to provide drinking access for European stock – as well as kangaroos, that bred to plague proportions. We spread out maps and charts, we experimented with poetry in many languages, we enacted battles and negotiated settlements. We were totally enchanted by this new form of education and waited eagerly for each day's session to begin. Sometimes we spent the afternoons preparing presentations for our captive audience. These included song and dance, tribal ritual, legal procedure and whatever else had captured our interest for the day.

The parents were so interested in each other's experiences that all four of them participated with great enthusiasm.

During the afternoon we played without obvious supervision. We stood at the rail watching the waves go by. We read books from the stock we had brought with us and shared the exotic literature provided by the Vincent girls. I vividly recall *The Bridge of San Luis Rey, Kidnapped* and *Robinson Crusoe*. We played deck games, cards and chess with liberal interpretations of the rules and frequent adaptations so that the smallest Vincent member of our group, who was barely six, could keep pace with the action.

At four o'clock each day we joined the adults in the huge glass cocktail lounge overlooking the front of the boat. Here, platters of delicious Italian pastries, *dolci*, were served. Bettina tried in vain to restrict our consumption on the basis that we could not possibly eat dinner after four, five, or even six pastries each. With angelic smiles we drifted through the crowd, every adult courteously ensuring we were offered just one more. Restraint was impossible. Briefly, my mother made a rule that we were not allowed into the cocktail lounge. It lasted one whole day. My father asked who would be looking after us while he was feasting in the cocktail lounge. In defence of our gluttony he pointed out that he had never seen us eat with better appetites. My parents were still concerned about my health and he felt that consuming a platter of *dolci* was much better than having to beg me to eat each sparse mouthful. Despite the *dolci*, by dinner time we were all starving again and ate generous servings of the delicious Italian food.

A Story Dreamt Long Ago

Dinner on board ship was very formal. My mother wore her lovely gowns and spent a long time getting ready. Our dresses were laid out by the cabin staff. So that we did not get grubby or crushed, we dressed at the last minute, presenting ourselves to our parents for inspection, just in time for me to fix Joe's tie before we set out.

We sat at the captain's table and this caused my mother some distress, because she now found it difficult to accept my father's habitual table manners. Throughout his life he had sat at the head of the table, not square and straight as she now thought proper, but with his long legs conveniently to the side. Furthermore, he had always drunk his tea from a saucer, so that it would be cool enough, and so that he didn't have to mess about with a fragile china cup handle far too small for his thick fingers. When he sat down to a meal he expected the tea to be set before him immediately; the most important thing when he came in from work on the farm was two or three cups of strong tea. Patiently, he explained to the Italian waiters that this was what was needed. Bettina tried to intervene. She set out to convince my father that tea would be served at the meal's end and that he should wait. 'A man might bloody choke' was his retort. The Italian waiters bowed, nodded and brought him a strange assortment of bowls, saucers, cups and dishes which he finally assembled to his liking. Elegantly sipping from a saucer, he performed his personal tea ceremony.

The captain, trained in the refinements, observed my father's habits and followed suit. He sat sideways at the table and occasionally drank his tea out of a saucer. My mother was not to be appeased. She pleaded with my father, but more and more of the men around the captain's table assumed side-on positions and ordered tea at the beginning of the meal, served with two saucers. I never discovered whether there was an acknowledged agreement among the men or whether the conspiracy was subliminal.

Oceania went through the Suez Canal. We were woken one morning to stand along the rail as the locks closed behind us and the ship slowly rose to the next level. Of course our 'lessons' had described this engineering feat and we were thrilled to be participants. We made a day trip into Cairo where the ladies shopped for exotic silks and perfumes, and where my father, with an associate, took us to see some belly dancing. Belly dancing immediately consumed all our energies for the next few months. Lacking competent instruction we could not quite master the techniques. Dad thought our efforts hilarious, and when we seemed to lose interest he would encourage us by demonstrating, with the straightest face, a new technique. Exotic wriggles ensued while my mother struggled to establish decorum with a warning: 'Joe!' To which he would respond, '*You* show us, Mum. How does it go again?' And she would laughingly oblige with a fair imitation. After consideration, Dad would say with a wicked grin: 'You don't seem to have the right knack for it, Betty. I like your Spanish dance better, the one with the shawls and the castanets.' This was undoubtedly her best performance, but highly dangerous in confined spaces. She used to perform it for us often on the farm, swinging a grey army blanket or a checked tablecloth, spinning and twirling and stamping her bare feet in the red dust as she clicked her castanets, bringing a gypsy world to us against the last glow of sunset.

A Story Dreamt Long Ago

One afternoon there was a knock on the cabin door. My father opened it to a shipboard friend. 'Come in, come in, the ladies are just belly dancing,' he said. The gentleman declined and retreated hastily. Dad winked at Mum and gathered up his hat and jacket for the afternoon deck games, which by now included lessons in tap dancing, with himself as instructor. At those 'concert' afternoons on the farm he'd often entertained us with his Fred Astaire routines. We had told the Vincent girls about them, and in response to our pleading Dad had given a demonstration. The report went out to parents, who first observed and then participated. Soon there were regular dance sessions around the deck. On this particular Lloyd Triestino voyage, society matrons and their portly partners followed flamboyant dance routines from a range of cultures and my father's imagination, mixed with tap and a touch of the Irish jig. However, as the ship drew nearer to Europe, my mother was becoming more and more conscious of her social obligations, and an agreement was forged that the sacred Viennese waltz be strictly reserved for the ship's ballroom, after dinner, when Dawn and I wore our organdies with their swirling skirts.

As we stood at the rail to watch the *Oceania* leave the Suez Canal Bettina told us how she had last seen her brother Otto in Cairo, before the war, in 1937. He was the one sibling she had been close to in her childhood. They had shared the nursery and Abby, their adored nanny. Through Bettina's darkest days in Cheltenham, Otto had visited. He had been there to console her through the death of their mother, father and brother. He was a rebel who dared to challenge his father's authority. He was a daredevil pilot and an inspired engineer. He was her hero, elder brother and good friend. Somehow, unexpectedly, at a social function in a crowded room, she had caught this beloved brother's glance. To the best of her knowledge he was living in Berlin, yet here he was in Cairo, coming towards her, laughing.

'Have you got any money?' he asked.

'What for?'

'I'm flying and need fuel,' Otto explained.

'Which side are you flying for?' Bettina wanted to know.

'The other side.'

'I'm sorry, I'm right out of cash,' she replied.

They never met again.

'Where is he now?' we chorused. We'd heard many times that he was 'lost'. Lost things often turned up unexpectedly. We were close to where she had last seen him. Perhaps he would suddenly drop down out of the sky or appear out of the desert, racing his motorbike along the bank of the canal. In our imaginations we saw him laughing, waving to Bettina, waving to us. But my mother didn't raise her arm to wave. She took a step closer to my father. In a quiet sad voice she repeated 'lost' in answer to our question. In our excitement we persisted. 'How can a grown-up get lost for such a long time? By now someone must have found him.' Bettina attempted to explain. 'In wars a lot of people get lost – sometimes you never can find them.' The concept was a mystery to us.

•◆•

One of our final adventures with the Vincent girls was our visit to Pompeii. There are faded photographs of us climbing in the rubble and of our parents posed against the ruins. My father picked up a small white marble chip as a memento. This stayed in the pocket of his sports coat for a long time. He would sometimes take it out and consider it as it lay in the palm of his hand. He seemed to be reading history in the texture of its surface. 'Just imagine,' he would murmur as he turned the pebble over. 'Imagine how they lived.'

Baby, whom we were instructed to address as 'Tante Maria', had come all the way to Genoa to meet us, travelling in a car provided for us, with a chauffeur called Uruski. She had been reunited with my mother two years earlier; this second reunion focused on the introduction to my father and to us children. Maria von Kozaryn was tall, straight and dignified. Her long, fine hair was pulled back into a bun. Bettina had bestowed the misnomer 'Baby' upon her as the most inappropriate nickname she could think of. She habitually spoke only in German or in fluent French, although we discovered that she could speak English well. She conversed comfortably with my father. My mother had decreed that Dawn and I were now required to speak French or German with everyone other than our parents. On that first meeting we were reduced to mutually curious smiles. Baby returned to Vienna by train to oversee the large amount of luggage while we travelled on by car, taking with us only what we would need on our journey.

We wound through the Alps, which towered above us, two-dimensional, like papier-mâché mountains with glittering snowy peaks. We drove through tiny villages with unfamiliar architecture. At night we stayed in quaint accommodation. Our eyes were glued to the car windows; we were fascinated by this strange, green, fairyland place. There were deep dark forests and castles on the hillsides. At any moment a dragon might appear.

At the end of the long drive we came at last to the outskirts of Vienna. Mother gestured at the familiar landmarks of her life, but it was all too much for us to follow. Finally the car turned into a wide driveway of cobbled stones overhung by trees. The house at the end of the driveway was three storeys high, with ornate ironwork on its lower windows. A statue of St Leopold, clad in armour, sword drawn, guarded the driveway. We stopped. Uruski, the chauffeur, held open the doors and we clambered out, gaping at the upper windows, where the rooms were obviously waiting for us.

My mother took a deep breath. 'So,' she said, 'we have arrived.'

5

Living in Villa Mendl

After the long boat trip, Dawn and I rushed around the house and garden like dogs unleashed. We poked and sniffed in every nook and cranny, we explored, examined and questioned. Then we took possession of our territory. The house had been divided into two large apartments. Aunt Mimi, the wife of my mother's brother Otto, and her two children, Hans and Eva, were living in one, while the other was to be ours.

Baby had worked hard to prepare our side of the house. She had implemented renovations and collected remnants of the original furnishings from storage and from what had remained at the country estates. The large rooms were bare but beautiful, with honey-coloured parquet flooring, high ceilings, tall windows and panelled walls disguising built-in storage. The bathrooms were an adventure in themselves. There were three. One was being used for storing coal. Apologies were made. Dawn and I marvelled at the size of it, the lavish black-and-white marble tiles, the steps down into the tub, the ornate taps and hoses that no longer worked. It stored a lot of coal.

The bathroom we used led off our parent's bedroom. It had *two* bathtubs, two hand-basins and ample space to waltz.

On the lower floor were the reception rooms, the foyer, cloakrooms, Mother's large office, which had been her father's, and the ballroom with its long wall of French windows leading on to the balcony, with steps into 'the Master's garden'. These were the rooms where the main treasures of the art collection had been displayed, before the Nazis had moved in.

By the time that we arrived in 1952, although the rooms were sparsely furnished, much of the aura of the home had been restored. The family living rooms were on the middle level. This was where my mother had wandered when she returned from Cheltenham, violin in hand, looking in vain for her mother. Elegant curved stairs with an enticing polished banister rose from the wide foyer. Kitchens, dining rooms, sitting rooms and studies formed a maze for us to explore.

The upper floor housed nurseries, staff accommodation and storage. Large areas of the house had been blocked off as war damage left it dangerous and forbidden territory for us.

Our lives soon fell into a routine. Bettina was required to attend business meetings almost daily. Dawn and I had tutors who attempted to remedy our lack of formal education. We studied German, spoke French to Baby and kept diaries in French which she corrected daily. To avoid the tedious chore I insisted there was nothing to write about – in French. Our mathematics tutor had a moustache and a fetish for decimals, which seemed pointless to us. We could not foresee the advantages of conversion to the metric system.

Despite the attempts to regulate our lives we lived mostly in the gardens, but as the weather grew cooler the ballroom was an especially favoured play area. Here we invented complex ceremonies for the coronation of Elizabeth II, which took place that year. We robed ourselves in musty curtains, devised crowns, wrote interminable speeches, designed rituals and ceremonies and shared the many roles required by this serious occasion. We ensnared whatever passing playmates were available to participate and allocated ceremonial roles of less importance than our own. I learnt more about the crowned heads of Europe from this pastime than in all my history lessons. There was, of course, much curtsying, at which we were adept.

We were delighted when it snowed. We built snowmen in the garden while we eagerly waited for our first white Christmas.

My mother had described for us the lovely little parish chapel where the Mendl family attended Mass each Sunday and where she and Otto had received their first communion. Shortly after we arrived she took us there to introduce us to the priest and to arrange for our instruction for communion. I remember walking down the narrow lanes, accompanied by my father or Baby, and the tedious discussions in awkward English and confusing German, as the priest went through the process of explaining the sacrament and our obligations.

In Australia, Dawn and I had barely been to church; we rarely visited town at all. Even if we had been familiar with Australian Catholicism, we would never have recognised it here. In Austria, Mass was a grand performance with music, incense and priestly robes. One could spend the entire hour just looking at the stories in the windows. There were statues and naves and fonts. Every surface was embellished with symbols and references to ritual. Even the few bare stones were old, some dating from Roman times.

Mass was a great resource for our coronation ceremony game; God seemed quite friendly too. We were happy participants and took our first communion with utter sincerity.

❧

From time to time we left Vienna to visit my mother's other properties. We went to the manor house at Velm, not far from Vienna, and we stayed in the mountain village at Veich where there was a dairy, forestry estates and hunting lodges all requiring some management decisions from Bettina and all providing magical playgrounds for Dawn and me.

During the summer and autumn we spent weekends and short holidays at the medieval castle, Itter, in the Tyrol, which was still in Mother's possession. This fortress stood high on a cliff commanding the approach along the narrow valley far below. Following the best traditions, the entry was by a steep and narrow access way blocked by a portcullis. The heavy iron bars threatened with their dangerous points as we went through. We had seen a similar portcullis in the film *Robin Hood* and were delighted to have one of our own. We felt that the inside of the castle was hollow, cold and inconvenient – not what we considered a 'good camp' – but there was plenty of room to play.

Itter was being renovated and was ultimately fully outfitted and staffed as an elite hotel, although Bettina later complained that people who were rich and famous frequently forgot to pay their bills and that the lavish enterprise was turning out to be a commercial disaster.

Now that we were in Austria, my mother was suddenly aware of our total ignorance of the family background, particularly her father's achievements that she had been reared to honour. She used every opportunity to fill in the details of the history which, until now, we had only vaguely understood.

My grandfather had been in the army when he was a young man. 'He served one year as an officer but he was very naughty in the army,' my mother told us. He played the guitar and could compose songs in an instant, and often they were about the high-ranking officers. He was sent off to Hungary where his German lyrics were less likely to be understood.

One of his friends was an engineer who had been employed by the government to study the dangers posed to workmen by new types of machinery that were becoming a feature of modern industry. This friend told my grandfather about the terrible way bread was prepared. 'You wouldn't eat it if you knew,' he told him.

The bakers worked long shifts and often slept at work on bags of flour. They peed behind the stockpiles of flour, then went back to kneading the dough without washing their hands. They had to immerse their hands in wet yeast dough for hours and their skin became infected. Scabs developed, and the scabs came off in the dough. There were rats everywhere. When the bread was cooked it was delivered on open carts and left outside the doors of people's houses, freely exposed to germs.

My grandfather decided that he wanted to introduce a new, healthier way of making bread. He decided to buy a small bakery in Vienna and went to his parents to ask for some money. But he had been terrible with money in the past, was unreliable, joked about everything and took nothing seriously. His parents said they wouldn't lend him any money as he'd only waste it.

Another one of my grandfather's close friends had recently inherited great wealth. This friend was a playwright and disinterested in his new fortune. He happily offered to lend my grandfather as much as he needed. My grandfather's parents, horrified at the possible scandal there might be if the venture was unsuccessful and he couldn't repay his friend's money, offered to provide the finance after all. In partnership with his brother Heinrich he bought the small bakery, which still operates under the name of the company he established, Ankerbrot.

After studying baking and organic chemistry, which he hadn't known much about, he set up a laboratory, produced bread and even designed the bakery's bread carts and ovens – they are still using his designs today. At that time people didn't have any idea of hygiene. My grandfather made the workmen sleep away from where they baked, and installed baths and showers for their use.

The bakery had only six ovens and operated flat out with three shifts a day. It was going so well that my grandfather had foundations laid for a huge bread factory. The challenge was how to build such an enormous roof when it would have to be able to expand with the heat from the ovens. He invented a concrete roof with a hinge in the middle to allow it to expand and contract without cracking. The new factory was a great success. There was nothing like it anywhere. People came from as far away as Russia to inspect it.

A Story Dreamt Long Ago

At the factory, it was a tradition to bake special bread at Christmas and Easter for the workers. Each man got a big, long loaf, but often, instead of taking the loaves home, the workers would trade them. People would wait outside the factory with goods they were willing to swap for a loaf of the fancy bread. My grandfather decided to start producing this special bread for sale. After that, the factory began to make Krakeys, little wholemeal rusks, and those sold very well. Then they made buns, and then they started to make cakes.

My grandfather had been shocked by the working conditions at the bakery when he had purchased it. 'If workers were treated like animals they would be better off,' he'd said. He bought the hill behind the factory and gave each of the workers a small garden about half an acre in size, where they grew vegetables and fruit. The gardener at Villa Mendl gave lectures to the workers on gardening, and supplied them with seedlings from the villa's garden.

Mother told us that as a consequence the Social Democrats hated my grandfather. He had taken the wind out of their sails. But he didn't do it for political reasons; he did it because he saw a need to change, and he really loved his workers. Dawn and I didn't understand the politics but we listened politely.

During World War I, Hungary and Czechoslovakia would not let Austria have any grain. 'They fed their pigs on grain while we were starving,' my mother said. A deputation was sent to Budapest to meet with the Hungarian prime minister. A very shrewd man, he elegantly entertained the deputation then sent them on their way with only a vague promise of some grain in the future. My grandfather, though he was not in a formal government position, had been put in charge of food distribution in Vienna. Seeing that the official deputation had had no success, he got in his car and went to Budapest himself. He met with Tisza, the Hungarian prime minister, and haggled for one train-load of grain to be dispatched from Hungary immediately. He then commandeered every available wagon and engine in Austria, engaged men to load the train and organised silos to receive it.

As a gesture of appreciation, the Emperor offered Fritz a title. My grandfather refused – he held that a person proved their value by what they did, not by the labels that they wore. Instead, the Emperor gave him a miniature pendant of the ancient Hapsburg Order of the Golden Fleece.

Even when the war ended, food was still scarce. The Mendls provided what they could to all the children in the district. They came with their plates and spoons and were given thick soup and bread, as much as they could eat. For some, it was the only meal of the day. The children sat down in the yard and the cook rolled out an enormous pot on wheels and dished out the food with a big ladle. There was not a drop of soup nor a crumb of bread wasted.

My mother and her brothers and sisters were not allowed to eat any more than anyone else. Even though my grandfather was in charge of the city's food distribution, his sense of fairness meant that his family was not given anything extra – it had to make do with little bags of bread, and sugar only once a fortnight, like everyone else. Occasionally the servants got extra food, and smuggled some to my mother and her brothers and sisters, but most days the children went hungry. Mother sighed as she recalled her childhood hunger and said, 'I'm really stunted. I'm smaller than other people. Big head, big belly.'

A Story Dreamt Long Ago

One day the Minister of Agriculture, Mr Yoland Fink, came to visit my grandfather. He was a handsome man with white hair and blue eyes. He was slim and very, very lively. He saw that the children were so undernourished. The next time he visited, his chauffeur rolled a round cheese as big as a cartwheel out of his big black car into the Villa Mendl courtyard. Mr Fink told my grandfather that it was for the children and the children only. Not for the servants. Not for the workmen. Nobody else was to have a piece, only the children. 'Oh, how we all enjoyed that cheese!' said my mother.

She also described her schooling at Villa Mendl. Lucie and Marianne had been taught by governesses, but by the time it was my mother's turn to be educated my grandmother had started a school in the garden of Villa Mendl. A modern school. She picked some young teachers under the guidance of a man called Yoden. He was an outstanding teacher, the uncle of Konrad Lorenz, who later won a Nobel Prize. He and his wife taught in the school as well. It was a fabulous school. According to my mother, a lot of the children who came out of it grew up to be world famous.

As a child, I sometimes experienced a sense of embarrassed disbelief as I listened to the stories my mother told. In my heart I accused her of tasteless dramatic invention; however, quite often irrefutable evidence proved she had actually understated certain things. But often I withdrew from sharing the experiences she recalled; it was as though I sat in judgment on her life, and only wanted to accept the clear, tidy, logical pieces she offered to us.

My mother explained to us that her father had planned to extend the family dynasty through his elder son and namesake. Young Fritz, seven years older than Bettina, was carefully prepared for his role, somewhat against his inclinations. Tall, thin with fine sensitive features, he wanted to be a painter and my mother told us he had studied under 'Kokoschka, who was quite a famous expressionist painter... he said that Fritz was very gifted. His paintings were accepted in the Salon in Paris and a friend of his exhibited them under a different name'. But young Fritz completely lacked his father's raw ambition. The politics and subversive tactics that opposed the development of Ankerbrot, from within the workers' unions and from the European political environment, confused him.

The stories Mother told us in Vienna were endorsed by comments and additions from Mucki and Agathe, who had shared the experiences. Agathe had been young Fritz's soulmate through this time. Often the intervention of the adults would extend the story into different shapes, then there would be a sharp reminder of our presence. '*Aber*, that's enough!' The adults would exchange meaningful glances and the 'children's edition' of the story would resume. Other times we would be sent to perform some chore while the intruding issue was more fully explored. We used the interjections to escape the complex, boring politics and drama that held so little interest for us.

Fritz senior was angry and critical. Rather than supporting each other through the difficult times, father and son blamed and avoided each other. Both clung increasingly to my mother as their trusted confidante and she loved them both. She was able to see their separate viewpoints but she could not heal the

A Story Dreamt Long Ago

breach. The growing tension following the death of his mother finally drove young Fritz to a nervous breakdown. My mother intervened in his treatment which she felt was worsening his condition and took him home for care. This made him entirely dependent on her to protect him from the cruel criticism of his father.

Fritz senior was increasingly frustrated by his own inability to continue to work effectively or to inspire his son to take full responsibility. Within two years of his wife's untimely death in 1928 he died from a heart attack. His heir, outwardly distinguished and responsible, operated behind a façade that relied heavily on Bettina's support. During sleepless nights he would wander through the house looking for her, often going to her room to wake her or to sit silently and watch her sleep. She found this invasion frightening. Fritz needed to know where she was at all times, suffering anxiety attacks when she was away from him. He became jealous of her friends and restrained her social contacts. While my mother understood these symptoms and lovingly hoped for improvement she felt trapped by family burdens. When relief came it took a tragic form. Hopeful of his improvement, in 1931 she encouraged Fritz to go away with friends for a week of skiing. He was a very good skier and the weather was perfect. Regaining some of his old daredevil mood, he accepted a lighthearted challenge to a downhill race. Something went wrong, there was a fall, Fritz was brought back to Vienna in an ambulance. There were murmurs of internal injuries, of inflammation, then – death. It was a brief eight months since his father had passed away.

Otto Mendl, Bettina's younger brother, was considered the

black sheep of the family. Despite the clear family resemblance to Fritz, Otto's nature was defiant and resilient. Early photographs show his features softened by humour, strengthened by confidence. He had become a brilliant aeronautical engineer, but ideological differences with his father had forced him to leave home early. In his first year of engineering studies he had filed the obligatory perfect cube, at that time the classic test of engineering manufacturing skill. Proudly he presented this to his father as a gift. Fritz Mendl measured the cube and found it a hair's-breadth out of square. This inadequacy enraged him. 'You must be either a liar or a fool to offer me such rubbish. I don't want either in my house!' The row flared out of control until Otto left home. 'We were all stunned,' my mother told us. 'Otto left the house without a word. He had worked so hard and this was the result. We were all upset but also knew that it was no good arguing with our father. Otto, of course, had not the guts to say anything. He never saw my father again. When my father was dying, Otto was in the next room. My father asked for Otto, and we tried to take him in, but he would not go. It was dreadful — they were both in agony.'

Otto finished his studies, but at twenty-one he dared to marry for love. Fritz seized on this as final evidence of Otto's irretrievable decadence. Citing genuine concern for her wellbeing, Fritz forbade Bettina to have any further contact with Otto. Torn by her loyalty to both, she could not entirely comply and guiltily visited Otto and Mimi at home and arranged secret street-corner meetings with Otto that echoed their escapades in England while she was at school. Her private justification was that she was trying to heal the family rift and that it was her role to maintain

Mendl connections for Otto and Mimi's adorable baby Hans. He was, after all, Fritz senior's first grandson. At this crucial time in their lives her connection with father and brother was marred by manipulation and lies. It was easy for Bettina to blame Mimi who had supplanted her as Otto's trusted companion and who revelled in her new position.

In about 1932, with his beautiful blonde Mimi, Otto moved to Berlin, a city that offered more scope for his passion for aircraft and flying, and an income to support his tiny family. Only the obligatory minimum share of the Mendl estate decreed by Austrian law was left to Otto, and ultimately to his children. Fritz senior had forbidden Bettina to have any contact with him and throughout her life she missed her brother dreadfully.

The death of her brother Fritz was the final tragedy that left Bettina the main family beneficiary. At twenty-two she had full responsibility and massive death taxes to pay. She was alone in Vienna without any experience of the business aspects of her new role. She felt keenly her obligation to her two married sisters, Lucie and Marianne, both of whom had escaped their father's obsessive ambition by marrying husbands he considered 'risky conveyances'. Like Otto, his elder daughters received only a small allocation from their father's estate in the form of shares in Ankerbrot. The dividend depended on Bettina's competence.

Bettina also felt her obligation to Otto, who had been the trusted companion of her childhood and constant visitor and confidant when she was at school in England. She was tragically jealous of Mimi. Moreover, she must have been aware that being an aeronautical engineer in Berlin in the 1930s meant working for Hitler's Luftwaffe. Perhaps she did not want to admit this to herself.

•◆•

In 1952, to prevent my father becoming bored while my mother was at her Ankerbrot meetings, he was sent off to the golf club, with a coach. He tried to take an interest and practised diligently to keep my mother happy and get some exercise. His coach reported that he was playing well, but my father resigned. His heart was not in it. He told my mother that he couldn't see the point in hitting a little ball all the way across the paddock and then walking miles to find it. But he did find another interest in Vienna that fascinated him. His old love, trotting. He bought a horse, a fragile little mare he fell in love with at a knackery sale. She was small and underfed and Dad raised his hand to bid – and found himself the owner. He called her Felsenquelle – 'a spring that flows from the rocks' – after the little spring-fed creek at Tarpoly.

Soon my father was going to the trotting track before daybreak each day. He was training, driving and grooming. He found a way to communicate with other trainers and attendants. Since the occupation of Vienna by the Allies and the need to communicate with British and American officials, most locals spoke some English. My father had taught himself some basic German so he was able to share strategies and tell yarns. I do not recall Felsenquelle winning many races, although subsequent horses did. She remained my father's favourite and gave him more satisfaction than many others with fashionable pedigrees.

My father came home in the afternoons to coach Dawn and

me at cricket which, he felt, needed some remedy. We could neither bowl nor bat with any skill despite his coaching. 'No matter – you'll come into it,' he reassured us. Because my legs were still not strong I was supposed to build up muscle and I had to learn to ride a pushbike. Dad coached me on the paths winding through the Master's garden and over the shuddery cobblestones. Dawn was by far the better rider, she did speed laps, she had wonderfully athletic legs and my father fancied she should be 'trained for the Olympics'; that's what he used to say to us when it was time to put the bikes away.

Often, in the evening, my parents would go out. They came to kiss us goodnight dressed in their elegant evening clothes, looking like royal personages from our coronation ceremony. Dawn and I felt warm and safe in the care of Tante Maria. We slept in the room my mother had shared with her brother Otto so many years before. As we drifted off to sleep it was easy to believe there were forces as unfailing as gravity to pull the world back into balance – even after a war.

•◆•

The Vienna of 1952 to which my mother took us was slowly recovering from war. No doubt there had been enormous progress with rebuilding and repair but to us, unused to scenes of devastation, the scars were everywhere. Barely a building stood without some evidence of bomb damage and in amongst the upright survivors, at frequent intervals there were gaps like missing teeth, sometimes boarded up to seal away the danger of the secret pits and pools that lay waiting to be repaired.

Vienna remained under the management of the four Allied

powers: England, France, America and Russia. The city had been divided into four separate zones, each one governed by a different power. These zones were marked like national borders; you had to show identification papers at each entry and exit. Each of the Allied powers demanded different papers in accordance with their own internal regulations. A simple trip across town required, as a minimum, four separate sets of identity papers. The entry into the Russian zone required a document referred to as a 'Grey Card' and the Russian barriers imposed the most stringent examination and inquisition. There were many stories of people asked to leave their vehicle, interrogated, kept hostage or bashed. Some disappeared, never to be seen again. We avoided the Russian zone whenever we could, but Ankerbrot was in the Russian zone and my mother went there to her office almost daily.

On those occasions when we did all cross into the Russian zone, our chauffeur, Uruski, handed out our Grey Cards as we approached the barrier. Everybody had their own card in case we were separated. Whatever happened, we were told to remain quiet and courteous and never to struggle or scream. Solemnly we would pass our cards to the guard when he approached the window. Inevitably we were waved through. As I sat waiting for the guard to examine my card, his face often a metre away from mine, I would observe the rough cloth of his uniform, his rosy pink face with eyes that sometimes expressed a childish friendliness. But their voices were always gruff.

'They're bits of kids; do you think they ever learnt to read?' my father would say.

On one particular day, upon leaving the Russian sector, the guards had taken our cards into the guardhouse and had just emerged and handed them back to Uruski. Suddenly Uruski in a calm, flat voice said, 'Please get down low. This could be dangerous.'

My mother, in the front, swung around and pushed our heads down. I glimpsed a pushbike rider coming up beside me, very close, apparently waiting his turn. As our car pulled away towards the opening gate the man started to pedal. Our car was now between him and the nearest guard. Uruski took his time. The pedaller kept up. I was sure he was holding onto some part of the car to give himself momentum. We seemed to be creeping through the fifty metres of open space between the Russian barrier and the next barrier leading into Allied territory. Then there was a shot from behind. I raised my head to see the rider's face grow pale as he dropped back. He fell from his bike and sprawled across the cobblestones. We glided to the next checkpoint. My father reached forward and rested his hand on Uruski's shoulder. Not a word was said.

•◆•

The war left other scars. I remember overhearing a conversation between my mother and Mucki, in which my mother was refusing to accept an invitation from an old family friend.

Mucki was saying: 'Surely, Bettina, you could be a little flexible; he so desperately wants to meet you again.'

'He can want,' my mother replied bitterly.

'*Warum doch?*' Mucki pleaded 'Why?' in her most honeyed voice. No one else would have dared demand a reason from my mother.

'He was an arch-Nazi,' Bettina answered. 'I will have no contact with him.'

Mucki dared the unthinkable. In pleasant tones she persisted. 'Could you be mistaken? I find it hard to believe. He was such a close friend of the family – of course, I was much younger then; I may not have understood.'

Bettina answered with a patience she reserved only for Mucki, but with a grim clarity. 'I am not mistaken, I was there, I saw him pushing people into trucks, he knows I saw him, he smiled at me – he need not imagine that he can seek my absolution now.'

Mucki dropped her eyes and murmured, 'I'm so sorry, Bettina. I did not realise.'

•━•

In the European spring of 1953, having resolved her immediate business matters, my mother seemed to have more time. In order to share my father's interest, she had been driving trotters in the many ladies' races. To his delight, she won the European Ladies' Driving Championship. She also re-established her contact with Colonel Alois Podhajsky, now head of Vienna's famous Spanish Riding School. Podhajsky had been one of her fellow tournament riders in the years before the war, and he and my mother had a deep mutual respect for each other's competence. They had also shared the social whirl of the pre-war equestrian scene.

Laughing, Podhajsky told me one day how Baby had vanquished an entire cavalry unit with one imperious wave of her arm. On one occasion, Podhajsky and a group of fellow cavalry officers, with their partners, had escorted my mother home for breakfast following a ball. They had removed their ceremonial swords and placed them on the table in the foyer. Midway through an informal breakfast, the Countess Maria von Kozaryn-Oculez appeared in her 'morning robe'. She was horrified by such undignified behaviour. In her view, an officer was either dressed – with his sword *on* – or undressed! Which did not bear thinking about and which she did not want to discuss. She gave an impressive speech on proper decorum and sent the visitors away.

During the bombing of Vienna, the riders and horses of the Spanish Riding School had taken refuge in the village of Wels; in 1953 they continued to operate from there. To re-establish her skill my mother enrolled as a student of dressage at the school, which took only internationally elite riders as private pupils. I wanted to ride too, and I realised it was not just a matter of climbing on one of the stockhorses. I was aware that in Europe horses served a different purpose. They were very expensive and leisure riding was an extreme luxury. I was enrolled at a local riding school and entered in local tournaments. Not many children of my age had had the opportunity to ride during the war so I immediately stood out. I was very confident from hours in the saddle on the farm. After galloping over gullies and jumping logs, a few carefully positioned jumps offered little challenge. I quickly gained a reputation as a brilliant junior rider. One day Podhajsky asked my mother why she was letting me mess around at a small local riding school when I could have been learning dressage within the formal training of the Spanish Riding School. She explained that she did not want to presume to ask Podhajsky to accept a child who had no record of international performance. He declared that that lack was about to be remedied. From then on my riding training started in earnest. I drilled three hours each day with three different instructors, all senior riders of the Spanish Riding School.

To counterbalance the dressage training, that summer we spent time in Verden, in Germany, where we enrolled for training at the Equestrian Training Centre at the German National Stud. Although we focused on cross-country and show jumping, every aspect of equestrian management was covered. Our farriery subject required that we make a set of horseshoes, complete with nails, from raw iron rods. We shod our allocated horses with the shoes and then completed the riding tests with the same horses.

Although the German horses were very big and I was very small, I had no problem with this test. I had been handing shoeing nails to my father since I was two years old. I knew every strategy; I could handle forge and tongs. I made some extra shoeing nails for Dad and packed them in cotton wool in a cigarette case. He kept them in the bulging pocket of his sports coat with his other special treasures. Bettina, Dawn and I were enjoying the best of international coaching and my father was an enthusiastic supporter.

•◆•

I remember fragments of discussion about travelling to Berlin. Bettina seemed both drawn to the city and repelled by it. She had visited Berlin often before the war. Otto had moved to Berlin following the deaths of Fritz senior and Fritz junior and had last been seen there in the final months of the war. A few weeks before he vanished he had managed to get home to Vienna. He found one of the faithful estate gardeners to whom he entrusted a message to Bettina. The gardener had survived the war and on Bettina's first return visit to Villa Mendl in 1950 asked to meet her. He faithfully delivered the message in the exact words Otto had instructed: *'Don't worry, I've had enough, I'm getting out.'* Those words had haunted her ever since. Now she was talking about going to Berlin. Had she decided to attempt to find him?

As tension had mounted in Berlin, Otto's wife, Aunt Mimi, placed Hans in a Catholic orphanage and left the city with Eva to seek refuge with relatives in the country. In the last few months of the war she had returned to Villa Mendl with Eva, having received a message that Hans had made his way there. Otto had fallen under suspicion by the SS; obscure threads linked him to Allied intelligence. Checks were being made – then he was on the run. Was this what he had meant by 'getting out'?

The villa in Vienna had been ransacked and was bomb damaged but it did provide some measure of protection. The Old Vienna Network provided information that my mother, the rightful owner of the villa, had married an Australian; this made her a British subject by marriage entitled to a British passport and the special blessing of full diplomatic protection.

In the first days of Allied control of Vienna, Mimi went to the British headquarters. Family mythology tells that she stood in a queue for three days to present her case – that the property was owned by a British subject and therefore she demanded British military protection. Within twenty-four hours British military police stood on guard around the clock.

Villa Mendl became a safe haven for those seeking refuge from the plundering mobs and occupying armies. The

Ankerbrot factory was able to provide some food, although irregularly and illegally. My father's name on documents seemed to hold magical powers. Bettina Mendl had become Mrs Joseph Thomas McDuff, a British subject whose property was entitled to the protection of the Crown.

Though she provided a safe haven for Mimi and her children, and despite the hardships that Mimi faced, my mother still held Mimi responsible for the separation between herself and Otto. The relationship between the two women was very cool. My mother did not consider conferring with Mimi. Bettina could well have gone to Berlin alone, but finally we all went together. She wanted Joe with her. I saw the ruins of the city, façades and walls and empty spaces where the bombs had fallen. I tried to imagine what it would be like to live the daily hell of war. I overheard snippets of conversation that seemed too horrible to invite understanding. My mother grew tense and distant. My father was sad. We left Berlin labelling it 'unsatisfactory'. Perhaps Mother's inquiries had been in vain.

•◆•

For a time we lived in Italy, accompanied by our usual entourage: nanny, chauffeur and Tante Maria. Over winter we stayed in Vipiteno on the Brenner Pass. We learnt to skate and ski, and briefly went to the local village school, where we spoke Italian. We lived in a typical Austrian-style chalet tucked tight into the mountain with a steep pitched roof, honey-coloured timber on the upper levels and solid rock enclosing the lower floor. Inside it was cosy and warm; outside there were mountains of snow, sometimes higher than the door. Visitors came often; they were hungry and exhausted. They crossed the border on foot. Sometimes we were put to bed early and heard voices talking late into the night. The voices were carefully controlled so that we could not overhear the words but the patterns conveyed a sense of urgency. No one explained who they were. One evening I came downstairs and, pushing open the door into the parlour, I saw my father seated at a table with two young boys, their dark hair bent over bowls of steaming goulash. I could smell it. My father caught my eye immediately and flashed the signal to get out. I retreated upstairs to find Tante Maria. At breakfast the next morning I asked my father who the two boys were. Before he attempted an answer Mother glared, forbidding challenge and said, 'No one, there was no one here!' Under the intensity of her glare I was almost convinced until during the day I overheard my father say: 'They were starving – poor starving little buggers!' and I knew that I hadn't dreamt the scene. Dad was restless till the next snowfall a few days later. He watched the snow clouds gather. He stood at the window and watched each flake come down. I sensed what he was doing. He was willing it to fall faster and heavier. Fresh snow covers tracks.

For a little while we moved to Milan, into a large hotel. Here Mother again went to meetings, and she and my father attended social functions. One night they were going to a masked ball – perhaps it was New Year 1954. They bent to kiss Dawn and me goodnight, she in a cream gown stitched with silver and a swirling dancing skirt, he regally attired in tails. We did not expect to see them until lunchtime the next day. Like Dawn, I drifted off to sleep.

Much later I heard noises from the hall. It was still dark outside. I crept into the room next door; through the connection

I listened to a hubbub. Peeping through the crack I saw my parents – and uniformed police. Tante Maria arrived in a dressing-gown. I understood the languages: Italian, German, ruptured English.

'Would you go over the statement once again, Madame?' – 'Sign the document now, please.'

Polite goodbyes. Doors banging. My father saying firmly: 'Settle down there, Mum. Spoilt a bloody good night. I can't see what the fuss was about.'

And Mother saying softly, wonderingly: 'I don't know. I don't know. I don't know.'

Then I heard Tante Maria comforting her. Soon I went back to bed and snuggled down to sleep.

Next day, inspired by cunning, I asked my father, 'What happened at the ball?'

He looked up at me from the *New York Herald Times*. 'Not much – home early – police got all excited – funny thing to happen. Someone asked your mother to dance. He was wearing a uniform – with a mask, of course, like everyone else. They danced a few steps and then the police appeared each side of him and took him away. Seems it's an offence to dress up as a policeman. Afterwards the real police wanted to know all about him. How would we know? He must have had an invitation to get in. I didn't ask his pedigree! He was a pretty good dancer. Your mother thought it might have been her brother Otto, the one that disappeared. She got upset and ran after him as they were taking him away, but she didn't get a chance to speak to him, and then she thought she might endanger him if he really had tried to approach her in some sort of disguise. The police advised us to come home – seemed to think there was some sort of threat. Spoilt the night. We should have stayed but your mother was upset – not much of a ball really.'

He folded out the newspaper, spread the pages wide and flicked it straight, leaving my questions conveniently outside his realm of interest.

The romantic image of the 'lost' Otto suddenly appearing at a ball to dance with my mother appealed to me but, despite my father's explanation, I couldn't see what this had to do with the police or why my mother didn't simply identify him and bring him home to meet us. Dawn and I agreed there was something missing from the story.

•◆•

We had been away for almost two years and were longing to return home. Despite all of the entertainment, we missed our farm, our pets, the very purpose of our lives. We received constant reports of the farm and animals but now, rather than reassuring us, they made us impatient to be there.

The many legal processes that involved my mother's property had either been concluded or else were at a stalemate. Finally we travelled north to Bremerhaven where we boarded the Swedish cargo boat *Tarn*. It had room for fourteen passengers, and with the sense of an adventure well concluded we settled in for the long trip home.

6

Getting a good education

We disembarked in Sydney. Our trunks and boxes were transferred onto rail for the trip back to Tarpoly. Meanwhile we stayed with Aunt Marianne and Uncle Gustav. Soon I would be twelve. Up to now I had received only haphazard schooling. During our travels in Europe the tutoring we received had been inconsistent. On a day-to-day basis we converted currencies, spoke several languages badly, and knew how to curtsy in the best of circles. We had collected fascinating insights into history and politics, but there had been no planning and no set curriculum.

My mother was totally opposed to boarding school. My father withdrew from the discussion, unable to reconcile his realisation that I did need some sort of education and the awareness that this meant separation. Nine-year-old Dawn calmly and persistently stated that she wanted to go to school at Tarpoly. This was greeted with a sense of relief from the adults but was not considered an option for me. It was finally agreed that I should return to Sydney, stay with Marianne and Google, and attend day school. Despite the fact that the school year had already started, I was to go home to the farm briefly before I started school.

In our absence, alterations had been made to the farmhouse. There were more rooms and the old corrugated iron kitchen had been demolished. In its place, part of the original building had been converted to a farm kitchen with built-in cupboards, laminex benches and room for a sturdy kitchen table in the centre.

Some of the material had been reused to build a generous shed behind the house. This had new rainwater tanks, a cement floor, efficient cow bails, a feed room for the horses, and an upstairs loft with pegs for the trotting harness. There was a trapdoor at the top of the access stairs.

Despite the alterations, this was simple accommodation after the luxury we had become accustomed to, but we didn't notice. We were delighted to be home and to re-establish connection with our beloved animals.

Aunt Marianne made the long trip up to the farm to pick me up and take me back to Sydney on the train. On the afternoon we were to leave, Dad had gone out fencing and as our departure time grew close he had not returned. I prowled and waited with growing impatience and a sense of dread that I would not have an opportunity to say goodbye. The grown-ups seemed to be avoiding my questions. My father's reluctance to send me off to school had been unstated, yet it hovered over us like a cloud.

Finally, unable to endure the growing tension, I bolted. I knew exactly where he'd be. I jumped the rocks and logs and thick grass clumps. I crossed the flat and flew over the hill, down onto the railway track, through the railway cutting where we were absolutely forbidden to go but which was a good short cut. He was a speck in the distance, heading home, his crowbar and axe on his shoulder. I ran as fast as I could.

'I thought you'd be too late,' I gasped rocketing into his side. 'I thought you might not get home in time to take me to the station. How can I go away to school if you don't take me there?'

He rested his hand on my head. 'I'll not go to the station this time, girl. You can go with your aunt. You'll do just fine. Mum and Dawn will be there to wave you off. You won't need me.'

I knew better than to argue. We walked in step along the railway track. The light was fading and I knew that time was running out. I felt Dad's hand on my back, pushing me on.

'You go,' he said. 'Run! Show me how fast you can run.'

I swung around to grab him at the waist, to hug him close.

Briefly he rubbed my shoulders, saying, 'You're a good girl don't be upset,' then 'Go' with a gentle push. 'Run!'

I ran. I ran all the way home. I didn't stop, I didn't turn to wave. I showed him how fast I could run, but my ribs ached. My legs ached. My heart ached even though I didn't know that I would never see him again.

◆

I had a uniform and all my books but the new school year had begun six weeks ago, so I was an oddity, a new girl arriving late. I sat at the back of the classroom. The day had started and the

A Story Dreamt Long Ago

lesson was mathematics. Money sums. Australian money. Pounds, shillings and pence in those days. I could do decimals and convert many currencies but this was new. I had never been taught 'money sums'. I studied the examples on the board. They did not make sense to me and could not be related to decimal calculation. I felt a rising panic. I needed help to work this out. Desperately, I hissed at the girl closest to me.

'What's the answer to the first one?'

'Two and six,' she hissed back, intending to be helpful. She meant 'two shillings and sixpence', a point I did not grasp.

With a great sense of relief I wrote down '8' just before the teacher focused on me. 'The new girl at the back, the one who has so much to say – what is your answer?'

'Eight,' I retorted confidently.

'Eight what?' asked the teacher. I didn't have a clue.

•◆•

I found school very difficult. There was not much to connect me with the normal lives of suburban Sydney girls. In art class we were told to paint a woman washing her hair. Responding to my experience in European art galleries I painted a naked lady and in my absorption did not realise that everyone else had carefully dressed their ladies in floral dressing-gowns. I was asked to explain myself. I stated that it was hard to wash your hair with clothes on because everything got wet. I was sent to the headmistress for my boldness. I remembered my mother's unacceptable painting of hell, at Cheltenham Ladies College.

I was everlastingly grateful for Tante Maria's dogmatic efforts to teach us her elegant French. My new French teacher seemed to like me and I made fair headway, although her pronunciation was quite different. She was Scottish and had her own variation on phonetics. I managed by recognising the written version, although I could barely write in English; no one had taught us that.

Uncle Google consulted with me every evening. What subjects had I done that day? Exactly what material? What homework did I have? He picked up on my evasions and quickly saw the difficulties I was having. He had almost predicted them. Kindly he explained that he would try to help me to catch up. He would arrange extra coaching from tutors. This was not meant as punishment but would make things better in the long run. I was sceptical. Google explained that if I did my lessons well, I could be rewarded with some theatre tickets. I might be able to go to music concerts like the ones in Vienna, or to the ice follies, or even go ice-skating myself with my cousin Valda McDuff. All these enticements did nothing to connect me with the normal eleven-year-old girls I sat with during school. I remained weird.

◆

In the midst of this restructure of my life, a month after I had started school there was an evening phone call from my mother. Dad had had an accident. I was to go home. Perhaps at that moment he was still alive but long before we caught the train he was dead, dead, dead. I did not consider this a possibility. I thought an 'accident' required treatment with liniment. Not even a doctor. I had never known anyone to die from an accident; *dead* did not enter my mind. Even when I saw the coffin, even when they shovelled dirt down, even when everyone was crying I did not think of Daddy as dead. The day before the funeral I asked Dawn where he was because he wasn't at home.

'He's fine. He's doing very well,' she said. Years later I challenged her.

'Why did you say that?'

'I really don't know,' she replied. 'I couldn't work out what was going on. Someone said he was with God; I thought that meant he was all right; I couldn't think of him as *dead*.'

It seems that my father had been greasing his trotting harness and hanging it in the new shed. Bettina had gone down to the kitchen to make a cup of tea and called that it was ready. My father came to the stairs. Did he slip? Did the stairs move? The bolts were later found to be loose. Did he grab the heavy trapdoor edge to steady himself as he fell to the cement floor? My mother found him, unconscious, lying in a pool of blood from a gaping head wound.

The telephone had not yet been connected. One horse stood waiting near the yards. It was Jinny's foal. 'The champion'. My mother didn't wait to saddle up. She leapt onto his back and galloped to the neighbours, jumping every fence on the way.

My mind's eye clearly sees her desperate leap onto the horse's back, her bare feet thudding on his ribs before she's properly balanced, the downhill charge towards the creek, the short cut, the narrow, stony cutting around the hill, the hesitation at the floodgate into the neighbouring property. The fence is low and weak. He's been led through there so many times before. He props hard but she drives him on. He clears it with a little hop. But now she's riding hard, pushing him dangerously on the treacherous narrow track where the stones roll out beneath his hooves.

She drives him harder still on the downhill side, until they reach the gate with the padlock that she could swing so easily without even dismounting – except that now, this one time, the padlock is clipped shut. She is trapped by the tight wire fence stretching on either side without a flaw. Doubling back is slow and dangerous, she searches left and right for a weakness, an opportunity. A branch has fallen on the fence a little way along. It will provide a marker, just enough definition to indicate the jump for an untrained and awkward horse. Desperately, as she passes by a gum tree, she rips off a strong green twig to use as a whip – a waddie.

She charges down the hill towards the fence. He swerves and baulks but her arm is waiting, raised; she brings the stick down on his rump once, twice, lying along his neck she roars 'Go!' into his laid-back ears. Then the split second in the air, curling into his body, clinging to his mane, gripping with her knees . . . She knows the landing will be awkward and rough – now just the hiss of a prayer to drive him on, one more stride till he's settled with his back legs bunched under. He's steadier now and they're still together as he crosses the flat with long, even strides. The rhythm is checked only by logs and gullies and – 'dear God in heaven, please, no rabbit holes'.

Two miles more, they are long and he is tiring – one more jump, just an old wooden gate. She raises the waddie but it's really not needed. He is beat and obedient. He bunches and leaps, staggers slightly but holds his stride to the house with the hedge and the neat garden gate.

My mother slides off, leaps the steps to the veranda and throws her weight against the door, which is lightly held by an

A Story Dreamt Long Ago

old iron stop. The door gives way to reveal the cool, dark corridor and Mrs George Raffan in her pretty Sunday floral frock, bringing drinks out to the veranda. My mother sobs for breath, ribs aching, tears streaming. She manages only choked sounds: 'Doctor – Joe – Ring up! Oh please ring.'

With agonising precision Mrs Raffan puts down the tray and turns to the telephone hanging on the wall. She winds the handle to reach the local exchange. Betttina leans against the wall and watches with fearful, pleading eyes. Mrs Raffan rings again – no answer – it is Sunday, after hours. Over her shoulder she calls 'George!' and again 'George!' until he appears from a back room with questions on his face. Through the open door he can see the horse, shuddering in distress, sweat pouring, head low, and my mother in the shadowy hallway, and then he hears the whispered 'Joe'.

Gasped and hurried explanations follow.

'Get the car.'

'No, don't move him.'

'Go to town!'

'Bring a doctor.'

'Ring. Try again. Just keep ringing.'

They make quick, muddled plans, George takes the car, my mother has to trust her chief tennis opponent to keep phoning, she steps down from the veranda into the bright glare outside to find the horse swaying and staggering away from her. It is being led by Colleen, Hilly's granddaughter – Colleen from my first schooldays, who is very scared of horses. Hilly's voice instructs her, 'Keep moving him about! Don't let him stand! That's a good girl. I'll be with you shortly.'

Then he appears around the corner of the house leading another horse towards my mother, who reaches for the reins. 'I've saddled you a better horse,' he tells her. Mother's fierce glare points out his mistake. There is no better horse than Jinny's foal.

'This one's fresh but you'll need to go through the gates. And Missus – take it steady – for the sake of the girls.' As my mother prods the horse into a trot, Hilly tips his hat.

Dawn has waited beside our father. She watched our mother ride away and came to find the reason. She sits with the dog, seeing the growing pool of blood, whispering *'Daddy?'* then settling down to watch the shallow breathing and to wait for Mum, who rides home carefully, under Hilly's ominous instruction 'for the sake of the girls'.

•◆•

There were phone calls and hours later, an ambulance, hospital and a little hope, but Joe left us in the night.

He did not wait to grow feeble with age, he did not wait to see us leave the farm, he did not wait to be irrelevant. I always knew he chose his time with the same calm honesty that he had lived throughout his life. The world had changed and so had we. We were on the brink of things he could not share and he had gone.

•◆•

Sometime during the week following the funeral Mother asked me to take a horse and check the sheep in the back paddock. Andy Regan, my father's favourite, cranky old stock

A Story Dreamt Long Ago

horse had come up to the yard for water. I tied him short to the fence to stop him biting while I saddled up. I took the heavy saddle from the rail where my father had left it and heaved it onto Andy's skinny back. I gripped the girth straps with my teeth to pull them tight. It seemed important to do this without help.

I checked the fences, floodgates and the dam. The water was receding and there were ewes and lambs trying to get access. The ewes were feeding half-grown lambs and were no longer strong; their wool was getting long and they were vulnerable to the cruel grip of the mud. I decided that the dam was risky. I dismounted and struggled to shut the wire gate to lock the animals away from that treacherous water. I wasn't strong enough but I knew how to use a tough old branch for leverage. I got it closed. Then I opened the gate to the creek, which still trickled through the rocks and gave safe access to clean water. I tied the gate with wire so that it could not swing shut again – stock would die of thirst if no one checked.

I felt I'd done things well.

As I approached the house my mother called, 'Phyllis, did you shut the gate?'

'No – I left it open.'

'Go back and shut it.'

I was still not properly within earshot. I would explain when I got closer.

'Will you shut that bloody gate!' she yelled.

'No, I've wired it open.'

'I want it shut!'

'I've left it open for the ewes to get to water.'

'Daddy left it shut.'

'That was a week ago. The dam's dried back and I've closed it off.'

I had dismounted from the horse and we stood glaring at each other. She could not retreat; this had nothing to do with grass or sheep or water. This was about blind obedience, which I would not offer.

She insisted, threateningly, 'Phyllis, go back and shut that gate.'

'No – we'll lose sheep there. If you want it shut, shut it yourself!' I told her with venom.

She turned and went inside.

Sadly, this set the tone for our relationship for many years to come. I concluded that she had no idea what she was doing and her judgment was not sound. She saw me as mean and defiant. She was right.

•◆•

Back at school in Sydney after the time I'd missed, I was asked to hand in a note of explanation. I kept forgetting. Finally, in the principal's office, I was asked the reason for my absence. Stammering, looking at my feet, I murmured, 'I don't know, we went away, I think my father died.'

The principal was disbelieving. She stated that if my father had died she would have been advised. I was to stay in, at detention, for the whole term for telling lies and being obtuse. This forced me to catch a later tram after school. Aunt Marianne wanted to know why I was later than expected and made me promise to catch the immediate first tram after school finished.

A Story Dreamt Long Ago

I was not to dilly-dally. I had to lie. I told her we no longer got out of school in time for the earlier tram. I never asked for a note. I did not want to have the words on paper.

7

Caught in a whirlwind

In the months following my father's death, Bettina struggled to establish purpose in her life. She tried to stay on at Tarpoly but found the loneliness unbearable. The house had been overflowing with family but when all the visitors were gone she was alone with Dawn. What had once been a blessed retreat must now have seemed like isolation from all humanity. On my first night home on a brief holiday from school I set the table for three places – it looked heartbreakingly bare. The room seemed empty, the chores had lost their purpose, the silence was a threat.

Within a few months Dawn went to stay with Aunt Lucie in New Zealand, while Mother returned once again to Europe to consider resettling there. Dawn and I were not in favour of this option. We simply wanted things to return to 'normal'. We wanted to feel safe; we wanted Daddy back.

That year Bettina, Dawn and I spent Christmas in New

A Story Dreamt Long Ago

Zealand. Mother had returned from Austria and decided to stay on, to continue to make Australia her home, to carry on with farming, with some concessions to doing it alone.

She bought a beautiful old house in Tamworth, quite close to the school. We lived here during the week and on weekends went 'home' to Tarpoly. A resident caretaker had moved into the house and we were weekend guests. Dawn and I both went to day school in Tamworth and struggled to bridge the gaps in our erratic education. For commercial viability, my mother purchased other properties. The planning and development of these kept her quite busy and we saw very little of her.

Before these arrangements were put in place there was an angry exchange between my mother and Marianne and Google. I feel sure my aunt and uncle would have protested against the new plan to disrupt the education they had so carefully arranged for me. Mother would have been enraged to have her authority challenged. I can imagine the ugly accusations – the wounds that did not heal. We were forbidden to have any contact with any of the 'Sydney' family again. I particularly missed their loving kindness, the wisdom and security they had offered, but I did not dare oppose my mother's edict. Years later, when I gathered courage and dialled the Mosman number I heard Aunt Marianne's voice and familiar endearments: 'Honeysuckle, I'm thrilled to hear from you, but I know it's not your mother's wish. I can't encourage you to go against her wishes. You must not ring again.'

•◆•

Despite her best efforts Mother could not settle down, or was it really the demands of the European businesses that called her back so often? There never was a school year that Dawn and I were able to start and finish with our friends. We were either arriving late or leaving early. We became adept at packing, shuffling documents, and entertaining ourselves in alien situations.

Typically, one afternoon when I was fourteen my mother burst through the door demanding, 'Phyllis, pack all the underwear!'

'*What?*'

'Pack all the underwear in the red suitcase. Everyone's. All together so that we can find it.'

'Why?'

'Because we're leaving straight away. The taxi to the airport will be here in half an hour. We'll miss the plane! Dawn and I will do the other packing. Hurry. Don't just stand there gaping!'

I followed her directions – it was easy enough. I stuffed the contents of three drawers of underwear into the red suitcase and put it at the top of the stairs leading from the front veranda through the garden to the street.

In due course the taxi came to the back door. We slung the luggage in. We caught the plane. We transferred to the international flight. We flew the eight-hour hops in the Superconstellation, arriving in Jakarta in the midst of a political upheaval that left us impounded in the no-man's-land of the airport hotel for three whole weeks. As it turned out, we did not have a single change of underwear between us; it was in the red suitcase, poised for take-off, at the top of the stairs on the front veranda back in Tamworth.

My mother grasped at this as further evidence of my mental decline. She was becoming desperate at my stupidity. It seemed

A Story Dreamt Long Ago

I could not follow the simplest instructions without a catastrophic outcome. She had seen me put 'drunk' milk bottles back into the fridge. Losing everyone's underwear was typical – what would I get up to next?

I had long since given up trying to defend my actions. My strategy was to survive by seeking cover. I retreated into daydreams. When I did consider my mother's accusations I had to concede that all the evidence supported her case. In fact, I had put empty milk bottles in the fridge, I had left our underwear at home. To almost every charge she made I silently acknowledgd my guilt. I saw no point in making a defence. It would not have been valid and there was no one to listen to it. When she pursued me too closely with her accusations I made bitter sniping retorts, which increased the distance between us and for a time left me safely out of reach.

On this trip we were not heading back to Europe. We were, quite suddenly, flying out to Egypt. Mother had developed an intense interest in Egyptology. I remember her absorption in a book called *Gods, Graves and Scholars*. We would see temples and pyramids and go to the Cairo Museum. I quite looked forward to it. I loved the stories of the ancient Egyptian rulers. I had read a lot about embalming, and sailing down the Nile on barges. I admired the workings of Shadoofs, which enabled farmers to lift water from the Nile into their irrigation channels. Perhaps I could dress up as Nefertiti. Egypt was a happy prospect.

Mother's promises came true. We spent two weeks in Cairo going daily to museums or on excursions into tombs. The tour groups were very small. Sometimes there were only the three of us, which gave us ample opportunity to ask questions and to linger over the more interesting discoveries. Bettina seemed to know a lot about items that had been removed to museums outside Egypt. She would often say: 'Oh yes, I saw that piece displayed in the British Museum! Scandalous! Thievery!' At which the guide would glance away, too embarrassed to agree.

After our stay in Cairo we went on to Luxor. We travelled by train, sitting cross-legged on the floor of the carriage packed with natives and their domestic animals. We chewed on stalks of sugarcane, as they did, while we chugged through miles of sand and past picture-book oases with a few palms offering fragile shade against the glare of the sun.

In Luxor we explored more temples until the stories merged and all the gods congealed into confusion. Mother decried my loss of interest. She lectured me on lost opportunities and how one day I'd be sorry that I didn't pay attention. I still marvel at Dawn's resilience; she was so much younger yet managed to remain cheerful through all the days of sunrise starts, interminable walks across the desert, hours of driving in overheating, smelly cars and eating peculiar food.

Finally we went to Aswan to see the dam, Karnak and the ruins of Ancient Thebes. Here the peculiar food curtailed our further exploration. We had been to the markets and Mother bought a generous bag of green dates, which we chewed on the way back to the hotel. The next day she was quite ill. We did not go out. She slept all afternoon and did not get up for dinner. In the morning she was worse. We couldn't make her understand that the guide was waiting. She tossed on her bed, sweating and moaning. Dawn declared that she was going to call a doctor. We went to the reception desk and demanded that a doctor should come to see our mother.

A local doctor arrived, examined Mother superficially and offered us white powder wrapped in newspaper. 'Very good,' he said. 'This will make Madame very good.' We gave him the money he asked for and stood staring at the powder after he left.

'I wonder what it is,' Dawn said. 'It might be poisonous.'

'We have to give her something,' was my reasoning. 'She's not getting any better.'

Dawn held Mother's head steady while I tipped the white powder onto her tongue. She coughed, moaned and rolled over to the wall.

Next morning she was worse still. She lay unmoving, sweating, her hair was matted and she smelt quite bad. With quiet determination Dawn, who was almost twelve years old, went to the reception desk and demanded to be put through to the British Embassy in Cairo.

'Are you quite sure, miss?' the desk clerk asked doubtfully.

Dawn was sure. The line was full of static and the voice we heard was faint. Dawn repeated over and over again, 'I am a British subject, my mother is very sick, you must send a plane immediately. You must take her to hospital or send her on to Vienna.'

There was disbelief and argument and questioning. Dawn was relentless. As we had been taught to do, she quoted her British passport number. She asked for the names and rank of the people she was speaking with. She wrote down phone numbers and instructions and refused to hang up until she was given an exact time to expect the plane.

'I will wait here while you check,' she said.

In due course the plane arrived – an English pilot came by car to pick us up. My mother, unconscious on a stretcher, was carried by native porters to the plane. In Cairo, she was given injections and we were all trans-shipped onto an international flight. Ultimately we reached Vienna and Mother went to hospital. Even then she barely survived; for almost a year she was weak and thin. She was suffering from an extremely toxic, tropical food poisoning and probably cholera.

Tante Maria settled the three of us into Villa Mendl, where, assisted by a nanny and Uruski, she took good care of us. Ellen Müller-Preis was a friend of Mother's from the tennis-party days at Villa Mendl. She was calm, purposeful and elegant, with a warrior's helmet of gleaming bronze hair. They had met at fencing classes which Mother soon abandoned. Ellen had won world acclaim. The friendship had endured. In July, as Mother improved, Tante Maria took us for a long Italian holiday with Ellen's two sons for company. We lived in a rented house on the shores of a lake and spent the days boating, swimming and reading while my mother recovered strength in Vienna. At the end of the month she was well enough to join us and we set off for a tour of Italy in the car, driven by Uruski. We spent magical days in Venice, prowled through St Mark's, rode in gondolas, visited galleries and palaces. We came back to Vienna through Florence and wound through the majestic Alps, driving short distances each day and spending the nights in quaint villages. At last the boys had to return to school and we returned to Villa Mendl – but we didn't go to school.

As the days shortened and winter approached 'Aunt' Agathe, Mother's friend who had written all those letters so many years ago, offered to take us to the mountains for some early skiing. A brilliant skier herself, she coached us both lovingly. We moved into a high mountain chalet and under Agathe's tuition we walked and climbed and skied each day. From the very beginning Dawn was more talented than I. When Agathe offered a challenge I declined and chose the easy option. Dawn grasped the opportunity to extend herself, tackling terrifying slopes at terrifying speeds. Soon Agathe was ringing my mother asking permission to engage a coach who could really challenge Dawn. Alois Zopf became Dawn's personal trainer and they worked together daily. After our return to Vienna, Dawn, Agathe and Herr Zopf made regular sorties to ski on different slopes and by the end of the season Dawn was winning most of the junior events. It seemed she had wonderfully athletic legs and was indeed 'good enough to train for the Olympics'.

By the time we got back to Australia eight months later a new school year had started. This time we knew we were going back to the lovely old house in Fitzroy Street, Tamworth, and to the familiar schools we'd left. We faced the challenge of catching up with our classmates.

·◆·

There were other trips to Europe, somewhat briefer in an attempt to fit them into or around a school holiday period. They all began with equal spontaneity. Sometimes we wondered how a business crisis could develop quite so suddenly; at other times we put it down to my mother's impulsiveness. There never seemed to be a proper plan, time to pack or to say goodbye, but we had become used to these strange patterns in our lives.

In 1957 there was a late-night phone call at a large house we rented on the outskirts of Vienna. I answered the phone; a bland male voice asked to speak to my mother. I handed her the phone and watched her change from the haphazard, impetuous person that I knew. In an instant she was governed by a new energy. White-faced, focused, she precisely repeated instructions: '*Sofort, allein* – immediately, alone, don't park, just pause at the crossroads.' She put down the phone and turned to me.

'We have to go out. I was told to go alone but I won't leave you both here because I can't be sure. Fetch Dawn, get in the car, lie down in the back; whatever happens don't make any noise and don't sit up until I tell you.'

'Where are we going?'

'Not far. I have to meet someone.'

We drove a little way and stopped at a corner near a high stone wall. A weak street light shone on the cobblestones. Soft rain fell. From the shadow of the wall a man stepped forward, hat well down over his face, dark coat collar turned up, no features visible. He took three long steps towards the window at the driver's side; he stooped.

'Bettina, what a pity you did not come alone.'

'Get in – get in – we need to talk.'

But he stepped backward, leaving one whispered German word dissolving in the rain: '*Schade*' – a pity.

Mother whispered, 'Please.'

'*Leider*, I am sorry.' He turned and disappeared into the shadows.

Bettina drove around the corner and pulled into the kerb. She slumped forward, arms crossed on the steering wheel.

A Story Dreamt Long Ago

'Should I go back?' she muttered. 'No, I can't go back, he would not wait, I mustn't make a scene. I'll go on home, then he might ring again.'

I could not contain myself. 'Who was it, Mum?'

'I don't know. I'm not sure. It's a long time since . . . Oh, you both might as well sit up. It has passed. It doesn't matter. It was nothing. Just a silly game. Forget it ever happened.'

We drove home. Bettina spent the evening silently prowling near the phone. I would never forget the glow of the light on the cobblestones, the shape of the man's hat, the length of his stride, the pain in the voice that said *'Schade'*.

It brought to mind the incident of the New Year's Eve ball in Milan in 1954 – the masked policeman who had wanted to dance with Bettina. I remembered her hollow voice as she whispered, 'I don't know, I don't know.' Recognising a similar emotion in this recent episode I asked her very gently, 'Do you think it was your brother Otto, Mum?' She looked directly at me, revealed her vulnerability, and sighed. 'How could I ever be sure, how could I tell? Go to bed. Forget about it.' But she hovered close to the obdurately silent phone.

I had a sense that people standing right in front of you could be 'lost'. It was all to do with the war.

8

The brief reign of the Ugly Duckling

I was growing up and questioning our lifestyle more and more. We moved out of the old house I loved into a brand-new one on the edge of town. I wanted to know why. Why didn't we have normal mealtimes and normal meals? My mother's system was to make sure that there was a box of fruit in the house, steak in the fridge and fresh bread in the box. We helped ourselves to unlimited delicious fruit in season, apples, peaches, apricots, grapes, and when inclined grilled a piece of steak to eat between two pieces of bread. This was not normal. Other mothers cooked. Other families sat down to eat together at the same time. The people across the road reverently listened to the news during their carefully timed dinner. I had witnessed this. This was normal. Why didn't we have holidays at Port Macquarie every year like our neighbours? Why was my mother always at the farm instead of making biscuits for us to come home to? Why did she swear and laugh and fight with everyone she dealt with? When she calmly responded that she had always been 'impossible' I wanted to know why.

I was worn out with being weird at school and dreamt that with some effort from my mother I could at least establish a veneer of normality. She drove a beaten-up VW beetle – the one she'd brought out with her when we returned by cargo boat in 1954. In Australia they were still uncommon. The back seat had been removed to better accommodate the farm tools and dogs, drums of oil, bags of feed. We perched precariously on this mixed load and at the school gate, with everybody watching, tumbled dishevelled from the back seat. Normal parents drove a Holden with four doors.

There was the matter of the lounge suite. We didn't have one. We sat on assorted cane chairs from the 'Eastern Emporium' which Mother loved. When I proposed that we buy a lounge suite, preferably like the one recently installed in the home diagonally opposite, Mother's eyes popped open. 'What?' she bellowed. 'Do you think I'm a lunatic? What would I do with a lounge suite?' I explained that it was, in fact, a maroon velour suite, extremely tasteful, all the parts matched. She swung around to Dawn and declared, 'She's mad! She hasn't a clue . . . we ought to lock her up. She's always been a bit skew-whiff.' She rolled her eyes and tapped her temple to illustrate my problem.

My adolescent conservatism put me in constant conflict with my mother. She would neither tolerate the questions nor provide answers I could accept. For the most part we lived in Tamworth, but we spent time each week on the newest farm at Keepit Dam. This property was at the junction of the Peel and Namoi Rivers.

The flats along the banks were planted with lucerne, watered by an 'irritation' system. Our lives were governed by its foibles. The pumps did not work effectively so that the pressure in the pipes often failed to build up and the carefully arranged network of sprinklers refused to spray and dance like ballerinas. Yet at other times the same pumps were suddenly over-enthusiastic, bursting pipes, causing wash-outs and bogs and urgent trips to town for parts. These teething problems seemed to go on for years during which our main social activity was 'doing irrigation'. We invited all our friends. They came to help us check, turn, adjust, change, and swear at the ever-expanding network of pipes.

A two-room fibro shack provided weekend accommodation at Keepit Dam. It had no bathroom, but there was a lovely view over wheat crops edged with willows fringing the wide, silver river that formed the boundary of our land.

The kitchen was a primus stove on a wobbly box and a tin washing-up dish, but the rivers provided swimming and fishing opportunities. From time to time they rose in flood, entangling wire and fence posts in the willows. It was tedious work retrieving them with pliers – and expensive to replace them. We sailed and water-skied on nearby Lake Keepit.

Meanwhile, once again the question of our education posed a problem.

By now I was so fed up with being out of step, behind the class, stupid, lazy, backward and strange – all familiar and regular labels – that I'd simply given up any attempt to cooperate with the education process. I'd spend hours gaping out of the window, scribbling pages of haute couture designs through all my notebooks and occasionally sitting in front of the headmaster's office 'cooling my heels', reluctantly waiting for yet another interview to discuss my inadequacies.

Despite all the languages and travel I could not find a single subject that inspired me. Nothing I had ever done or seen connected me to the geography or history lessons. Music was a painful cacophony, I couldn't spell Tchaikovsky and I couldn't sing in tune. Maths was intriguing and delightfully logical but because of my frequent absences there was mysterious missing information that prevented any real success. I loved geometry and theorems, which I could learn, understand and apply. These were trustworthy individual segments of information akin to poetry, which was another favourite. Theorems and poems could be stored in the head without the agony of trying to write – in an uneven childish scrawl, in fractured sentences with words grossly misspelt. I was surrounded by a chorus of adults who yelled, whispered or pleaded with me, 'Try, Phyllis – try!' My silent, belligerent response was: 'Try what?'

It was with a sense of enormous relief, even delight, that I heard the sternly spoken news at sixteen that I was to be sent to boarding school. An intervening angel in the form of the wife of Bettina's solicitor had observed my struggle with my mother and with school. She had made inquiries on my behalf, approached my mother and approached the school. Bettina was sufficiently desperate that all of her former objections to me going to boarding school dissolved. I was sent off to Sydney to Brigidine College, Randwick – to peace and sanctuary and sanity, to as much poetry as I wanted to read, to modern and ancient history that fascinated me and gave connections to my own experiences, to French that was familiar, to days and weeks that followed recurring patterns, sometimes to smiling approval – to bliss!

Although eventually Dawn followed me to Brigidine, initially she continued in Tamworth and boarded with a local family in town during the week.

Brigidine so improved me that my mother regained hope. Her constant trips to Europe influenced her to think that I must be introduced to 'society'. She bypassed Australian society at Sydney Airport. We no longer stayed in Sydney. We had no 'connections'. We received no invitations to grand functions – I'm sure Bettina would not have accepted any. To her, society meant one thing: Vienna. Tante Maria, Agathe and Mucki all advised that, of course, the only correct way to 'enter society' was to be a debutante at the Vienna Opera Ball.

The separation from Mother while I was away at school, together with my improved reports, did wonders for my confidence and for our relationship. We were both ready to bury our respective hatchets and embark on new enterprises together. Mother enthusiastically presented the Opera Ball project and I was happy to accede.

Her genuine enthusiasm touched me. She was enthusiastic about something we would do together and she trusted me to 'make a good impression'. It was a vote of confidence. I wanted to please her.

Brigidine had re-established for me what I had learnt on the Tarpoly farm; if I calmly focused on a project I could complete it sucessfully. It gave me confidence that I could do the debutante season justice. It was fortunate that our visits had given me established friendships there. My weirdness was easily forgiven, viewed as exotic because I lived in Australia and because I was the daughter of the widowed Bettina Mendl, much admired as the beautiful, wealthy head of a huge corporation. I knew I would be surrounded by Tante Maria, Mucki and Agathe and that when I fell out with Mother they would negotiate a solution. At a more pragmatic level how could I *not* do it? How could I say 'no' to Mother?

True to form, Bettina and I left Australia a week before the end of my final year at school. I didn't get to sit my English honours exam although I had worked hard for the whole year and my teacher held expectations of a very good result. This was easier to forfeit than to jeopardise Bettina's delicious proposals.

At Brigidine I had become fascinated by Greek and Roman history. The first stop on our voyage was Athens, where I retraced the steps of the heroes of the textbooks, paid homage to ancient gods and gloried in the views from sacred hilltops. My mother had formed a close friendship with a Greek financier she had met during a visit to Bad Gastein where she owned a lovely house. I was expecting to be introduced to him. I did not expect to be quite so impressed. Constantine Eftaxius was tall, slender, silver-haired, elegant and utterly charming. On our first night in Athens we were collected and taken out to dinner. After a languorous sightseeing tour of the city we approached a restaurant which hung above the water of the port of Peiraias like a glittering glass bauble. From our table we saw the harbour laid before us, outlined in twinkling lights.

In his perfect Oxford English, Constantine described for me the strategies of ancient battles, the names of ships, the stories of the leaders of the fleets that sailed the dark, mysterious waters more than a thousand years ago. I fell desperately in love, with

Constantine, with Athens and with life. I whispered prayers of gratitude to the nuns at Brigidine who had taught me ancient history with so much passion and thus equipped me for this conversation. I felt totally at ease, enchanted and enchanting.

The next day we shopped for shoes. My mother and I shared a shoe fetish. We both loved to be either barefoot or luxuriating in the most elegant of shoes. Appropriately, long before I'd owned a pair of 'town shoes', one of the first poems I'd learnt at Tarpoly school was:

New shoes, new shoes –
red and pink and blue shoes.
Tell me, which would you choose –
if they let us buy?

I'd dreamt of going to a shoe shop and buying some of every kind. I doubt I ever voiced this lust but I knew the few Sydney shops where one could buy imported shoes – Italian – obscenely expensive.

Suddenly in Athens these 'Italian', soft, multi-coloured, strapped, bowed, buckled, folded, ruched, studded, flat or heeled shoes were available by the thousands. 'As cheap as chips' Mother said. 'You'll need good shoes, you'll be walking miles, you'll be dancing all night. Whatever you wear you must have suitable shoes.'

Under the influence of my recent convent experience, I chose a pair of simple navy court shoes with a chisel toe which, I reasoned, would be serviceable and elegant. 'You'd better choose a few more pairs,' Mother advised. I chose beige. I did not dare to look too closely at the carmine sandals or the sky-blue needle toes or the silver with the rhinestones in the heel or . . . 'Just try a few – just check that you can walk in them,' my mother said. I paraded up and down, towering and wobbling on ten-centimetre heels. Lizzie's careful training was not wasted. I could dance in *anything*! There was not a single shoe that could defeat me. The pile of boxes grew. The tissue paper mounted higher. There were shoes strewn in a wide circle around me and on the adjacent chairs. I was trying to select the most useful, the most suitable. 'Are they all comfortable?' Mother asked. 'Could you wear them all day? Do they pinch? Do they rub?' Those that did were set aside and still there was a sea of shoes. At last my mother said, 'We'll take these.'

'Which did Madame choose?' the shop assistant asked.

'These,' said she with a wide circular gesture taking in the whole array of shoes around us, excluding the little pile of pinching, rubbing rejects.

'All these?' questioned the shop assistant in disbelief, copying the gesture.

'All these?' I echoed.

'Well – in Europe you can't go anywhere without shoes,' was her explanation.

The assistant packed thirty pair of shoes. She built the boxes into towers. She tied the towers with string. We looped the ties over our fingers and with the string cutting deep, we exited the door obligingly held wide by the smiling staff.

We stepped out of the cool shop and were blinded by the white glare of Athens at noon. We turned left into a narrow, shadowed alley. At the end we turned right, hesitated and looked at each other. 'I think we're lost,' Bettina said. We glanced up and down the street and slowly became aware that there wasn't another soul about. All doors were shut, every window shutter was firmly latched. We doubled back to the shoe shop we'd just left, only to find it closed, but we were not quite sure – the shutters hid the window display that had drawn us in. Mother put the boxes down, rummaged and checked her docket. Yes, this was the shop we'd started at. 'Think!' she said. 'Think! How did we get here?'

The shoe selection had consumed all my concentration. I hadn't the least idea. In the unfamiliar northern hemisphere and without shadows in the bush or any other familiar guide, my navigation skills deserted me. My mind and face were blank. Bettina's voice was tense now. 'There must have been a revolution,' she stated.

'*What?*' I was trying to keep up. Was this all a consequence of buying far too many shoes?

'Everyone has disappeared! They've locked themselves in! There is some sort of marching in the street! A revolution!'

I could only continue to gape.

'Shhhhhh – listen – try to hear which way they're coming!'

I listened carefully and could hear only a hot, threatening silence. Then I caught sight of a large black car gliding around a street corner some blocks away. 'Mum – let's get a taxi,' I suggested, and immediately realised that there was not another car in sight.

'We'll walk – we'll find someone – the hotel must be this way.'

Mother set out in the opposite direction. At the first intersection she stopped short, pressed her back against the wall, peeped into the street she was about to cross and waited for me. As I reached her she hissed, 'It seems to be all right, hurry and keep up!' We dashed across the street and hurried on until she doubled over. The tower of shoe-boxes dragged along the footpath as she bent below the ledge of a large uncovered shop-front and scuttled to the next corner. I thought it best to copy her.

We crossed three streets and were careful to avoid uncovered windows until, at last, we saw the familiar sign above a cinema two doors from our hotel. Exhausted, we pushed against the revolving door of the hotel, and fell into the lobby amidst the clatter of boxes as the strings on our tower packages gave way. The lids fell off. Shoes spewed out across the floor. We lay panting on the cool tiles in drifts of tissue paper. The room was heavy with silence. Not far away three gentlemen in suits sat reading newspapers over which they discreetly peered at us. The porter rushed forward to gather us up. For long seconds we offered no explanation. There didn't seem to be one – in Greek or any other language. A bellboy came forward to gather up the boxes and shoes.

At last, fully erect, my mother asked the porter, 'Has there been a revolution? Has anyone been hurt? Have you been listening to the radio?'

'I beg your pardon, Madame?' The porter looked puzzled and seemed to doubt his comprehension of English.

She continued to explain. 'The streets are all deserted – the shops are boarded up – we couldn't find our way –' Her explanations wound down as she realised she had reacted in panic.

'No revolutions, Madame. No revolutions today – it is the siesta time – till two o'clock, Madame.' He mustered us, the bellboy and shoe-boxes into a lift and pressed the button to send us up to have a good lie-down.

She must have known about siesta; she must have experienced it on many of her travels.

Despite our relief at finding ourselves safe, my mother did not lie down. She unpacked the shoes from their boxes in an attempt to fit them into our luggage. Then she declared, 'Now we have to get them all through customs. They are not supposed to be new – you will have to put marks on the bottom – just take them down to the street at the front of the hotel and scratch the soles.'

For the next hour I went back and forth through the lobby, under the increasingly suspicious glare of the porter. I carried five or six pairs of shoes at a time and stood in the street outside, changing my shoes at brief intervals, scratching like a chook and feeling immensely grateful that the neighbourhood was utterly deserted.

I wanted to know what earlier experience had triggered my mother's panic. Why did she immediately think of revolutions? But I couldn't taint our adventure with my questions. Not now, so early, not when the days were full of promise.

•◆•

For the rest of our week in Athens, Constantine sent flowers regularly and collected my mother for outings. I was provided with a charming companion, a junior version of Constantine, perhaps a nephew, cousin or godchild. He was tall, slender, elegant, with crisp black curls – and also spoke beautiful Oxford English. He took me to quaint restaurants in caves overlooking the city. Here we ate goat's milk cheeses, olives and sun-dried tomatoes. We listened to zither music and discussed democracy. We attended a service in a Greek Orthodox cathedral, which lingers in my memory as the most profoundly touching religious ritual I have witnessed. Relaxed, charming and attentive, my companion was at all times utterly decorous.

It was with some regret that I left Athens, but Vienna beckoned and I hoped that we might meet these two charming men again. Alas, it did not happen.

·◆·

Viennese society decreed that one became a debutante for a whole three-month 'season', attending a number of formal balls selected from a list. The invitations came according to one's status and pedigree. A debutante was also obliged to entertain sister debutantes with stylish parties and to attend formal teas with the older generations. All these obligations, with dance practice sessions, dress fittings, skiing weekends, theatre, concert and gallery outings – with informal parties given by the artistic community – had to be crammed into those three short months. We met the leading performance artists of plays, opera and ballet, as well as painters and sculptors, and we were expected to understand their work, interpretations and philosophies.

The final, formal grand occasion was the Vienna Opera Ball where 200 debutantes were presented to the 'City of Vienna' in an all-night extravaganza. The celebrations took place throughout the seven separate auditoriums of the Opera House. The last dance, at 6am, was a waltz played on a single violin. By then the debutantes were wilted, wind-blown blossoms swirling across the gleaming floors, along the long halls, down the curved stairs and out into the snow.

A partner for almost all of these occasions had been found for me. Peter was the son of one of my mother's oldest friends. Peter's father had partnered Bettina at her debut in 1926. Peter's grandfather had founded the respected building firm that had built Villa Mendl, designed by Grandfather Fritz. It was appropriate that the families continued their connection into the next generation. Peter and I had already met on my previous visits, but as he was five years older than me, we had not formed a close friendship. Peter was chosen as a 'veteran partner', which meant that he knew all the protocols and could be depended upon to supervise me – in case I slipped up. He demonstrated how I should hold my flowers – 'not like a cricket bat'. He whispered titles into my ear precisely when I needed the reminder. It was fortunate that my father had taught me to waltz so well; I could balance and twirl, pivot and reverse, and add my own graceful, rhythmic variations. Dad and I had practised on the veranda of the Tarpoly house, at the school tennis parties, on the deck of *Oceania*, mostly to the beat of old Irish melodies he sang.

Peter was a magnificent dancer and he was determined that I should take the whole debutante procedure as seriously as it deserved. I was confident I would not fail him. We were required to provide a gracious spectacle and prove ourselves worthy of inclusion in Vienna's inner sanctum of grace, charm, art, intellect and culture. We were always punctual for practice. We were courteous to *everyone*. We were considerate of the Mendl chauffeur – that same Uruski who had met us at Genoa on our first family visit to Europe. The unstated fact was that our chauffeurs were highly trained bodyguards. Apart from other considerations, we all wore family heirloom jewellery on most occasions. The greatest sin was not to respect the subtly stated suggestions of one's chauffeur, made in the interests of safety. They spent hours waiting to drive us to our next appointment and it was considered 'gracious' to arrange informal 'relief rosters' by sharing cars so that the chauffeurs could get some sleep.

•◆•

Otto Schönthal, the man who had guided Bettina through her worst despair and had been her business adviser since before the war, the man who had encouraged her to return to Vienna and reclaim her property, remained her confidant in Cold War Vienna of 1959. This was the era of the Iron Curtain that sliced Europe in two, a mere 100 kilometres east of Vienna. The Cold War was palpable. Three years earlier the Hungarian population had suffered a brutal suppression of an anticommunist revolution. Suspicions and accusations permeated the atmosphere. There was a great fear of Russia: there was talk of mysterious disappearances, there was dread of a Communist plan to push east and annex Austria, or at least claim Vienna as the old capital of the Austro-Hungarian empire.

Uruski's family was from Eastern Europe. Soon after we arrived, my mother became aware that every time she was to travel in the car he altered the position of the Ankerbrot logo on the front of the car before they left. She discussed Uruski's behaviour with Otto and they came to the conclusion that Uruski was being pressured by the KGB to provide information concerning her activities. By now Uruski had worked for Ankerbrot for over ten years through difficult times. Bettina decided to place her trust in his continued loyalty. She told him that she knew of his activities and the forces pressuring him. He remained in our service but the logo was removed from the car. No doubt Bettina and Otto took other, less obvious, measures to ensure our safety. I didn't have to know what these were but I was deeply saddened to learn how fragile Uruski's loyalty was, and that I had to monitor what I said, especially about my mother, while I was in the car.

•◆•

I met Hector at a function to welcome young international visitors to Vienna. The formalities had been rigorous and I had braced myself for a dull and pompous evening when I overheard Hector's hilarious mimicry softly hissed in English. I tuned in and the evening magically changed. At its conclusion Hector grandly offered to see me safely the few blocks to my hotel. By the time we arrived we were firm friends.

Hector was a student from Mozambique whose Greek family owned large breweries there. They had sent him to Vienna to study beer technology. Possessing a horror of all things to do with beer, he used the generous fees his family provided to enrol himself in the school of fashion, where he was happily studying textile design. We became inseparable and on many of the less formal occasions of the season, Hector would act as my partner, leaving Peter free to study. Hector and I had much in common. We were both 'colonials' and although we came from 'very good houses' we were not expected to be quite as formal and correct as the local debutants. He was a safe companion who shared my own interest in textiles, design and fashion.

Hector had a wicked dry wit and dropped delicious gossip among the matrons – just enough to get them twittering. He recklessly allocated titles to names he introduced – precisely calculating his effect. 'I would like you to meet Leo – Count von Popskavinsk, daaarling – a very old line.' He was unreliable with noughts on bank accounts when reporting financial positioning and he could dance a deadly tango – with a rose in his teeth.

The immediate challenge on my arrival was to commission 'the Gown'. The formal debutante regalia was designed, not merely to look pretty for one single occasion, but to withstand the rigours of an entire season of dancing. It was considered crass, even *common*, to have more than one formal gown – although some girls admitted having a copy made of the original. Night after night, week after week, these gowns were worn, cleaned, adapted and repaired. Close inspection of any outfit on the final grand occasion, the Opera Ball, would reveal debutantes in tattered dresses with cunningly hidden patches and stains and subtle renovations to save sagging seams and hems.

Success was founded on appropriate design. Tulle and fine lace were out of the question. They disintegrated far too easily. Heavy satin and heavier laces were far more suitable. Strapless gowns were risky, regardless of how well they fitted at the beginning of the season. The hours of dancing, skiing and walking meant that everyone lost weight, risking unseemly sagging and gaping. Peter's own mother, the doyenne of style, told stories of having endured this embarrassment when she had done 'something reckless in a strapless' in the 1930s. She did not recommend it.

It seems that at a regal diplomatic function she was to partner an impressive young dignitary. His bloodlines were impeccable, his prospects were illustrious, his preparation for Vienna was immaculate. His traditional Viennese waltz was flawless with flashes of brilliance. Peter's mother, Maria, had returned from skiing to fulfil her social obligations and had chosen the hapless strapless. Having lost a little weight she carefully positioned padding underneath her breasts to create the required cleavage. Towards the end of a particularly vigorous bracket of waltzes she became aware of a lump under her left armpit. Horrified, she recognised the padding and quickly snatched it in her right hand. The diplomat immediately took it from her and placed it in his jacket pocket without the least hesitation in his waltzing rhythm. Maria beamed a 'thank you' and murmured, 'I'm just a tiny bit worried about what might have happened to the other one.' To which the waltzing diplomat replied, 'Madame, do not be concerned. I'm holding it firmly in my right hand, centre back.' Maria went on to say that had she not actually already been engaged she would have considered 'encouraging' that young man.

The foremost haute couture salon in Vienna was Fahrenhammer, which provided all of my mother's clothes – as they had done for her mother. One made an appointment for a showing and selected from their seasonal range presented by house models. One then discussed adaptations and variations in colour or finish. The individually created item, which represented a substantial investment, was then constructed, and even after delivery was cared for by the salon. All cleaning and repairs were carried out in house. This was most convenient for me, as

Bettina, relaxed at the entrance to her house in the spa-resort town of Bad Gastein.

The pendant Bettina is wearing, handed down from her mother, was identical to a brooch worn by famous American society hostess Elsie de Wolfe, wife of Sir Charles Mendl. Bettina's mother and Elsie almost certainly had been connected.

Bettina was a formidable international equestrian competitor from the late 1920s and an obvious choice for the 1936 Olympic Games in Berlin. She 'didn't like the politics' and refused to participate.

My father, Joe McDuff, astride his favourite stock horse, Andy Regan, at Mostyn Vale, the farm my parents bought in 1945.

Left to right: My sister, Dawn, Bettina and me, about the time we moved to Mostyn Vale, near Barraba.

I intended to be a circus rider when I grew up. I practised constantly. Regardless of temperament or suitability, any horse standing around fell victim to my risky experiments.

Just before Joe, Dawn and I accompanied Bettina to Europe, she told us about Villa Mendl where we were to live, close to the heart of Vienna. She described its enormous garden, 45 acres of lawns, orchards, and stables. The main entrance to Villa Mendl was a wide driveway of cobbled stones, overhung by trees.

The view of Villa Mendl from an access lane, which was an ideal bikeway for me to strengthen my weak legs in 1953.

My parents, Joe and Bettina, exactly as I remember them, around 1952–53.

Dawn, Joe and me experiencing our first deep snow at Vipiteno, Italy, near the Brenner Pass. For a time we lived in Italy, accompanied by our usual entourage: nanny, chauffeur and Tante Maria. We learnt to skate and ski and briefly went to the local village school.

Bettina thought I must be introduced to 'society', and to her 'society' meant one thing: Vienna. I was among 200 debutantes at the Opera Ball in Vienna, February 1960 – the flawless result of an intense preparation to deal with any social situation our future lives might present.

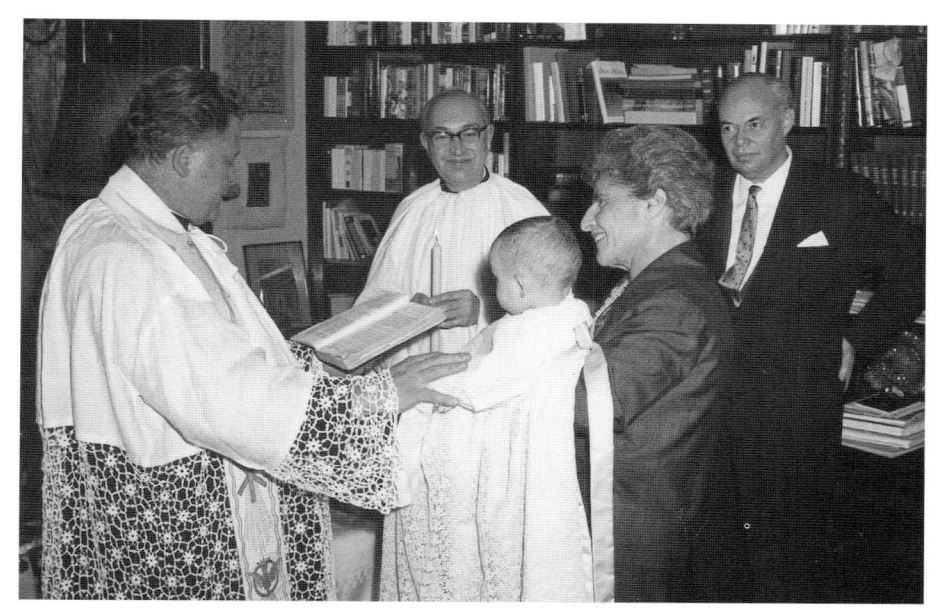

Bettina was godmother to Otto Schönthal's daughter. Otto watches the christening from the far right of the photo. He was the man who had guided Bettina through her worst despair and had been her business adviser since before the war, the man who encouraged her to return to Vienna to reclaim her property.

The castle in my dreams, Schloss Itter in Tyrol, where Dawn and I revived jousting matches, ransomed princesses and chivalrous knights from ghosts of long past.

Bettina was one of the foremost dressage instructors in the world. She was both feared and famous for her passion and for demanding immediate perfection from her students.

Bettina in Australia, aged in her sixties.

on this trip we resided in our suite at the Hotel Kaiserin Elizabeth, across the road from the salon, and conveniently in the centre of Vienna.

I loved the subdued elegance of the old hotel. It definitely was not a 'brass and marble chook house', which was how my mother described the larger hotels. Hotel Kaiserin Elizabeth was discreetly tucked into the narrow Weihburggasse and offered vintage staff. They knew the names not only of the guests but of their visitors. They knew the cars and chauffeurs of each guest. They knew our timetables and reminded us of details in our schedules that we might have overlooked. All this was done without any seeming effort. The most unlikely occurrence was managed as though on oiled ball bearings. On this visit, alone with my mother, I did not miss Villa Mendl, which had been transferred to Otto Mendl's family. Because of the frosty relationship between Mimi and my mother it was now strictly out of bounds. Mother offered no explanation. Sometimes friends asked why we were not staying at the villa and I would have liked to understand more fully. Perhaps because of the stories my cousin Hans had told me I liked and admired Mimi, a fact I dared not disclose to Mother. I wondered why we had no contact with Hans, formerly quite a favourite of my mother's. At carefully chosen moments I slipped prompts into the conversation to glean explanatory information. My mother always responded with a wave of her hand and a dismissive 'They are quite impossible'.

Fahrenhammer designers were called in to suggest the ideal debutante gown. Hector and I muttered over the suggestions and made our adaptations. We decided on a heavy guipure lace with a high neckline.

'Simple and virginal,' Hector said.

'Do I want to look virginal?' I asked.

'Might as well – while you can,' was his opinion.

We decided on little cap sleeves, to hold the whole thing up, and a simple bell skirt to let a bit of air up my legs so I didn't overheat. The whole effect was to hinge on the quality of the lace, which had to be robust but elegant, heavy but not burdensome, ornamental but not prissy. We searched the whole of Vienna and could not find a particular piece of lace that took our breath away. My mother suggested that Hector and I should fly to Paris with her where there would be a wider selection. We spent a weekend in Paris and despite walking miles in well-shod feet we were exhausted and did not find the lace we sought. A helpful merchant suggested that he could have it manufactured and we weighed up this proposal. My mother felt that we should try Harrods first, so she and I flew to London. Just as she had predicted she found the elusive ideal lace at Harrods. We purchased huge quantities – a whole suitcase was needed for the wide bell skirt. We did not see a single gallery or museum. I did not even take a drive through London. We stayed one night, saw an exquisite play based on the life of Shelley, *The Aspern Papers*, bought the lace and then returned to Vienna, where momentum was already building and obligatory social events could not be ignored.

My one 'normal' activity during all this time was to ride every day. My mother kept her horses at stables in the Prater, the vast parkland on the outskirts of Vienna. A mare purchased from the German National Stud had been trained for me by Irbinger, senior rider of the Spanish Riding School. Each afternoon at two o'clock he coached me in dressage. The mare had been carefully developed and was capable of tests of the highest standard but I could not fall in love with her. Her size and cranky nature did not trouble me; I was used to cranky stock horses at home. I resented the limitations of riding within the arena. Outside, the snow was deep on the ground so we stayed inside and practised advanced movements that I considered forced, artificial and graceless. It all seemed to be about control and discipline, and, despite continued success at competitions, I could not give my heart to this equestrian form.

Once the Christmas festivities were over, the ball season claimed all of our energy. Decisions had been made as to which balls I would attend. Dates and invitations were fixed for the round of debutante parties. My diary was full to desperation. Often I was obliged to leave a party at midnight to make an essential appearance at another gathering on the same night. Some mornings I hosted a lavish 'English Breakfast' at the Hotel Kaiserin Elizabeth. Guests came straight from their balls in evening finery. We had huge helpings of ham and eggs, sweet grilled tomatoes, toast with berry jams. This was a way of fitting in just one more obligatory function, but consequently I didn't get to bed until after 10am. It was fortunate the breakfasts were curtailed by debutantes having to go home to have their dresses processed by the cleaners. Often I had to cancel riding to get sleep before preparing for the next ball, concert or theatre party. Days and nights flashed by. Nerves were shredded, tempers flared but somehow we kept on dancing, enchanting – 'Smile! It has never been known to kill you. In every circumstance be gracious; send *thankyou* cards; remember flowers. Use your team . . .'

Tante Maria made phone calls, ordered meals, arranged transport, all within required protocols. Uruski carried a small leather case in which I kept several changes of shoes. During the night I could slip out to the cloakroom to change from the initial very high heels that Peter insisted were necessary for the best dance routines, to sequentially lower heels, until I went home in soft flat ballet slippers carefully hidden under the long dress. Sometimes we chose to walk the last few hundred yards barefoot in the snow – just to cool our feet.

My gown held out night after night. Cleaning after cleaning, it was returned in a flat box packed with tissue paper, ready for the next occasion. The lace around the neck grew tatty so we cut it back with nail scissors, once, twice, then made a new deep scoop. Hector bumped against me with a glass of red wine in his hand. It spilt and soaked through the lace on the front panel. The next day the front was redesigned and a satin panel was inserted. By now the dress was substantially different from the original design, but so were all the others and I rather liked the variations. At least mine had not unravelled in layers, as had other people's.

There was no time to catch our breath before the final grand occasion. The Opera Ball was upon us. We were on show to the world, we performed without a quiver: we were veterans. I was infinitely grateful to, and slightly in love with my partner Peter, who had been inspirational. Through the whole process he had mentored, protected and encouraged me constantly without restricting my enjoyment. Night after night I silently revelled in my good fortune to have the absolute best partner in the room. His height, good looks, dancing style and social savoir faire gave me enormous confidence while he achieved all of this without any hint of arrogance. Bettina was pleased that we got along well. She had deliberately chosen the perfect partner, son of her own partner for whom she still had great affection. The attributes were hereditary.

The morning after the Opera Ball, a cellophane florist box arrived for me. It contained a large mauve orchid, a lavish tropical bloom resting on fragile greenery. It had been sent by Alexander, easily the best-looking man I have ever met. He was superbly built with golden skin and bedroom eyes. A week earlier I had been invited to a business function in honour of my mother, given by Alexander's father, who did something with oil. Alexander had been a pleasant enough companion, although somewhat preoccupied with the angle of his jawline. Now he was sending orchids and further invitations.

Hector, who had cruised by to 'check my pulse', objected to the orchid.

'Gross!' he declared. 'He simply has no class. How can anyone with a minimum of refinement send *orchids* to a seventeen-year-old? Purple! What *can* he have been thinking?'

I tried to defend Alexander. 'Perhaps he *likes* orchids. Perhaps he asked his secretary to order it. It's not that bad. I rather like it. It was nice of him to send anything at all.'

Hector could not be calmed. He paced and banged his fist. 'It is the *tone* of the whole thing. Quite off! You should send it back – immediately.'

I would not agree to do that. I did not want to give offence. I knew that anything other than a gracious acceptance of the orchid would cast a shadow over an important business connection of my mother's. Hector left, outraged. He refused to stay in a room with 'other people's orchids'. Hector and I had defined our relationship as 'passionately platonic'. We had a deep affection and trust in each other but our lives clearly had separate destinies. I ignored his tantrum. It was easy to forgive him. He was under pressure. His parents were expected to arrive within the week. This would be the first visit in three years and there was every likelihood they would discover that their son, heir to a substantial brewing empire, was about to complete his studies in textile design. I quaked on his behalf. 'What will they doooo?' I wailed.

At first he was offhand. 'Poppa will roar – that's never been a problem. He roars so often and so loudly that I just can't hear him.' Then he continued sadly, 'But Mummy – Mummy will weep – and the weeping breaks my heart.'

I had a sense of Hector's childhood. I saw a small boy with large, sad eyes, alone in a room, listening, as the sound of his mother's quiet weeping seeped through every wall.

In the next weeks calm descended. The hotels slowly emptied as the internationals went home. There were farewell phone calls and trips to the airport. The Vienna debutantes went back to studies and visited now in boots and leather jackets with books under their arms. The partners, who for months I had only seen in tails, appeared in corduroy pants as young professionals struggling to get a foothold on slippery careers. The carefully suppressed romances were acknowledged; spring was just around the corner; love was in the air; parents were tightening their faces against 'inappropriate connections' – and I had absolutely no plans for the future.

More out of habit than for purpose, I trod the familiar short walk from the Hotel Kaiserin Elizabeth to Fahrenhammer. Not knowing why I was there I stood around and poked at things. I loved Atzi, the owner and chief designer. I was so filled with admiration for her elegance and grace that I barely dared to speak to her. When she asked, I shyly told her why I'd come. 'I'd like to work for you,' I said. 'I want to understand the business. I want to work with textiles and to design.'

Atzi was amazed, perhaps even embarrassed. 'You are always welcome to visit,' she said.

'But I don't mean just to visit – I mean to work, learn, understand. Not here, at the front of the shop; I mean out the back where the machines and buttons are – out there where you do the cutting.'

'We will see. I will talk with your mother. Would you like to stay now – for a little while?'

In the end an arrangement was made that I would work at Fahrenhammer in the role of a house model. The deal was struck because I was appropriately tall and thin, and, as a well-known debutante, was something of a social coup for Fahrenhammer. As frivolous as the title sounds, the work was gruelling and I loved it. We were drilled in presenting garments to individual clients. The work was much more intimate than parade or photographic modelling. We had to 'maintain image' the whole time we were with the client, who sometimes included us in discussion or beckoned us nearer to examine a pleat or button. We must not bend or sit or gesture in any way that did not 'advantage' the garment. These impromptu interviews could go on for an hour. When asked for an opinion we had to be utterly discreet.

Behind the scenes, we pinned and picked. We ironed and steamed and pleated. We hand-stitched rouleau edges on miles of gossamer fabric. We learnt how to use lead weights to give weight and flick to a hem, where to anchor invisible supports to prevent gaping as the body moved – every millimetre of fabric was controlled. What was to be revealed? What must remain concealed? Buttons were sent from Rome, Paris and New York. The matching and balancing was a science. They were in bone and bronze and pearl, in wood and stone and finely plaited hair. The materials alone were magical components. This wondrous experience reminded me of the happy times I spent with Cousin Lizzie at the factory in Sydney. It was she who had first aroused my interest in textiles.

I saw very little of my mother but when we met she seemed pleased that I'd found something to absorb me. She was confident that whatever I was doing under Atzi's supervision would be good for me. Fahrenhammer was a haven and I was also riding every day. The patterns of this lifestyle almost satisfied my craving for a normal routine but by the time three months had passed I began to long for home. I missed Dawn, who was now a boarder at Brigidine. I missed the farm. I could not see the purpose of the life I was leading in Vienna. What would it lead to? What would I do if I went home? I remembered how Uncle Google had always hoped I would become a barrister. I would go home and study Law. I had regained confidence, and, once again, I believed that I could do it.

I advised my mother that I was flying home to go to the University of Sydney. I knew that her business obligations would keep her in Vienna a while longer and I had arranged for residency at Sancta Sophia College. Although the year was well under way, I was confident I could catch up – I always had in the past.

My first disappointment was that because of the late enrolment, I was not accepted into Law. I was advised to enrol in Arts for the first year and then to consider changing. I hated Arts. I hated languages. Although my spoken German stood me in good stead, the study and analysis of Kafka turned my stomach. In English lectures I could not grasp that a room full of responsible adults spent hours analysing whether Hamlet was mad or whether Shakespeare devised his madness, and what techniques he used to do this. I felt this interminable analysis was surely the pathway into our own madness. I dreaded the lecture rooms where I felt choked by the air of unreality. Without a true mission I was overwhelmed by my old shyness. I could not speak. I could not write essays because my pen still blobbed and scratched. Again I heard the chorus whispering, 'Try, Phyllis – try!'

Six weeks later, on my eighteenth birthday, I came back to my college room to find a present – a large cellophane florist box – with a card sent from Vienna. As I peeled aside the tissue eighteen immaculate white orchids were revealed. There was a tiny card from Hector with the words '*Hi Doll*' – and for a while this contact made the decision to come home to university a little easier to bear.

As I gazed into the box of orchids on their bed of tissue paper and ferns, Vienna seemed so close that I could not imagine I would not see Hector again or that it would be more than thirty years before I returned there.

9

The years go by

Eighteen years after the Vienna Opera Ball of 1960, life had changed significantly for both my mother and myself. Mother was leaving Keepit Dam to move closer to Dawn, who now lived at Tarpoly, the old farm of so many childhood memories. This was when I acquired my two drawings signed 'Picasso'.

That glaring November day when I headed north to Brisbane in my overloaded car, the two Picasso 'Shearers' were still in their simple frames, loosely wrapped in sheeting, softly chattering on the back seat.

The signature on the drawings indicated that they must be valuable. If the drawings were valuable they should be insured and that required a valuation. The valuation would depend on some sort of verification of their origin.

Someone must have suggested the Philip Bacon Gallery in Brisbane. I telephoned and asked to speak to Philip Bacon. I was asked the reason for my call. Carefully I explained that I was looking for advice about how to proceed with identifying two Picasso drawings. The responding silence was longer than I had anticipated. I repeated my request in the belief that my listener had not heard or had not understood me. I was then told that Mr Bacon was not available. I asked when I could ring again and was informed that Mr Bacon was extremely busy. As a result, I did not call again until a month had passed.

This second call followed a similar pattern. I was slightly more insistent. I inquired whether someone else might be able to help me. I was asked whether the drawings were originals or prints. They were originals, I said. My adviser replied that Mr Bacon's opinion was that the drawings I referred to were probably student copies of Picasso's work. (Later I learnt that such artifacts surfaced quite frequently around Brisbane in the 1970s.) I tried to explain that the drawings were signed and dated, did not originate in Brisbane and that I had been familiar with them since the late 1950s. The conversation was firmly terminated. I never did get to speak to Philip Bacon. I would have to find somebody else.

I removed the drawings from their frames, confidently expecting to find their full history and identification conveniently affixed to the back. I was momentarily frustrated that there was no such information there. However, this did not shake my confidence that the whole matter would resolve itself in a few hours as soon as I established to which authority I should show the drawings. I put them under the bed and set the research aside for a quiet moment sometime in the future.

Phyllis McDuff

My *real* life went on at quite a pace. I was married to a Brisbane bookmaker, and I was preoccupied with a house full of young children. I had met my husband during an impulsive trip I took to Cairns in 1962. Ron was tall, dark and debonair. He was fifteen years my senior and as well as coming from Queensland's mysterious and uncharted north he already had glamorous silver threads in his sideburns. As a bookmaker he was the living prototype for every riverboat gambler who had appeared on screen. In keeping with this image I made him a waistcoat of antique French silk brocade that I'd discovered in a little shop in Paddington. He wore it to the races with panache. We married in St Mary's Cathedral in Sydney, barely a year after we met. I chose my father's brother, my beloved Uncle Clarrie, to give me away. He was aged and a little fragile now but as I linked my arm through his he drew himself up very straight. From my sideways glance at this tall figure dressed in tails, I recognised how very much like Joe he was.

We set off down that long, long aisle, our steps silent upon the deep pile of the red carpet. Some way ahead I saw the brass edge where the carpet runners met. I wanted to be sure Uncle Clarrie noticed this hazard. Discreetly pointing with my finger I whispered, 'Mind the join, Uncle.' – 'What's that, girlie?' he responded. I repeated the warning but with the same effect. We were drawing closer and Uncle Clarrie was walking so very straight and tall that I was certain he had no idea that hazardous brass edging was sticking up to trip him in his next stride. I braced myself to steady him and hissed more urgently, 'Mind the join ahead!' – 'I can't hear what you're saying, girl. We'll talk about it later. Meanwhile' – in a dear familiar voice so like my father's – 'don't go arse over head!' And he indicated the join with his pointing chin.

A Story Dreamt Long Ago

Through all the years I lived in Brisbane with my growing family Bettina visited us. Our home was a rambling, old timber Queenslander perched on long legs with creaking joints. We lived on acreage with a menagerie of ducks, geese, goats, cows, dogs and, most importantly, horses. I was using my European training to coach dressage and show jumping, which had only recently attracted a following in Queensland. Bettina coached my star pupils and had an elite following of her own clients. She inevitably brought chaos and delight. She would arrive late, in a rush, half-packed, with urgent phone calls to attend to. She left late, scrambling to the airport with an unconfirmed ticket and negotiating last-minute detours across continents to make desperate connections.

On one occasion she was leaving for Hong Kong and I was about to drive her to the airport. We were running late, rushing down the stairs, when she turned to me and said accusingly, 'You haven't said what I should bring you.' Nothing was further from my mind. Although she often arrived bearing exotic treasures – sari silks, leather jackets, brass ornaments – there was no formula for wish lists. I never thought of stating what she 'should bring' me.

'You have to tell me,' she demanded. 'I hate shopping when I don't know what to get.'

I was halfway down the stairs with a small child on each hip, heading towards the car with the keys clenched between my teeth. When at last I had a free hand I said, 'Pearls, if it's convenient and you're in Hong Kong – perhaps some pearls.'

'What kind of pearls? It could take all day. You have no idea what shopping in Hong Kong is like. I need to know *exactly*!'

As I loaded the luggage into the car I considered her question and remembered that Ellen, Mother's close girlhood friend, who visited me from Vienna from time to time, had a lovely string of blue-grey pearls. She had insisted that I wear them to a concert we'd attended together on her last visit.

'A string of black pearls would be lovely,' I said as I started the car and prepared to deal with traffic, bearing in mind that time allowed us no margin for error.

Suddenly and uncharacteristically my mother brought out a notebook and was busy writing. She asked, 'How long?'

'Just long enough for around my neck – not too tight.'

'I want to know in centimetres – do you want to tie a knot? How many times around your neck?'

'Just a simple strand of pearls, Mum, nothing obvious, perhaps a little over a foot long – about eighteen inches I think would do.'

Mother wrote: *'One-and-a-half feet of black pearls for Phyllis.'* Then she asked, 'What kind of clasp?'

The circumstances did not allow me to design a clasp in my head. Nothing came to mind.

'Perhaps without a clasp,' I said. 'Just a continuous strand of pearls to pop over my head.'

'It will have to be longer. Your head is bigger than eighteen inches. You'd never get them over your head. You can't go anywhere with pearls jammed over your ears. Perhaps you need two feet of pearls.'

'Perhaps you're right,' I said, thinking about the traffic and the squirming kids in the back seat and trying not to give offence by seeming disinterested in my mother's generosity.

She crossed out the note she'd made and wrote something I didn't see.

A Story Dreamt Long Ago

As she leapt from the car at the airport I remember saying: 'Don't go to any special trouble for the pearls, Mum, but they would be lovely if you see something nice.'

•◆•

A month later my mother rang from Frankfurt. This was an era when international phone calls were quite difficult. They had to be booked in advance and were constantly interrupted by telephonists of various nationalities and languages inquiring whether you were properly connected or whether you were 'extending' the standard three-minute limit. The gist of her concern was that she was having trouble with the pearls. Did I really mean *black*? They were very hard to match; the jeweller would have to send away for more. He was doing his best but they would not be ready this week. I tried to reassure her, repeated that I did not want her to go to any special trouble and asked why she was buying them in Frankfurt and not in Hong Kong, where I imagined she would have found something suitable on almost any street corner.

'Hong Kong!' Mother exclaimed. 'You can't get *decent* pearls in Hong Kong!' The phone crackled and hissed – I wasn't sure how much of this was due to her frustration. When the line went dead I hung up, a little relieved but with a sad sense that I had been 'difficult' . . .

•◆•

Weeks passed peacefully until Mother rang again from Munich. The pearl problem had still not been resolved. The pearls that had been ordered in Frankfurt did not match; they were the

173

wrong colour entirely and had been sent back. The jeweller was now waiting on a consignment from New York. Mother had to leave. She could not spend her life in Munich waiting for pearls. She was on her way home now and in due course the pearls would be sent. Would I please let her know as soon as they arrived so that she could be sure they had not been lost?

By now I was feeling very guilty at the trouble I had caused and dared not even imagine the expense. I assured her I would let her know as soon as the pearls arrived, which in due course they did, embedded in white tissue paper and packed unobtrusively in a plain blue plastic box.

I fell in love with them as soon as I removed the lid. They were the perfect size; they gleamed with a living iridescence, a 'Christmas beetle' sheen, beautiful beyond anything I'd imagined. As I reached into the box to pick them up the strands uncoiled to reveal a continuous length of 180 centimetres, nearly six feet. I could not believe it.

I rang Mother, not only to let her know but to find out how I'd received this unbelievable length of pearls. Were they really mine? To keep? Was I perhaps to share them with Dawn and our cousins? That didn't make much sense but I hadn't expected such a lavish piece of jewellery. Perhaps they were fake? Perhaps it was a joke.

When I asked Mother she declared, 'Phyllis, you're impossible! You never say exactly what you want, you wouldn't say how many times around your neck, you did say one-and-a-half metres, and then we said it had to be a little more, so that's what I got.'

I tried to defend myself. 'Remember, Mum, I said one-and-a-half feet – eighteen inches, and a little more to go over my head.'

'Well,' she said, 'you can't send them back. I can't afford the insurance! You'll just have to wear them as they are!'

Which I do, often.

•◆•

The next time I saw my mother she withdrew a leather pearl pouch from her bag. It bore the gold stamp of the famous Viennese jeweller, Köchert. I had seen so much of my mother's jewellery in the familiar Köchert boxes. She had brought my little pearl pouch all the way from Vienna — I could imagine her discussing it with Köchert with more intensity and care than she had applied to the pearls themselves. Now she explained to me: 'You must keep them in this pouch; they like the feel of chamois, and you must wear them often. Pearls get sad when they're neglected. They love the touch of skin.'

I reflected on the strange contradictions in her nature. She could barely focus on the particulars of the pearls but she could not contemplate them without the correct pouch. Her most absurd endeavours had a purpose and completion.

Years later, among the scraps of paper that I sorted through in my attempts to understand my mother, I came across fragments of a poem in her handwriting:

All of my life is a sing-song
a story I dreamt long ago.
Although the days do not last long
each one is a pearl in a row.
Softly they gleam or glitter,
some of them blink like a tear,
in memory of times hard and bitter . . .

Perhaps, if I had caught her in this mood she would have answered questions. My questions would be different now. As I've come to understand the circumstances she lived in and the challenges she faced I would now pose the questions in a gentler tone. Perhaps one day I'll understand exactly what it was she wanted to pass on to me in the plastic box with the beautiful pearls.

•◆•

For years my relationship with Bettina had revolved around horses. I had started working as a show-jumping and dressage coach during the years when professional coaches were banned from Pony Club and viewed with suspicion by all equestrian administrators. It was felt that the sport should be kept 'pure' and only 'genuine amateurs' included.

On the one hand I had hundreds of enthusiastic clients, mostly competent riders, who wanted to embrace the new forms of Olympic competition. On the other hand there was the stiffest official opposition to any form of professionalism making insidious inroads into the Queensland equestrian scene. Barely five years earlier, in 1960, Australia's three-day-event team, captained by Bill Roycroft, had won gold at the Rome Olympics. This inspired the nation. Pony Club officials, inevitably parents, begged me to coach their children – secretly – while they themselves went off to meetings to endorse the passionate moves to keep the sport 'clean'.

For myself, I could not afford to spend upwards of fifty hours per week doing voluntary coaching, then 'finding myself accused of favouritism if any child missed out. The normal fee-for-service system seemed an intelligent alternative. I did not anticipate the strange revulsion that surged through committee gatherings.

I simply soldiered on, ignoring all of the gossip that surrounded my activities: analysis of whom I might be coaching, discussion of whether judges were justified in disqualifying riders suspected of being coached by 'professionals', whether parents could be restrained from this new and dangerous cult influence. Ultimately the desperate will to win, with all its risk and costs, became the overpowering influence. More and more pupils enrolled – and admitted it. They even flaunted their success.

Bettina came on visits and participated. She coached the more advanced riders and was both feared and famous for her passion. She was utterly intolerant, demanding immediate perfection. Any deviation was interpreted as a deep character flaw, a shadow over one's sanity and a question of one's breeding. If a rider's hands or heels or knee positions were not perfectly aligned and sustained, the rider risked subjection to hysterical and abusive criticism, which today would probably see my mother jailed. Throughout the 1960s, 1970s and 1980s she not only got away with it, she was loved for it.

I lagged behind. I applied, quite strongly, some principles of educational process. I sought to encourage rather than destroy. This meant that my mother and I were constantly at loggerheads while often achieving the same goals. Her surviving pupils were as hard as nails, were indomitable competitors; under pressure their performances were heroic.

Despite our differences we often worked with the same clients, travelled together and judged at the same venues. Even when this was not officially arranged we often went together and argued the pros and cons of each judge's decision during the long drives home.

On one occasion we were guests at a major indoor show-jumping competition. This type of venue was new to Queensland and made unfamiliar demands on horse and rider. The indoor courses were tight, requiring more control; the surface was deep, requiring enormous impulsion. There was little opportunity of gaining points for speed; precise footwork offered the only chance of trimming split seconds from the times.

My mother and I were honoured with seats in the glassed-in judges' box and watched the riders meet this challenge with mixed results. Bettina's frustration gained momentum; viciously she critiqued each rider. She carped with increasing venom until I was forced to offer a defence for one particular rider whose horse was making valiant attempts. The rider lurched, miscalculated and mistook the course. Bettina rolled her eyes and groaned. I intercepted her remarks. 'He's not that bad, Mum; he hasn't much experience; he'll settle into it in time.'

'Experience! He doesn't need experience! Brains are what he needs! He's got no brains at all! He hasn't worked it out!' she raged.

I tried reason. 'Even when you work it out you can't always pull it together. Things go wrong. You need time to experiment.'

'Experiment! What about the horse? How do you think it feels about this experiment? That horse did everything he could to lift the lumpy imbecile – and they still crashed three fences. The horse deserves a medal – and that rider should be shot.'

I tried to quieten her, although it didn't really matter. The microphones were carefully controlled and the officials in the judging room knew my mother well. Most had cut their teeth on her poisonous commentary.

From our privileged viewpoint the irritating rider could be seen outside preparing his second horse. Theatrically, Bettina shuddered with revulsion and muttered, 'You talk about experience. He's been at it for years — ten years ago I had him in a group at Pony Club. How many horses will he ruin before he gets enough *experience?*'

I was exasperated. I wanted to end the conversation. I drew a purposeful breath and hissed, 'He needs time and more experience, Mum. Lot's more. *You don't go to bed one night and wake up in the morning with experience!*' How could I have known that at that moment the technician had recklessly turned on our mikes?

My words of wisdom rang out through the silent stadium. There was a breathless moment then uproarious applause. For years afterwards people I barely knew sidled up to me at barbecues to offer me the sauce and to question with feigned innocence whether, in my respected view, a particular horse or judge or coach had sufficient experience?

The changing shape of our mother–daughter relationship was brought home to me on one of my last visits while Bettina was still at Keepit Dam. She was a crack shot, familiar with many styles of firearms. She knew their range and specifications and could clean and assemble guns with ease, almost with affection. She attributed this competence to years of stag stalking on her father's mountain estates. This passion, shared with her father amid the Alpine scenery nurtured their growing intimacy and after his death this interest continued, indeed intensified. Among the many photos showing her amongst an entourage of keepers and with various firearms, there are none with her siblings. Only my mother, in her twenties. Here and there an image of Maria von Kozaryn clad in sturdy walking boots proved that she had joined the hunting party to share a festive feast. My mother told us of the week-long sorties made into the mountains, camping at night in isolated huts. The purpose was to cull the deer herds and to provide venison for the dining table.

My father had respected Bettina's marksmanship and her professionalism. His experience had been different, and although competent with the firearms necessary in the bush he avoided them as much as possible. One of his brothers had longed for a .22 rifle for his sixteenth birthday. This was the classic weapon for shooting kangaroos and foxes for their skins and the means of earning handy extra money. The family considered it appropriate and clubbed together to provide the rite-of-passage gift.

That afternoon, two of the brothers went to test the weapon. The birthday boy, though thoroughly instructed, shot his brother dead in a split second of carelessness. My father knew, first-hand, the anguish of over-familiarity with guns and was fastidiously cautious. From time to time he'd clean his gun and say, almost to himself: 'I ought to teach the girls. They should know how to handle firearms. They'll need to know.' But he always put it off and by the time he left us we had never touched his gun.

While, as a child, I'd been in hospital with osteomyelitis, my mother missed visiting me only once. That particular day she had gone with my father to buy a horse. She chose a brown thoroughbred filly of medium height, reasonably well built with refined head and legs. Although the body was not exquisitely proportioned my mother loved her and rode her in preference to all others. Did she remind Bettina of her beloved tournament horse Bubunut? The mare was called Biddy and slowly aged in my mother's loving care.

On this visit to Keepit Dam to see my mother I arrived in the early evening. Now in her late sixties, she was distracted, rummaging through drawers, barely acknowledging me, unusually withdrawn. At last she asked me to help her find the box of bullets she'd misplaced – and was forced by way of explanation to say: 'Biddy's down – she's been weak for days. I coaxed her close to the house and tried to feed her up but she's got down in the gully and I'll have to shoot her before it gets dark – I don't want her down and alone through the night. I don't want her to lie in the sun tomorrow.' While she made this calm and reasoned explanation the tears streamed down her face.

Not thinking, I reached for the gun, which she surprisingly relinquished. She had a moment's hesitation. 'Can you manage?' she questioned as she slid the bullet into the chamber. At that moment I still felt confident and hugged her briefly with my spare arm, trying to transfer comfort. I went out to find where Biddy lay while Bettina waited alone to hear the shot.

I went to the head of the gully and followed it along to find the mare. This gave me too much time to think, to remember all the versions of Biddy I had known. First the flighty young mare I had avoided riding as a child. She'd seemed too fast and slippery. I had not felt safe on her until I was bigger and she was older. Then the years of solid workmanship when mustering cattle or running the horses home. 'Take Biddy' had been a daily solution to some unexpected escape by poddy calves or intrusion of the neighbours' cattle. The years of coming home to find Biddy's newest foal in the paddock by the house. A series of long-legged, soft brown fillies that went on to serve the family as general saddle horses, or to take our kids to Pony Club.

Now the light was fading and I was hurrying to find the Biddy who was too weak to get up. What if I couldn't find her? Would that excuse me from my reckless offer? I didn't entertain the thought. I knew my father's rules for animals too well: 'If you know you can't help it, shoot it. You owe them that. They serve you well enough.'

I came upon her lying quietly, like a shadow, already disappearing into a fold in the earth. I squatted down beside her to stroke her face and look into her soft brown eyes. She nickered – was it out of habit? Or was there something she wanted me to understand? I wanted her to know that what I was about to do was being done with love, with deep respect and was a difficult thank you for the years of service.

Then I realised that I had no idea how to aim and fire a gun. My father's fear had kept me well away from firearms. I had no confidence that I could shoot to kill at any distance. The light was fading fast. Where should I aim? I knew from seeing skulls of long-dead horses that the obvious centre forehead was a solid bony plate. In my ignorance I couldn't calculate whether my bullet would penetrate. I couldn't bear to frighten Biddy with an ineffective shot. I felt my mother's tension as she listened through the darkening evening. I struck a deal, explained to Biddy that I had to hold the gun, gently, to the groove above her eye. I stood behind her head and pulled the trigger. Biddy's soft eye closed, she let out one long sigh. Then I sat beside her, stroked her still-warm neck, and watched the stars come out.

I went into the house quietly across the back veranda. My mother was making herself busy in the laundry.

'She's gone,' I said.

'Thank you,' she answered simply. Her bland response echoed in my head: *'Gone – thank you – gone – thank you.'* We were both hollowed out with sadness.

•—•

Around this time I broached the Picasso matter with my sister. Carefully, so as not to trigger memories of my 'difficult' behaviour in the past, I asked, 'Do you remember the Picassos that Mother gave you for your wedding? Do you still have them? Have you had them valued? Do you know their history?' – all in a gush to get the questions out and avoid a rebuff.

Dawn laughed. 'They're not really Picassos; we took them to an expert. They're uncatalogued, valueless. Apparently they're student copies.'

'Oh,' I said. 'I asked because I have the other two. The ones that Mother used to have hanging on the wall. They're signed and dated – I took them out of the frames and they are originals, pen and ink. The student must have been quite ambitious to sign and date them so carefully.'

Dawn poured another cup of tea.

Dawn prompted me into remembering Bettina's delight when she first showed us the drawings in their frames. 'They're absolutely beautiful,' she had announced. Dawn and I could not quite see it but didn't want to spoil her mood. We recalled how she had held the drawings high against the wall, measuring the light. We took turns to hold them while she stood in front assessing, her head tilted to one side. 'No not there – here perhaps.' We held the frames in place. Eventually one of us was sent to get the hammer from the shed and we stood on a rickety fruit box to bang the pin into the wall. That day she had only hung the 'Shearers'. The two drawings that were later given to Dawn had been stored away.

Dawn's information discouraged further research. More practical and urgent matters consumed my days; for ten more years my drawings stayed under the bed – as I moved house, as the family grew up, as I left home and returned.

•◆•

Those were the years I spent coming to terms with the guilt of the traditional Catholic divorce. The healing process drew me closer to Dawn, who was now living on the Tarpoly farm where we had lived with our parents so long ago. I visited this territory with my children who knew little of my background or of the life I'd lived there. They barely knew my father's name and certainly did not understand that this was where I'd spent my childhood with him or that they were playing on the exact spot where he had fallen in his fatal accident.

I remember a cluster of cousins happily playing in the shed. There were seven little bodies immersed in the construction of a grand prix raceway for their matchbox cars. This was modelled from clay dug from the creek bank and hauled up to the shed in buckets when Dawn and I insisted it was time to come inside out

A Story Dreamt Long Ago

of the scorching heat. The sun-brown bodies were clay-streaked, their heads towards centre circle, they kneeled and stretched and murmured as the construction progressed. The adults went inside to boil the billy. Soon a five-year-old arrived to gather food. He held his shirt out to be filled with plums and biscuits. As he happily turned to go I asked was everything all right out there in the shed. Were they happy playing all alone? 'Oh,' he said, wide-eyed, 'we're not alone. Joe's out there looking after us!'

In the stunned silence that followed, Dawn's husband had the presence of mind to say calmly: 'That's good. What's Joe doing?'

'Just having a smoke and telling us stories,' came the cheerful, confident reply.

Confronted with my adult problems, I had forgotten that 'Joe was out there looking after us'.

Dawn's husband poured the tea and, glancing up with a half-smile, asked, 'Was that message clear enough?'

Years later I came to understand the Aboriginal belief that 'the old people' live among us, to help and to guide and when needed they materialise to bring their healing message.

10

Connecting with the past

Now that I had time to reflect, I became intrigued by the inconsistencies that surrounded my mother's life. I longed for explanations. Whispered voices in the hallways of my childhood. A hastily packed suitcase. The 'lost' Otto. A masked ball that ended abruptly. A man stepping from the shadows. *Schade*.

Nothing Bettina ever did was pointless; every gesture, every outrageous, smart remark lured me away from issues she considered dangerous. She would enchant us into abandoning a line of questioning that could bring me into territory she did not want explored. In a prim voice she would say: 'Ladies do not discuss money, politics or religion.' She would smile charmingly, perhaps ask me to pass something or inquire after one of my friends to steer me off course. She might tell me a delicious piece of scandal – she kept a store of these for the right moments. I remember one cunning incident when I was about eleven. She'd had enough of my questions and said, 'Do you know what I just found out? Grace Kelly has to wear contact lenses to make her eyes look normal.' '*What!*' I squeaked, successfully ensnared. 'Yes, she is cross-eyed, very badly cross-eyed.' At this point Bettina crossed her own eyes, hilariously. 'She can't see where she's going. Strange combination, cross-eyes and knock-knees don't you think?' She baited her hooks shrewdly. She knew Dawn and I adored Grace Kelly. We had watched *The Swan* and she was the epitome of the princess we both aspired to be. Bettina knew how passionately I'd respond to this salacious titbit. 'It's not true! You can't say that!' Diversion accomplished.

Finally, if I pursued too closely, her anger dropped down like a portcullis.

•◆•

Bettina aged, her body weakened, she went into a home and relied on a wheelchair for transportation. Ankerbrot had been sold a long time ago, in 1969, and the other European properties had passed on to new owners. It had been some years since she'd been able to travel back to Europe to visit friends of her youth with whom she had maintained contact. I knew their names from childhood memories and the many, many letters that had come to Australia. They were like characters from storybooks. At last, at the age of eighty-three, Bettina asked me to take her home again just one more time, to say goodbye.

So now I looked up the addresses, and for the first time I was the one who wrote letters, made connections, fixed dates until the storybook took on a tangible form that linked with faint memories – and real recollections emerged of buildings, episodes and faces buried under thirty years of daily family responsibilities.

I would never have left Australia otherwise. I had grown up and married here and felt no curiosity about Europe which I had last visited when I was seventeen. To an extent I had enjoyed the parties and the holidays beside the lake, I had enjoyed the skiing and the balls. But Australia was home, safe and familiar. I felt no lack of options in my Australian life.

However, I could understand Bettina's wish to return to Austria one last time. I looked at the wheelchair and decided on a fitness-training program for myself. I knew I needed to be fit to get myself and Mother, wheelchair and luggage around Europe for thirty days. I walked for miles. I did stretches. I carried backpacks. I knew I needed to be strong, lean and sharp and I knew I could achieve that. It was simply a matter of being focused and prepared. It was just like riding a cross-country course.

We landed at the airport in Vienna on 9 September 1992. Mother's birthday was actually ten days later, but her dear aged friends had mistaken their calculations and assumed the arrival date coincided with her birthday. They had gathered a large group and organised a welcoming birthday party. About thirty people were gathered in an airport VIP lounge complete with red carpet along which Bettina entered with complete aplomb. There were bouquets of flowers, buffet refreshments and the 'Blue Danube Waltz' playing in the background. Mucki's was the first face I recognised. There were many that I did not know at all. The room buzzed with a sense of reunion while I was kept busy noting in my diary 'bookings' for visits with Bettina.

A Story Dreamt Long Ago

Among the reception was a faintly familiar figure, tall and gracious. Why did his shape and gestures seem so familiar to me? He seemed to take the form of a knight in the castle of my dreams.

As he took leave of the gathering, he bowed formally over my hand looked into my face and said, 'Madame, if there is anything I can do to assist your visit, I am, as always, at your service.' And that's when I remembered. Gaping back at him I heard my voice: 'You were a knight in a castle — is that a dream?'

His eyes lit up. 'Madame, I remember fondly the castle where I visited each summer when I went down to the Tyrol to report to Madame Bettina.'

Scenes came flashing through my mind. 'You were a knight in the garden and we were princesses, Dawn and I. There were robbers and wolves outside, we climbed the stone walls and ran away. We had sword fights! We had coronation ceremonies! Jousting matches!'

'Yes, yes,' he said. 'You were most energetic young ladies, bush princesses. You could climb anything — trees, walls; I feared you would be hurt. As we played in the garden I invented the Rescuing Knight to try to preserve your lives. I was not used to such energy. Your father thought it only natural; he could not imagine that you should sit quietly and read, or play draughts. He felt you should run and climb as much as possible. So I was privileged to be the Knight.'

'And was there a real castle?'

'Of course, Madame, Schloss Itter, in the Tyrol — no longer in the family's possession. You may be interested to visit there — you would surely be most welcome.'

With that he handed me his card, bowed one more time, repeated 'If I can be of service', clicked his knightly heels and left the gathering. I looked at the card – it was Engineer Heinrich, who had been on the board of Ankerbrot and was a close associate of Bettina's through all those years.

Later I telephoned him. We visited and sat in a long room overlooking his garden as he and Bettina reminisced over mutual acquaintances. Then a quiet fell across the room.

'Tell me,' I said, 'tell me the whole story. About Ankerbrot, about the castle. Please tell me.'

'Madame, surely you know more than I. Surely your mother has shared the family history.'

I smiled and said that I knew that my mother had come from a well-established family in Vienna, that her father had left her well provided for. I knew the name Ankerbrot and something of its history, but that there was much more I would like to know.

The Knight turned to my mother, inclined his head and said, 'With your permission, Madame, I am happy to share my memories.' The request was courteous but firm. My mother was unprepared, perhaps outmanoeuvred. The Knight clearly intended to place the family history in the keeping of another generation. She was forced into pretence, nodded her agreement, and with a muttered 'It's all so long and boring' gave limited consent.

The Knight described the Mendls' magnificent private estates. These included pine forests that were systematically replanted and harvested. Timber from these forests was brought down to the valley by teams of draught horses. The saw mills, dairies, horse stables and the manor house were in the valley surrounded by vegetable gardens and orchards. The produce from the gardens was bottled, dried or pickled and supplemented the produce from the gardens of Villa Mendl in Vienna. One of my mother's closest friends had been a man named George Lippart, who was also a friend of Otto Schönthal. The two men would visit Villa Mendl to play tennis, enjoy private concerts and attend dances and parties. Lippart, however, turned out to be an enthusiastic supporter of Adolf Hitler. In an attempt to curry flavour with his Nazi colleagues, he arranged for Villa Mendl to be requisitioned. It was to become the residence of Dr (Baron) Gustav Otto Wächter, the incoming head of the SS, the dreaded 'Special Staff' of the German occupation force. This was a betrayal my mother would never be able to forgive.

When Wächter withdrew from Austria, he looted the Mendl family's treasure, including their art collection and antique crystal glassware. He took everything except the Bösendorfer grand piano. In the years after World War II, attempts were made to bring Wächter to justice for war crimes. These did not succeed: it seems that Wächter used the loot from Villa Mendl and other similar properties to purchase safe custody within the Vatican, where he lived under a new identity until his death.

As the war drew to a close, assets were stripped; generations of timber were felled without replacement planting; milking herds were slaughtered for army supplies; wineries were plundered for precious vintages or booze for the night. All the machinery on the farms and at the bread-making factory was run-down, had been misused, and was technologically outdated. Debt had been accumulated against every asset and demands for payment were overdue.

At the war's end, management of the Mendl properties went

to administrators appointed by international committees. There was no motive and no capital to restore the assets. The 'solution' offered was that the properties should be nationalised and compensation paid on the pitiful current values of the dysfunctional estates.

The Knight described how on my mother's first trip to Austria, when I had missed her desperately as a child, she had fought tenaciously. Penniless, she dealt and wangled, swapped and promised, first to have the assets restored to her in her own right, then to redeem the debt, then to restore the assets to their original profitable state. In doing this she faced powerful opposition. Every possible obstruction was placed in her way. Fees, levies and back taxes were demanded. I'd overheard her telling her sister Lucie: 'The vultures circled waiting for me to lie down.' At the time, I'd considered the comment a dramatic outburst. Now I understood. The vultures were the would-be buyers at the meagre prices that the valuations of the day indicated. These low valuations made it impossible to raise the necessary finance to rebuild.

No one doubted the long-term viablility of the properties but everyone wanted a slice of the action. They calculated that the more desperate Bettina became the more she would sacrifice. She faced a wall of opposition and bluffed her way through it. She hocked the jewellery Tante Maria had hidden. She was discreet; no one should be aware how short of funds she was. With a few small loans from loyal trading associates she talked big. Without being specific she radiated the impression that she'd married the man who owned Australia. Using clever misinformation she convinced her opponents that they

A Story Dreamt Long Ago

were doomed to fail. They began to see advantages in alliance with her and her mysterious commercial backers. One by one they came with secret offers of support, breaking the finance cartel. She drove hard bargains, demanded low interest, delayed repayments, made profit-share deals to key associates – but they would have to wait! She trusted no one – except Otto Schönthal, her fellow conspirator. They were often a whisper away from disaster but they held their course and as Europe slowly healed the Mendl empire stood on firm ground once again.

Bettina sat impassive throughout these revelations. From time to time she quietly questioned the Knight – 'Is that how you saw it?' – or she would shrug dismissively at the description of a victory. I felt a growing sense of relief that the seeming chaos of our lives, for which I'd blamed her, had had some reason. The afternoon awakened a sneaking admiration for her dogged, creative determination. I now appreciated my mother's role in the scheme of things.

•◆•

A week later, accompanied by our dear friend Mucki, I drove under the portcullis of Schloss Itter. As we approached, I feared the ancient mechanism might choose that fraction of a second to collapse, to drop the gate, to spear me in my seat as I passed beneath it. Bettina was in the car with me, slightly annoyed that I should insist on this diversionary visit to Itter, and that I was sufficiently a peasant to be intrigued by ownership of castles and histories of great estates.

In fact, Schloss Itter had frequently appeared in my dreams of childhood spent in Austria, in summer, in the mountains of the Tyrol, playing in the castle gardens with Dawn. I remembered what we wore, the layout of the grounds, the texture of the stone, the exact density and moisture of the grass beneath my feet – perhaps because it was so different from the dry white grass of the Australian countryside. The castle was more than a dream. It was a place and a reality and I had lured it out of its mysterious past and made it real. And because it stood there, stone on stone enrolled in a book of title stamped with dates, I knew that I had made connection with more than dreams – it was with a real past that somehow had connection with the life I lived now.

My mother had not waited for her prophecy of commercial disaster to overtake Schloss Itter. She had successfully placed the Hotel Schloss Itter in other hands, and it had since passed into private ownership once more. We were welcomed by the owners on the terrace. They were a small, round gentleman of approximately sixty years and his young blonde wife. They were honoured by our visit, they guided us about the rooms and told of renovations, they served us tea and asked if we would come back for another visit. With a gracious, distant smile Bettina replied, 'Probably not.' Wordlessly she exuded the impression that there had been enough indulgence of a daughter who had nothing more pressing to do than view an ancient castle simply because it was a former family asset.

Despite my sense of victory and delight, the visit could not be termed a complete success. The new owners had been extremely anxious to please us but became preoccupied with the large, clear sign on the back of my mother's wheelchair. '*Achtung!*' it stated in letters ten centimetres high. 'Stolen property!! This chair is the property of the Innsbruck Hospital. Anyone sighting this property outside the hospital grounds should report the theft immediately.' As I stood behind the chair I obscured the sign until we were safely seated for tea. Once revealed it fascinated our hosts who were so preoccupied with the implication that they were suddenly unable to conduct a normal conversation. After I became aware of the signage I did not want to embarrass Mucki (who had lovingly made the arrangements for my mother's visit) by making any reference to the chair. I offered no explanation.

As the tension settled unresolved into the afternoon I recognised the view, through the internal rooms, of my beloved garden. 'There it is!' I shrieked unexpectedly. I pointed, waving my arms until everyone at the table turned in the direction of my gestures. Nothing they saw justified my excitement but I kept on pointing, waving, shouting, 'Outside, just as I remember. It is there.' At last I managed to say the words 'The garden'. And with a relieved and gracious smile the host stood up, and offered to take me into the stone-walled garden that had so excited me.

As I burst through the door leading into the garden I saw the swimming pool that must have been added since my childhood and which was now under maintenance. It was surrounded by hoses and pipes. In places, the garden had been dug up to expose these workings. I rushed past to view the valley beyond the old stone walls. This left the host hurrying along behind – until I heard a yelp of pain. I swung around to see the small, round man rolling in apparent agony clutching at his ankle. I knew exactly what to do. I had done years of St John's

Ambulance training. My children had survived their childhood accidents. This crisis was entirely my fault; I'd been far too impetuous and I would find the remedy. I turned on the water full blast, and despite the vigorous protests from the owner, I removed the shoe and sock from the swelling ankle and proceeded to apply the hose.

The screams and my urgent instructions brought his wife hurrying from the house to witness the scene of her husband writhing on the ground in protest while being hosed down by an over-zealous guest. This, coupled with the *'Achtung!'* signage on the wheelchair, triggered an obvious loss of confidence in her visitors who, all things considered, left soon after.

•◆•

During that trip we had other lovely jaunts, sometimes with the 'aunts' Mucki and Agathe together. Tante Maria had died long since, and my mother admitted that she missed her terribly. We met mother's old flames, on walking sticks and in their eighties. With shining eyes they reminisced about the tennis parties and the balls, about the frivolous flirtations and the tragic romantic betrayals. Sometimes as I left the room I sensed a change of mood, as though some secret was threatening to get out. Their eyes locked with a new expression, voices changed, the laughter dried up and I was left outside.

Sometimes a comment was half-made to be halted in midsentence by a sharp glance from my mother. Sometimes this happened on the presumption that my German would not follow the detail of the conversation; but the glances were reminders that I must not be included.

A Story Dreamt Long Ago

Increasingly I knew that things were being communicated, arranged, negotiated that I was not to know of. There were too many changes of pace in conversation. I knew that I could trust my German-attuned ear to understand the nuances of tone and inflection that revealed the desperation and intensity of conversations masquerading as merely social and lighthearted.

I began to sense smiles, nods, slick changes of tempo and conversations winding full circle... Suddenly there was a blunt interruption to the pattern — we were told there was a message for Bettina to be delivered to her in person at a meeting at Martin's house the next day. I did not know who Martin was but took down the instructions and arranged for a taxi to deliver us to the address.

A tiny, creaking antique lift carried my mother in her wheelchair up three levels while I ran up ahead to assure a safe exit at the top. The afternoon was like so many similar afternoons we'd spent. Familiar faces served us with cakes and tea, witty reminiscences, elegantly reported scandals.

Then the question hanging in the air. 'Bettina, now that there is better information from the East, what have you heard about your brother Otto?'

'Nothing — I tried to find out, but nothing, no contact.' I thought this a strange response considering that my mother knew that the 1954 Red Cross report had officially reported him dead, a prisoner of the Nazis.

Then Martin said, 'You know he crashed the plane?'

My mother shrugged; I could not gauge whether in dismissal or in disbelief.

'He crashed the plane and he was killed. I've had reports

confirmed quite recently by a substantial witness: the co-pilot, who escaped. He himself died just a few months ago, in the East. He wanted you to know – arranged for us to tell you.'

My mother betrayed no emotion. 'I may have heard something . . . One hears all sorts of speculation.' And she turned the conversation to another topic.

In the taxi on the way home I could not wait to question her. 'What plane? You never mentioned a plane. Is that why you suspected he might have been somewhere in the East, behind the Iron Curtain?' When I stopped to draw a breath I realised she was very quiet.

'Don't believe everything you hear,' she said with a sigh. Suddenly she seemed too tired to continue the conversation.

A few days later there were other messages from Martin – never Martin personally – but intermediaries telephoned wanting to arrange another meeting. My mother was reluctant. 'I've met him already, I've heard all he has to say, I'm not interested in seeing Martin again.' But he was insistent and she relented. I arranged another taxi to wind through those narrow, cobbled streets.

This time we met in a tiny apartment with just Martin and his housekeeper. Her role seemed to be to keep me out of earshot of the conversation by requiring my assistance in the minuscule kitchen. We took a very long time to make a simple afternoon tea. When we joined Martin and my mother they were talking about Otto. Martin smiled inclusively at me as he said, 'There is a possibility that Otto survived the crash. He may have taken the co-pilot's identity. When the person who was supposedly the co-pilot died just a few months ago he was most particular that Bettina be advised.'

A Story Dreamt Long Ago

This time on the way home I sensed a deep calm in my mother. With a happy smile she whispered, 'He did get out, and he lived. I knew he lived. I knew he'd fly away.'

I didn't want to spoil her pleasure but I needed to ask, 'How can you know for sure the messages are genuine? Anyone could make those stories up. Even Martin wasn't sure – he said "a possibility".'

'No,' she replied, 'you won't understand but that last message was from Otto. I know it was from Otto.'

At that time I put her belief down to her desire to resolve the questions around his death to suit herself.

'What about the Red Cross report? That seemed quite definite,' I persisted.

My mother looked straight at me: she seemed impatient with my simplistic thinking. 'But of course, that's exactly what they were paid to do!'

She would say nothing further, and I was left shocked at her calm, ruthless manipulation.

My mind went back to the strange trip to Berlin in 1953. At the time it seemed to have no purpose and no plan. I considered the possibility that Bettina had been gathering the last shreds of information about Otto and arranging his 'death' to meet legal requirements, so that his family could inherit. This would give him cover in whatever new life he'd gone to.

The last fragment of the puzzle fell into place when I later read the diary that Abby, Bettina's nanny, had kept. It had been given to me from the pre-war treasures rescued by Tante Maria. There were many items that Bettina had not brought home to Australia, particularly documents, and Tante Maria had assumed the role of archivist. It must have been a burden to her. In the limited space of her tiny flat I'm sure she pared down the bulk to its minimum. I was touched to find this very personal diary still treasured thirty years after Tante Maria's death, when it was handed on to me.

I knew that Abby had been the beloved nurse shared by Bettina and Otto. She featured in so many of the stories of Bettina's first memories and she appeared in happy childhood photos as a radiant young woman. The photos were not posed; she was inevitably snapped as she made some caring gesture. She radiated warmth. I remember meeting her just once. During our visit to Vienna in 1953 we drove into the country and briefly met a plump, faded woman in her sixties. Only when she smiled did I recognise the radiance of the old photographs. This was indeed the Abby of the stories.

After Bettina's death I had more time to rummage. I took the diary out and read the careful copperplate script on the first few pages. The writing was interspersed with photographs, the whole work designed with utmost care. It was Abby's gift to 'her children', Bettina and Otto: her fond memories of their childhood from which their mother, Emily Mendl, had been chiefly absent. Perhaps Abby feared a separation. Without her diary, who would reveal their stories? Who would cherish their first identities?

The diary started in 1907 and described Otto as a baby. I was surprised that Abby seemed to be his wet-nurse. I used a dictionary to check the German word *stillen*; I was not mistaken, it did not mean to calm or pacify, it meant to breastfeed. This implied that Abby had had her own child – what had become of it? I was mystified. I continued to read about the baby pranks and shared experiences as the children grew. I sensed Abby's concern over their minor accidents and illness.

Then I read a passsage that struck home. The children were older now, perhaps nine and eleven. Normally an eleven-year-old boy would not have had a nurse and perhaps Abby was kept on for Bettina. Certainly the photos show them all together almost until Bettina went away to school. Abby wrote of her dread of Fritz Mendl's stern discipline. All of his children were quite brutally 'belted' to enforce his rules. This ritual took place in his study and spread anguish throughout the house.

Abby wrote: *'Thank God the children seem to have a code. When they are questioned by their father they let each other know what alibis they've used. Something in their words informs the other what is fact and what is a convenient story. In this way they protect each other from those beatings that are agony for all of us.'*

Perhaps this was how, in 1992, Bettina knew the difference between the first message indicating that Otto had been killed when his stolen escape plane crashed and the second message revealing that it was the co-pilot who had died and that Otto had assumed his identity and lived out his long life 'in the East'. It is too late now to seek an explanation from Bettina.

·•·

Bettina's friend from the tennis-party days at Villa Mendl, Ellen Müller-Preis, had come and gone to Australia, visiting me almost every year since 1972. With each trip she pleaded with me to go to Europe, to find some culture, to research my family, to get in touch with 'people'. I hardly understood her urgency, and, tied by my own family and duty, I was not inclined to follow fantasy. The here and now had dominated me twenty-four hours each day. I had visited the house where my mother was born. A nice big house. Dawn and I had played in the garden with Ellen's sons; these were fond memories but I had had no reason to go back.

For thirty years I had refused to be ensnared into the mystery of my European heritage, but now here I was, and Ellen fought to break the silence. She fought with me and with my mother and the wall of years that helped to obscure the information she wanted me to have.

Ellen wanted me to investigate my mother's bank accounts. She was certain there must be some of the old family money still in Vienna and she wanted me to have it. Yet my mother was totally dependent on me; I could not leave her for an hour. How could I possibly go from bank to bank around Vienna, asking for information?

Ellen made several visits to our hotel and insisted I use her brief half-hour presence to make some attempts. Unable to withstand her insistence I zigzagged to the familiar branches where I'd had pocket-money accounts in 1960. To my surprise I was offered encouragement and support. Bank officials gave advice on how to trace old accounts. At one bank I was told: 'We believe we may be able to help but you must supply account numbers and your mother must personally visit to arrange authority for you to access the account.'

Ellen would not give up. She remembered how Mucki had withdrawn money from my mother's accounts for small shopping errands. 'Sometime in the 1970s she bought Bettina riding gloves,' Ellen remembered. 'They were posted out to Australia. Mucki must know the account numbers.'

Under pressure, I broached the subject with Mucki, who amazed me by agreeing with Ellen. Yes – she had shopped for my mother from time to time, but not recently. There was a bank account she was authorised to draw from. The number was written on the back flap of a white envelope with other family papers in a carton, kept for the last fifteen years on a top shelf of a storage unit in the attic. She would have the housekeeper bring it down and I could sit with her and help to go through the documents.

While Ellen sat with my mother, who was always impatient at my brief absences, Mucki and I sorted through the box of family paper fragments, neatly piled in chronological order, starting before the turn of the century. Many of the contents had been left to Mucki by Tante Maria. There were letters from children whose adult lives had now long since ended. There were old housekeeping accounts, lists of instruction to house staff in the castle where Tante Maria was born, inventories of the personal possessions of relatives who died at war, at sea, at home. I held very little hope of finding the triangular back flap of a white linen envelope; yet, in due course, without the least surprise on Mucki's part, there it was. Just a clearly written number with absolutely no other identifying link.

I rang the bank and spoke with the clerk who had been so helpful. 'Oh yes,' he said, 'that matches my records; please bring Bettina Mendl here with her identifying documents to authorise transactions.' I lied. I told my mother that Mucki had suggested that she might like to use her 'shopping account' and had offered me the number as I didn't have it. If she wished, I could take her to the bank to make withdrawals. My mother thought this was a grand idea; the account held the equivalent of $5000 Australian dollars – a convenient addition to the budget for our trip, but more importantly it was symbolic – it proved Ellen's theories sound; there was still family history and family money in Vienna about which I knew absolutely nothing. Ellen passionately wanted me to have access to both.

•—•

Towards the end of our adventurous month we stayed with the Winklemans, old friends in Munich. I had met Helmut Winkleman in our teenage dancing years when he had come to Vienna with his sister to be part of my debutante group at the Opera Ball. Now, at their Munich home, we stayed up late, drank too much wine, reminisced and told stories of our long lives since our last meeting. Of course, my mother had been constantly in touch, visiting often in the thirty years since I'd last been in Europe. At 4am on our final night we said a wine-wobbly goodnight in the foyer as we went off to bed.

Then Sybille, the wife of this good friend, turned back, touched my arm and said, 'Phyllis, you'll forgive my asking, but your mother's beautiful Picasso drawings – you still have them?'

I laughed, then sighed. 'Oh yes, they're underneath my bed. But they're not Picassos, they're some sort of student copy, without merit or value – or so it appears.'

Sybille did not smile; she shook her head and said, 'No, I know Picasso's work, I know those drawings. I saw them in Vienna. I saw them in Australia. I know where they fit in the

A Story Dreamt Long Ago

context of his work – when I visit the Musée Picasso in Paris I know the sequence they are missing from. The two drawings of the 'Man with the Lamb' are absolutely definitely Picassos.'

With that she reached up to a bookshelf and took down the catalogue of a Munich exhibition of Picasso's work she had visited. She pointed out the many similar sketches, the dates, the signatures, the paper sizes and the fact that most, though not all, were identified by their Zervos catalogue number.

Christian Zervos, an art connoisseur and friend of Pablo Picasso, had embarked on the mammoth task of cataloguing all Picasso's known works. Picasso himself had initially supervised this catalogue raisonné. It should have been a complete and irreproachable inventory; indeed, many experts did rely on it entirely.

Among the sketches in the exhibition catalogue before us was one bearing the familiar date *26/9/43*. It had no signature, but there was a Zervos number. The subject of the drawing was the lamb – the same lamb that appeared in my drawing of that date. I thought what a dedicated student it must have taken to create anew a Picasso-like drawing, to set perfectly in context not a copy of an existing drawing, by which one might learn new techniques, but a fabrication created from intimate research *and signed*, while this acknowledged work was not.

The student-copy theory seemed too innocent to cover all these circumstances.

'Well then,' I said aloud, 'it will be a simple matter to follow that up when I get home.'

11

Meeting Sara Murphy

Safely back in Australia, I had a focus for my investigation. At last the drawings emerged from under the bed. Now that I had been back to Austria I had glimpsed the hidden patterns beneath the surface of my mother's life, and the drawings took on a new vitality, a new urgency. They lured me to ask questions, to dig deeper.

The insights I now had into family history made the forgery theory seem preposterous. And since hearing from the Knight how much my mother had struggled while reclaiming the Mendl family assets after the war, I felt certain that she had not impulsively purchased the drawings. The only explanation she had ever provided to me was that they had been given to her by Otto. No one had seen her brother Otto since the war. That left Otto Schönthal. But from 1943, the date of both the drawings, to 1959, around the time I remembered Mother bringing them home, she and Schönthal had been relatively short of money. Whatever money they did have they needed to use effectively, not to buy expensive Picasso drawings. Where had the drawings really come from?

I yearned to discover the provenance of the drawings: a history, a step-by-step explanation that connected me, the owner, with the artist, the creator. There should have been a series of transactions with appropriate documentation. Even if some paperwork was lost there should have been some document kept by either party. But I had nothing to explain the existence of these drawings. When I pressed my mother for more information she said she did not know, could not remember, repeated endlessly the skeleton response that the drawings had been given to her by 'Otto' and that he had got them from Picasso.

She gave no dates, her statements appeared to lack logic, and under pressure she turned away. 'Why these incessant questions?' she asked angrily. It was entirely unimportant; could she not have some peace?

The drawing that Sybille Winkleman had shown me in her catalogue, and which was so similar to mine, was a sketch for a sculpture called *Mann mit Lamm,* and I suspected that my drawings were also sketches Picasso had made in preparation for the sculpture. I spent every spare moment I had scouring books and exhibition catalogues, making comparisons with other Picassos, checking dates. I learnt quite quickly that finding out who had drawn the pictures and who had bought them was not going to be a straightforward process.

Authenticating a Picasso is complicated by the fact that not all of Picasso's works made it into the Zervos catalogue, and even the dates written on the drawings are open to interpretation. Many of Picasso's works were not signed or dated at all, and Picasso was known to sometimes sign and date a work long after its completion. The date might indicate not when the work was done but rather the time of a sale or preparation for exhibition or cataloguing.

I contacted auction houses and fine arts experts, museums, galleries and historians around Australia and across the world. No one could give a definitive comment. No one was sufficiently interested even to look at the drawings. However, they did refer me to other experts, other historians. Meticulously, I followed all the leads.

Finally, it seemed that the trail was leading somewhere promising. I had the address of Picasso's daughter Maya, who is the officially authorised expert in her father's work. I carefully prepared a letter of explanation outlining what I knew of the drawings' history. I enclosed a small photo of each drawing, hoping for instructions on further images and detail Maya Picasso would require. Her reply, dated 10 April 1995, was prompt, polite, brief and left me breathless. She told me she was sorry but the drawings were not her father's work – the head of the girl was a reproduction, the sheep were also copies, and the two men with the sheep were created by whoever had drawn the pictures. She said she knew nothing of who had made the sketches or when they had been drawn.

Her firm rejection curtailed my inquiries for some time. Having eventually recovered, I telephoned Dawn to find out more about her Picasso drawings – one was a sketch of the head of a girl, the other a group of dancers. Dawn gave me the correspondence

A Story Dreamt Long Ago

from the experts she'd approached, who had all concluded that the drawings couldn't truly be Picassos because they did not appear in the Zervos catalogue – a catalogue that I now knew was incomplete. Intriguingly, one of the experts noted that the drawing of the girl's head was similar to an unsigned, undated Picasso that was in the Zervos catalogue. My mother had always said that there were two of them, and to my mind this proved she was right.

It had been years since I'd seen Dawn's drawings and I felt that if I could see them now, it would help my search. Even over the telephone I could sense that Dawn gave a characteristic shrug. 'I don't know where they are, we've moved a lot since we were married.'

'Well,' I said, 'if they turn up I'd like to have another look.'

A short time later Dawn's husband, Peter, rang back. 'I've found the one of the girl's head. It's here with some old files. I can't find the dancers. They might have been left at a gallery for framing and for some reason we never picked them up. Or they could have been thrown out with an old briefcase by mistake.'

It was a pity that the dancers were nowhere to be found, but at last I could look at the picture of the girl's head once more. At first, to Dawn and I she had just been a pleasant ink sketch of a girl's head – until she was upgraded to being known as 'THAT Girl's Head' following an incident one quiet Sunday when I was in my late adolescence, at home on school holidays. Dawn and I were hanging around the house when we became aware of our mother thumping about with increasing agitation, muttering as she went from one room to another. She never suppressed her emotions.

Subliminally we knew that if she didn't find her boots, put out the dog, or kill the crawling insect, any one of which might be the cause of her present agitation, very soon that agitation would expand and we would be needed to resolve the problem.

It happened. My mother burst through the door. 'I can't find it anywhere!' she wailed.

'Find what?' in unison.

'"The Girl's Head". My drawing.'

'Why do you need it?'

'It's a Picasso.'

'What are you going to do with it?'

'I just want to find it. I *have* to find it.'

Mystified silence from her two daughters.

My mother's anguish built up momentum. She glared and wailed, 'I know I had it. I saw it – in amongst some papers. I was looking at it thinking how good it was. Now I've lost it. I'll probably never find it again. I've lost a bloody Picasso! Well, that's the trouble with this place. It's such a mess. I never know where anything is. We'd better clean things up. Put stuff away. Where we can find it.' Then, hopelessly: 'It might turn up.'

There was no use arguing. The day turned into the biggest clean-up of my life. The rambling house, the result of haphazard extensions to the original two rooms, was put in order from floor to ceiling, room to room. Picasso was cursed with increasing venom as the day ground on to an exhausted evening.

Finally, as we were all collapsed around the table, Bettina announced, 'It's probably in my bag. My case! My crocodile case.' This was the repository of her most treasured items. A small and beautiful crocodile-skin document case with heavy brass locks. It was crammed full, bulging with letters recently received, birth certificates of associates long dead, photos of hunting trips on the Alpine estates where she grew up, last month's phone bill, some unused Australian air-letters, old cheque books – and, we hoped, just one medium-sized Picasso.

Grouped around the table in weary reflection, we became aware that despite an inch-by-inch cleaning frenzy none of us had sighted 'the case'.

Like an overtired child Bettina bleated, 'My case is gone! My case is gone! What will I do without my case? I had everything in there. Everything I really *neeeeed*. Someone must have taken it. It couldn't just go. Someone came and took it. Who could that be? Who would come into the house and take my case? I'd like to know!'

Dawn and I followed an age-old formula. It must have been born with us. Where else did it come from? Certainly not from our mother.

'Mum, when did you last see the case?'

'When I took it to the accountant.'

'When was that?'

'When he wanted to see the documents.'

'When *exactly*?'

'When I went to town – that's right, I went to town and saw the accountant and gave him the documents he wanted.'

'*When?*'

'I saw "The Girl's Head" then, at the bottom of the case, I couldn't find what I was looking for and had to dig through the papers; that's when I was looking at it. I showed it to the accountant. I said, "Would you like to see a beautiful Picasso?" He wasn't very interested; he hardly even looked at it. That's when I last had the case.'

'Did you find the documents he'd asked you for?'

'No. I couldn't find them. I can never find what I'm looking for. I left it there. The girl was going to find it. She was going to go through all the papers and dig out what he needed.'

The inquisitors persisted. 'You left it there? You left the case there for the girl to sort through the documents?'

'Yes.'

'Well, that's where it is then.'

'I'm not quite sure. Better ring him up. Ring up and ask has he got my case and is the Picasso in it.'

'Mum, it's Sunday!'

'He won't mind. You'd better phone, Phyllis. You're the oldest. You sound quite sensible. He lives just up the road from the office. He can quickly go and see if it's all right.'

'Muuum – no! – he'll think we're mad!' I had trouble coming to terms with family eccentricity. I struggled with the limitations in the thinking of a small country community. I was not about to prove our raving insanity to a respected, stable accountant.

I negotiated. I think I actually pretended to dial and then declared that the accountant was not answering. Subsequently my mother rang and was reunited with her crocodile-skin case and its precious contents.

I hadn't given 'THAT Girl's Head' much thought back then. Now, years later, Peter visited me in Brisbane and brought the drawing with him. I slid her from the manila folder in which she had spent over thirty years. It was a simple black-ink sketch of the head of a young woman, her softly curling hair pinned back. She wore a hinted, calm, reflective smile.

No one could ignore the large, clear *'Picasso'* at the bottom. The question was, had he actually signed it?

Since I had started my search I had discovered that Picasso had signed his name many different ways throughout his life. I had stumbled on a book about Picasso that contained a whole section showing his various signatures. Flicking through the pages I saw a familiar signature with the number 23 – presumably meaning 1923 – beside it. It was very similar to the one that appeared on 'THAT Girl's Head'. Perhaps this meant 'THAT Girl's Head' was drawn in 1923 – twenty years before my *'Mann mit Lamm'* sketches.

I shared my musings with my good friend Kath, touching on my frustration with my lack of library skills and my lack of art-research education.

'Picasso!' Kath said. 'What a hoot. We'll do it on the internet, we'll find out in an hour – everything's on the internet. Come to my place on Saturday.'

I decided to keep the project simple and to research only 'THAT Girl's Head'. I knew nothing of its history. Who was the girl? The only clue was the curl and slope of the signature that bore similarities to the other signatures of 1923.

I suggested we try the Museum of Modern Art in New York, where I knew there was a current exhibition of Picasso's portraiture. I rummaged in my bag to take out my photocopy of 'THAT Girl's Head' and laid it flat on the desk beside the keyboard while Kath found the website.

'We're looking for something like this,' I said. 'I don't know names or dates – try to find something from 1923 just to look at signatures, if nothing else.'

Kath clicked a sequence of options; Picasso pictures appearing on the screen in rapid succession. Then, a thumbnail-sized picture of 'Portrait of Sara Murphy', in oil, dated 1923, came into view. Kath clicked on it. Slowly there appeared a coloured image of a familiar face, soft curls held back, slightly heavy brows. I lifted the photocopy of my drawing from the desk to hold beside the screen. The head in the drawing looked from left to right. The painting was reversed. They looked at each other. 'Hello, Sara Murphy,' I whispered. 'Look, Kath, there she is; it's the same face.'

I felt the certainty of recognition. I knew the face like an old friend with a different hairdo.

12

Collecting fragments of the past

The heat was unbearable. It leaked in through the large, west-facing windows of the room where my mother's remaining belongings had been stored when she moved to Nazareth House, a nearby nursing home. I was sitting on the floor, having emptied every drawer and box of papers, creating a large mound in the middle of the room. I was determined to sort, file, check and label every document that lay there in my attempt to find evidence that might explain my mother's mysterious 'double life': her life here, in Australia, as my mother, and that strange pre-war existence that had touched us from time to time. Within a few weeks I would leave for Europe again – only a year since my visit with Bettina – and I wanted to finish this work before I left. On this journey of exploration I needed to follow up every clue that existed within that mound of paper.

Phyllis McDuff

I spent some hours each day with Bettina in Nazareth House. She made no objection to my trip. Nonetheless, I sensed her vulnerability and unspoken dread of my being so far away. I remembered the separations of my childhood and struggled to hold to my course. Ironically I also felt her support, her determination bracing me, her pride that I too could be dogged in the face of difficult decisions.

I groped for clarity as the heat numbed my mind. I reached for one more piece of paper. There was a single fold across the middle of the page, which had no letterhead and held just two typed lines in German that translated to: '*Madame, the enclosed documents set out the details you requested*' and a signature. It was a name I recognised – Eduard Schulthess. Yes! I had met him once, when I was fourteen, in Zurich, at the bank. He had been introduced to me as the manager of my mother's accounts. The enclosure he referred to must be somewhere within the mound of papers before me. I was stunned by my sudden recognition of his name on that bland piece of paper, but it seemed impossible that I would be able to find and recognise the enclosure.

As I leant back to stretch my cramping body, I glimpsed the framed photo of Grandfather Fritz Mendl hanging on the opposite wall. The grey-haired patriarch stood calmly saluting me, holding an upraised wineglass. 'Give me a hand here, Fritz; it's your little Bettina I am trying to discover,' I said aloud, then shook my head at my own foolishness and glanced away to the other side of the room. Over there a folded page lay on its own. Did it imagine it could escape my systematic sorting? I picked it up in my right hand – in my left hand I still held the two-line communication from Bank Leu. The folded grooves slid into one another. This second page, like the first, had no letterhead, no name, no number, no identification of any sort. It was the listing of a share portfolio with an attributed value of 1.2 million Swiss Francs. This was another confirmation of Ellen's claims. My mother had a life about which I was absolutely ignorant. Again I had stumbled on the evidence by a strange series of coincidences. *Thank you, Grandfather Fritz.*

•◆•

The next morning I visited Bettina again. I knew much better than to question her directly. We talked of my Aunt Lucie and her family in New Zealand, and this allowed me to introduce the family myth of a bag of gold coins that Bettina was supposed to have brought from Zurich when she left Switzerland in 1938 on her way to New Zealand. She laughed at the old memory.

'But where did you get them?' I asked her.

'From the bank, of course. I went in and asked for them.'

'Which bank? Did they know you?'

'Oh yes, they knew me. My account was there. Crédit Suisse – you remember it, in Paradeplatz, where the trams turn around.'

There were times now when Bettina forgot that I had not shared her European past. Sometimes she was impatient that I could not remember street names or incidents from before my birth. If I protested Bettina quickly recovered, saying: 'Of course, of course, you weren't born then.' This time I did not protest. I led her on. I was curious to know what her lapse would reveal and whether the old myth would stand up to examination.

'And then,' I went on, 'where did you go? How did you travel with a big bag of gold? Did someone help you?' I was trying to impose practical considerations on what seemed like another fairytale.

'No,' she replied, 'I was alone. I walked from the bank over the bridge to the hotel where I was staying. I put the gold in my suitcase and went by train to catch the boat.'

I needed to be able to verify the details; she did not seem to think this held any danger now.

'What was the name of the hotel?'

Confusing the generations, she replied, 'You know, the one on the lake where we always stayed.'

'Oh,' I said, 'The Hôtel Baur au Lac.' We had stayed there as children; it was the only Zurich hotel I knew. I didn't want to break her focus. I desperately wanted her unusual willingness to talk about the past to continue.

'No,' she answered, 'not Baur au Lac – too ostentatious. The other one, smaller, around the lake a bit . . . let me remember . . . Hôtel Rive au Lac, that's it!'

I sensed that she was enjoying this memory of her adventure and asked her to draw a map of the locality. 'You never know, I might go there on my trip,' I said.

She took the pen I offered and drew a map showing the bank Crédit Suisse, Paradeplatz, the bridge, and the Hôtel Rive au Lac. 'With the columns at the front,' she said, marking them with four strokes of the pen.

By this time my mother was feeling weary, so I left her to sleep and went off to the travel agent in Tamworth, where I made inquiries about hotels in Zurich. I asked them if they could book me a room at the old Hôtel Rive au Lac.

A Story Dreamt Long Ago

The assistant opened a thick hotel guide, flicked through it, and checked the spelling with me. 'It's not listed, but perhaps I could help you with an alternative hotel. Oh – excuse me.' Her phone was ringing, and as she picked it up she pushed aside the hotel guide so that it perched precariously on a stack of travel manuals. The assistant was caught up in her phone call; slowly the thick volume slid towards me, its pages turning through Switzerland, where it had been left open. It stopped at 'B': there, in the lower right-hand corner of the page, was an advertisement for the Hôtel Belle Rive au Lac, with a drawing of its façade, enhanced with Doric columns. I could not believe my luck. I drew the guide towards me and noted the address.

In Zurich a few months later, I trekked the path from Paradeplatz, where the name Crédit Suisse was still displayed across one of the buildings, past the tram terminus towards the lake. I continued on around the lake's edge in search of Hôtel Belle Rive au Lac. It was a bleak day and the wind blew hard against me. I had walked a long way and was ready to give up. I rested on a park bench, watching the nannies beside the lake with their gleaming waist-high prams and toddling charges. There was no need to find the hotel – it had nothing to tell me now, neither had Crédit Suisse. My attempts to discover connections here had led to nothing. I had wanted to assure myself that the story of the gold coins held some truth, that it was not a fantasy. But now it seemed sealed in the past, beyond my reach. I decided to give up my probing here and go on to Vienna.

I stood and turned towards the roadway, where a large building faced me. The lower floors were in the process of reconstruction; there was a gleaming new auto showroom. I looked up across the top level was a faded sign: Hôtel Belle Rive au Lac. I remembered my grandfather's photo image, wineglass upraised and almost heard him say *'Salut'*.

Thank you, Grandfather Fritz. The myth that I had always held to be another of Bettina's fantasies had shown its substance. I walked away.

•◆•

The train winds beside fast rivers, through dark forests at the foot of the snow-covered, papier-mâché mountains. Through the windows I watch each new scene unfold. I know that I am retracing the steps of my Aunt Marianne and her family's frantic midnight journey out of Austria in 1938. I am going back.

How strange it seems to arrive in Vienna, alone, with a bundle of papers and a bundle of questions. I feel my way around the language. In the intervening years I have so rarely used it. For the most part it still fits my mouth and now I'm learning a whole new vocabulary, the language of the financial and legal world. Trusts, estates, company structures, transactions, deposits, dividends: the new words for these trip off my tongue.

I am made welcome by people who have never met me, some of whom have only recently heard of my existence. Doors are flung wide open, stories are told. Some simple memories of youth, lovingly offered, have no connection to my questions. My mother's girlhood friend Agathe, now fragile and aged, brings me a silver serving spoon, begs me to take it, apologises with embarrassment. It was left with her in 1938 by a servant girl from Villa Mendl. When the villa was taken over by the Nazis a box of silver had been packed and hidden on a farm outside the city, only to be found and looted sometime later. The large serving spoon had not allowed the lid to shut, so it had been hastily removed and discarded in a corner of the cellar. After the box had gone the servant girl discovered the spoon and ran through the streets to take it to my mother's trusted friend. Through all the years it had waited for me to come to this formal afternoon tea with Agathe for lengthy explanations revealing insights into the desperation of those times. Of all that household treasure, one silver serving spoon was all I needed.

Another distant 'aunt' gives me a blue ceramic plate that once belonged to my grandmother's 'morning service'. Nothing else remains. It was found in the rubble at Villa Mendl at the end of the war and was recognised and rescued by Tante Maria. Absurdly, now it is packed in plastic bubble-wrap. Perhaps I should glue a little story to its back in case it gets lost again. Holding the piece, I can so clearly see tall, thin Tante Maria noticing the plate among the rubble, hoping for its completeness as she stoops to pick it up, cherishing this symbol of survival, a treasure to give back to my mother, who may or may not survive as completely as that flawless plate.

On all her visits 'home' my mother had refused to accept these fragments of her former life. She had told each custodian to keep them, had declared they were too heavy for the light luggage she was carrying.

I take the tram out to Villa Mendl, where the next generation of cousins is now living. The building has changed almost beyond recognition. Even the approaches are quite strange. I remembered shady cobbled lanes with few buildings around, but the garden has been subdivided since I was here in 1953.

A high fence blocks the entry to the drive so that you do not immediately enter the embrace of gardens and buildings. Now you press a bell. There is an intercom.

My cousins and I compare our myths, we eat and gossip in the remaining garden, inching over the scar tissue where deep family wounds have healed. This is easier for me. I was far away in Australia during those days of persecution. I am not my mother. I am innocent of her decisions to sell estates, to live her independent life without reference to her 'social obligations'. The family is generous, kind, and trusting with their stories.

The afternoon wears on and shadows steal across the garden. We settle into comfortable discussion. There is a mutual reluctance to end the visit within an accepted social time frame. 'Stay,' they say, 'we'll go inside. It's getting cool.' Gathering up the coffee cups and wine bottles we resettle around the large, pale wooden table. More coffee is brewed and revelations begin at a new level.

I remembered my cousin Hans Mendl from 1953, when we all lived in this big house containing various family apartments. He was my mother's nephew, son of her beloved brother Otto and the beautiful Mimi. Hans was twenty-three when I'd first met him. He was tall, thin, pale, quiet, kind. Painstakingly he had taught me German, carefully demonstrating the strange sounds, correcting me over and over again. Yet I had never felt inept. I thrived on his attention and developed an enduring feel for German. I spoke without a foreign accent, but also without reference to grammatical rules. Sometimes people newly introduced to me thought I was a local until I managed to make some glaring grammatical gaffe.

A Story Dreamt Long Ago

Now Hans tells stories of his childhood. He reveals the torments of his separation from his family. He explains how he'd survived the war in Berlin. He was sent into hiding in a Catholic orphanage; his blond angelic looks offered some protection as he sought sanctuary in church, stooped in prayer, hating and plotting revenge before the altar rail. According to the reports he'd gathered after the war, his father had been hunted and exterminated, his mother and baby sister last heard of alive and in hiding, but there was no certainty that he would ever see them again. Who might tell him where they were? Everything depended on trust and he had no one to trust. He transformed his fear to strengthen slender bone and muscle. In 1944, at fourteen years old, he left the Berlin orphanage. Clinging to fragile information and faded memories, he made his way to Vienna. Now he does not speak of details, his face is drawn and white, his hands tremble around the coffee cup. But he continues in a voice stable with determination. He made his way to Villa Mendl and found it deserted and bomb damaged. With his freezing, fragile artist's hands he dug a hole in the rubble to accommodate his body. The stones would keep him warm – or he would die there. He was home.

Villa Mendl chose to bless Hans. Somehow information reached him confirming the survival of his mother and sister, my aunt Mimi and cousin Eva, who in their turn reached Villa Mendl. There was a family reunion. It was not quite a sanctuary, for starvation threatened; Hans broke into a chemist shop and stole powdered milk. Mimi, balancing trust and caution, made contact with Ankerbrot, now under Nazi management; there she found a loyal family connection. Food parcels were secretly delivered. Sometimes.

At this point Hans sighs with relief and exhaustion. Excuses himself. Leaves.

His two sons turn to me. 'He has never ever spoken of those things. We never knew. We knew only his anger, his frustration, his inability to risk emotional connection.'

Soon the focus moves to Fritz, the patriarch; documents and dates are checked, stories rounded out. Then someone asks, 'Where is his grave?' Each had assumed that someone else within the family knew, but as we glanced at each other around the table it was evident that no one did.

•—•

Thomas, Hans's second son, was assigned the responsibility of looking up the parish records, entirely without success. Another day was spent combing the local cemeteries in search of Mendl vaults, but no record of Fritz's death could be found.

Thomas arranged to meet me at the main Vienna cemetery. We didn't realise that the grey November day we chose was All Souls' Day. I had come by tram, navigating from a tourist map with a sense of unreality. The Harry Lime theme from *The Third Man* kept running through my head. Thomas arrived with bundles of family documents reaching some generations back.

Thomas had a plan of the cemetery; leading me through rows of headstones, finally he stopped to read out inscriptions. Family names with which I had recently been made familiar appeared on monuments. Lines on the outspread page connected me to each burial plot – my mother's aunts and uncles, death certificates proving relationships. Thomas looked up from examining his documents. 'Phyllis, do you understand where you are?' he asked.

A Story Dreamt Long Ago

'Of course, I'm in the cemetery.'

'Which cemetery?'

'The main cemetery in Vienna,' was my confident reply.

'Which part of the cemetery?'

I looked around for clues. I did not understand his question.

'This is the Jewish part of the cemetery. Strangely, contrary to Jewish faith, these memorials are quite grand, ostentatious even. They are some of the leading families of Vienna, and these are our relations. Do you understand that now? This is why my grandfather Otto Mendl was killed. This is why my father was hidden in a Catholic orphanage for most of his childhood. This is why Bettina had to leave: because all Vienna knew of these connections.'

I had heard no hint of a Jewish background. All the family rituals had revolved around Catholic traditions. It had been my understanding that the escapes were necessary because of my mother's overt and political opposition to Nazism. History had been distorted to accommodate inventions. Slowly I came to an understanding of what he was telling me. Another heritage had claimed me. I think that without the evidence of tombstones and old documents I would never have believed in those kinships. I think without his gentle explanations, without the familiar outline of his face, I would not have accepted them.

As we moved toward the gate and the cold November mist fell across the cemetery I considered the significance of my Jewish background. I felt both enlightened and pitifully ignorant. A veil had been lifted to reveal the logic in Bettina's secrecy and fears. I recognised the interest I've always had in Jewish history, writing, achievements – all this from *outside*. Still I am emotionally immune to what it means to be a Jew – and what it meant in 1938.

Despite our searches we were never able to discover the three immediate family graves. My mother's parents, Emily and Fritz, and her brother Fritz all died in Vienna in 1929, 1930 and 1931 respectively. They left no trace of their last resting place. Bettina and her retinue of friends, all young adults at the time, mysteriously swore they had no knowledge of the burial ground, attended no ceremony, did not know. On reflection I realise that Bettina herself must have made the arrangements for her brother's funeral. She would have followed her father's example of her mother's funeral and his wishes for his own. Yet she had never even hinted at her role and, when I finally asked her, she could remember nothing, as though all this was done entirely without her collusion. I speculate that in his heart, Fritz senior, in spite of his Christian conversion, had been reclaimed by his Jewish faith. Perhaps three discreetly unmarked graves exist on one of his former estates. Bettina would have followed her father's example in making arrangements for Fritz junior.

The documents that Thomas had brought with him to the cemetery led to further discussion. In the closing dusk of the afternoon we sought out a comfortable *Gasthaus* and continued our analysis over bowls of steaming goulash. My preoccupation with the Picasso drawings prompted me to question what had happened to the family art collection. Was there any trace or evidence of the other household treasure?

Thomas told the story. Simon Wiesenthal had tried to bring Wächter to justice as a war criminal. He established that Wächter, having moved into Villa Mendl, had taken personal possession of all the contents. At the end of the war Wächter used the Mendl household loot to purchase safe custody within the Vatican. He used the escape routes through Italy set up by ex-Obersturmbannführer Rauff, who had designed the Nazi gas chambers. Rauff had negotiated safe passage for himself and other key Nazis with one Catholic Bishop Hudal. Hudal arranged interim private accommodation in Milan for those escaping war-crimes charges – Milan, where we had stayed as children during the winter of 1953. Now I wondered why we'd been there. What trail was my mother following? She may have been tracing the last evidence of the stolen Mendl treasures.

It was commonly accepted that when Wächter reached Rome, he went to live in the Vatican under a safe, new identity as 'Father Otto Reinhardt' until his death in 1949. I wondered when this information had first come to light. Aware that he was terminally ill, Wächter made a full confession of his identity and of his part in the extermination of 800,000 Jews. Simon Wiesenthal requested his files from the Vatican, but was told by Bishop Hudal that these formed part of Wächter's confidential confession. Hudal considered himself 'a priest, not a policeman'. This remained the official Vatican response to Wiesenthal's request. Wächter was survived by his wife, who had been summoned to the Vatican during his final illness. He was survived also by his daughter, who lived in Paris – surrounded by small remnants of Mendl domestic treasure. Thomas Mendl had casually met the daughter: by coincidence, they were university students together in Vienna. They had compared histories and realised their connection.

Among the documents Thomas gave me was a letter that Tante Maria had written in 1946 to the lawyer representing my mother in her claims for the restitution of her property. He required as accurate an inventory as possible of the assets, including the artworks, that had been present at Villa Mendl before Wächter plundered it. She wrote that she still had accounts for the silverware that had been taken by Wächter's wife on her husband's instructions; Tante Maria also believed that Frau Wächter had taken my mother's two fur coats. The only artwork Maria had managed to rescue from Villa Mendl before Wächter swept in was a painting by Hieronymus Bosch. She wrote that she had taken it to her own apartment for safekeeping. Like so much else, the attempt to rescue the Hieronymus Bosch painting was in vain. Whether removed deliberately or in ignorance, it disappeared from Tante Maria's apartment before 1945.

Tante Maria also talked about Bettina's valuable jewellery collection. Before my mother left Zurich in 1938 she instructed Tante Maria to withdraw the jewellery from the safe where it was held. Tante Maria had managed to hold on to most of the collection, but sent some pieces to a German lawyer who had claimed he would send it on to Bettina – he had done no such thing. In the letter she also mentioned that she could not give a full inventory of what was in Villa Mendl before the Nazis came because from July 1938 she was denied access to the property. In fact, the day after she had removed the Hieronymus Bosch painting she had returned to Villa Mendl demanding the right to make an inventory. As was to be expected she was denied entry. She persisted until she was arrested for creating a disturbance. She was briefly imprisoned until influential friends of Bettina's

A Story Dreamt Long Ago

arranged for her release and begged her to submit for her own safety.

•—•

In an attempt to verify the Wächter story and perhaps to confirm some inventory of items from the Mendl art collection that had been taken to the Vatican, I sent a fax to Simon Wiesenthal's office in Vienna. I felt his research since the war might reveal more than I knew from family sources. I identified myself and asked for an appointment. I received a prompt reply and invitation to discuss the Wächter matter with his assistant, since Wiesenthal himself was away. I walked through the narrow streets of a downtrodden section of the city. Here the buildings were not the ornate, charming pre-war houses but utilitarian concrete, built in 1950s style.

I was admitted to a simple apartment stacked from floor to ceiling with files. Mr Wiesenthal's assistant poured out coffee while she listened to my queries. She seemed familiar with the story, checked files and asked over her shoulder, 'Where is your mother now? Did she get out? What of the other family members?' Gradually she grasped the picture. She sighed and said, 'Those that survived are lucky – these files are full of stories – dreadful stories – new ones are added every day – tales of torture and death. We do not have the resources to investigate property matters. I am sorry.'

'There is no urgency for my inquiries – it all happened so long ago. It almost seems like idle curiosity. I would like to understand what happened, but you are right – my mother escaped, we've had good lives, we were the lucky ones.'

'We seldom hear that. People demand, accuse – all about property, property. They can't feel the human suffering, they don't feel another's pain. Genocide still continues: it is going on right now across the border – Bosnia is only 200 kilometres away.' She raised her shoulders in a helpless shrug. She obviously had pressing work to do so I gulped the last of my coffee and departed.

•◆•

I had been in touch with the manager of my mother's Austrian accounts. She is now retired and I am surprised that she's agreed to meet me. Unlike the Swiss account manager I contacted – also retired, who claimed he could not make any comment on his professional contacts.

We have arranged to meet at the Park Hotel: it is close by the train station. The year is coming to its end: it is cold, snow has fallen and melted and fallen again. I walk from the station in my thin Australian boots. They will need to be replaced if I am to stay much longer.

Although the name is quite familiar from my mother's diaries, I have not met Frau Le Grün before. The questions I have come to ask her are of a personal nature, nothing to do with money or accounts. I want to know how my mother handled her affairs, how she conducted her business. Had it been haphazardly, spontaneously – as she had claimed to avoid offering us explanations? Or did she form strategies and plans?

Arriving early, I waited, settling into the atmosphere of the coffee lounge with its ornate brocade wall coverings, obligatory gold-framed mirrors, plump-cushioned furniture. Very Vienna –

A Story Dreamt Long Ago

I didn't have to look to know what pastries would be offered from the glass cabinets. They would be rich with chocolate, cream and hazelnut, dusted with snowy powdered sugar.

Frau Le Grün arrives and recognises me immediately. She tells me I have my mother's face. This has been said before, but this time it feels helpful, comfortable. I sense she likes my mother; seeing my face she responds warmly, without reservation and the courteous suspicion I had half-expected. I begin my explanations. I tackle the difficulty of telling her, convincingly, that I would like to know my mother. That I would like to understand her other life and obtain some insight into her business persona.

Frau Le Grün explains that her contact with my mother for nearly thirty years was always professional. She did not know her 'privately'. That's the precise point, I explain. Over those long years, in so many different situations, without family loyalties or emotional considerations, *who was Bettina?*

A picture emerges that I cannot recognise. The Bettina that Frau Le Grün knew was calm, strategic, confident. She gathered information carefully, she laid complex and effective plans which she carried out after weighing opinions and advice. My mother was totally in control. This is not to say she had no sense of humour, Frau Le Grün tells me: she had great personal charm and captured loyalties by her touching response to other people's needs and interests. She agrees that taken to extremes this could amount to manipulation, but it was never overt and offensive – people felt honoured to be 'manipulated' by Bettina. As an example, Frau Le Grün explains her own passion for Picasso. My mother knew about that passion. She kept her beautiful Picasso drawings in the bank's strong-room, which was not in any way connected to Frau Le Grün's responsibilities.

'One day she showed them to me – just because she knew I'd love to see them. We went down together to the strong-room and spread them out one at a time. It was an enormous thrill for me. Although our relationship was always professional, it was somehow . . . warmer after that day.'

I take the photos of the Picasso drawings from my handbag. I'd brought them on the off chance, not really expecting to glean any detailed information from this meeting. 'Are these the drawings that Bettina showed you?' I ask Frau Le Grün.

'Aah, yes. I've never seen them since, not in any exhibition nor in any publication. Where are they now?'

I do not like to say 'under my bed'. It seems irreverent. 'She brought them to Australia,' I reply.

There are other questions I feel only Frau Le Grün can answer. 'You would have met Bettina's associate, Otto Schönthal?' I ask.

'Constantly. He was included in almost all of our discussions, certainly when a major strategy was being considered.'

'And how did you see that relationship? Did Bettina follow Otto's advice? Did she question him? Which of the two made the decisions? Where was the power?'

Frau Le Grün does not hesitate. She smiles as she answers. 'Bettina controlled everything. He did as she proposed – to the letter. She checked everything. She sought his advice and she respected it but it was she who made the decisions.'

'I thought she may have been under his influence,' I suggest.

Frau Le Grün shakes her head. 'I can only tell what I concluded. It was long ago but I don't think I can be mistaken – we were in contact for many years, not only when Bettina was here, but when she was in Australia or America. She would telephone; in the old days that was quite a project. She would give detailed instructions and authorise Schönthal to make certain transactions, but always he had to wait for her consent.'

'I was under the impression that he had the authority to manage affairs in her absence – that perhaps she was unaware of details.'

'No. I think you are mistaken. She is not the sort of person who would relinquish power.'

That, at least, rings true.

Otto Schönthal was the one person who could have revealed my mother to me but in 1978 he had died quite suddenly and with only casual comment from her. It was true that she took her losses well. Despite her regular dramatics over trivialities she bore the tragedies of her life with calm nobility. Even so, I reflected, it was hard to understand her apparent acceptance of this loss. Otto had been her guide and her companion for more than forty years. They seemed to have no secrets from each other. The constant letters and phone calls revealed their shared sense of fun. Otto had stood as confidant in place of her two brothers, and his clever management had helped her recover and retain her properties. She had always given him full credit for achieving this. But she did not mourn.

On this trip I again visited the Winklemans in Munich. Our conversation took up where we had left off last time – with the Picassos.

'Where did Bettina say she got them?' Sybille asked.

'From Otto,' I replied.

'When?'

'When she returned to Europe – to Austria, after the war.'

'When exactly?' Sybille persisted.

'I can't remember exactly. I actually don't know when she received them. They turned up in Australia some time in the late 1950s. She loved them. She was terribly excited about having the two 'Shearers' (that's what she called them) framed and hanging in the farmhouse. There was some mention that they were not to be exhibited for fifty years. We felt that that was one of my mother's mystery stories and couldn't see any reason for that degree of secrecy.'

'The drawings were not to be exhibited for fifty years from when?' asked Sybille.

'Who knows? It could be the dates on the drawings, or it could be fifty years from the transaction when my mother acquired them. Of course there is the fifty-year copyright following the artist's death. But it sounded like a more personal instruction, as if she should hide them for fifty years. But why?' I shook my head, then continued. 'It seemed to me she wanted to display them; she loved to look at them. She implied that because they were in Australia they were safe. For her that was a personal and powerful experience. Then suddenly she changed – completely lost all interest, didn't want to have them in her house after she moved. That was in 1978, just after Otto died.'

'Bettina indicated it was suicide,' Helmut Winkleman remarked. 'She was here, staying with us. Otto rang and she would not take his call. They'd had some falling out. He rang over and over again and she would not go to the phone. Finally, as a lawyer,

A Story Dreamt Long Ago

I asked her to take his calls: nothing could be resolved if she would not talk to him. Of course she refused. That was the night he died. Later, Bettina indicated he had overdosed – or perhaps she only suspected it.'

'She seemed to take the news of Otto's death very calmly,' Helmut continued. 'Were you ever told what Otto wanted to discuss?'

'No, I wasn't told – but I could still ask her,' I replied.

•◆•

After this trip to Vienna I would have a lot to ask my mother. I had arranged a visit to Mucki in Vienna. It wasn't surprising that my mother had always loved her. Mucki's energy radiated through those childhood months I had spent in Europe. She was small and brown with laughing eyes. She was an anchor through many changes and confusions, a provider of good food, soft words, warm hugs, reasonable explanations, reliable promises.

Now, in my fifties, I was on my way to see her, following her directions, tramping through the snow and trying to avoid the magnetic pull of the shop windows decorated for Christmas. I passed a chocolate shop then doubled back, lured by its glittering promise. I relished the long selection process at the counter. But I was already late and this delayed my arrival further.

At last I stood in front of the huge, ornate double door with its frosted glass behind wrought iron. To one side was a panel of buttons for intercom access. Above the door was the numeral in brass – 19, my mother's birthday number. I heard Mucki's voice and the door opened magically into a hall with a marble floor and a wide stone staircase.

Far above, a speck connected to the balustrade, Mucki was leaning over and waving. '*Komm, komm!*' she called.

She was flustered because I was late. 'What kept you so long?' she exclaimed, ushering me into the apartment. 'I waited and waited. I thought you were lost. I told you the right tram to catch. I thought you might not come at all, I thought I might have told you the wrong day –'

I tried to calm her. The walk from the tram stop had taken longer than I expected, I had stopped to buy chocolates for her, I was sorry she had been worried, but we had all the afternoon before us.

The walls of the apartment's *entrée* were hung with long silk swathes and artworks of recent origin, clearly valuable, though somewhat at odds with the furniture I glimpsed through the wide double doors that led into the reception rooms. There stood lovely curved and polished pieces I remembered well: tables, couches, tapestry-cushioned chairs that sometimes appeared in my dreams – my mother's furniture that I had known in childhood when we stayed at Villa Mendl.

I wondered at the strange relationships that brought me here. It was unlikely that my mother's mother would have had the time or energy to invest herself in guiding her spoilt, rebellious daughter. It would have seemed equally unlikely that the strict, religious and naive Maria von Kozaryn would be successful in this role. Yet perhaps my mother's father, Fritz, knew both Maria and his youngest daughter better than one might imagine, for their connection was immediate and profound. In spite of their contrasting personalities, which often brought them into temporary conflict, through years of separation, war, deaths and betrayals Maria and my mother kept intact their deep and trusting faith in each other.

Mucki's mother had died when Mucki was a child and Maria had helped to look after her, taking her on occasional visits to Villa Mendl. Bettina was charmed by the little girl and Mucki was sometimes included on summer visits to the mountains of the Tyrol. She also attended better schools than her father could have afforded; the fees were paid by my mother, who also provided her with a generous dowry later on so that Mucki married well. My mother's final provision for Mucki was this apartment.

Now Mucki wrung her hands and leant towards me. 'I am so embarrassed,' she said anxiously, 'I don't know how it could have happened. I thought I did everything correctly after the war – the documents, the property . . . I did everything I could to help Bettina. I would have kept nothing she did not intend me to have, but now I find . . . I am so sorry. I have discovered something –'

Nervously she continued, 'You know Tante Maria was very proud of the fact that she was born in a castle. Not that such a thing makes any difference. Many people born in a Schloss serve out tragic lives. Castles are cold, draughty places and swallow vast amounts of money to maintain. The von Kozaryn estates were gradually reduced, there were huge taxes, the family was impoverished and eventually everything was lost. Except the title.'

I nodded. What had this to do with my mother?

'Vincent, my three-year-old grandson, now inherits the title,' Mucki went on, 'and I went looking for the deed to pass on to him. Everything must be done appropriately, you see. It is engraved on vellum and kept in a heavy leather document case that came to me when my father died. A few days ago I opened the case for the first time.

'I can only imagine that what I am about to show you was put there by Tante Maria. She was the keeper of the title for many years. It was the family's most sacred possession. She is the only one who could have put something inside the case. She has been dead for over twenty years, and until now no one else has opened it. I have found – oh, Phyllis, will you open this envelope with your mother's name on the outside? Neither you nor I have any idea what it contains.' She extended one hand towards the coffee table in front of us, and for the first time I noticed the large, aged waxed envelope that lay there. On the outside, in Tante Maria's distinctive copperplate handwriting, were the words: *'Bettina – to be opened after my death.'* The flap lifted easily, without tearing. The pages inside were stiff and yellowed. The headings in ornate calligraphy slowed our reading but the content was clear. I spread them out so that we could both read them; in this way Mucki and I learnt their content at the same time.

The documents were dated 1935. My mother was twenty-six then. Emily and Fritz Mendl, as well as their elder son, Fritz junior, were all dead. Her trusted companion was Maria von Kozaryn, and there before us lay a series of ornate, formal documents showing that Bettina had rejected the Anglican religion of her birth, and, after instruction, been accepted into the Holy Roman Catholic Church. Well beyond her own life span, Tante Maria had guarded another of my mother's secrets by storing this information. During the Nazi regime this document might have endangered my mother's life had it disproved whatever background story she was using.

A Story Dreamt Long Ago

I was astonished, amazed, and the expression on Mucki's face echoed my own feelings. Against the documentary evidence that lay before me I had memories of the stories my mother used to tell about her 'Catholic' family and the Masses every Sunday in the church around the corner from Villa Mendl, the church where my sister and I had made our First Communion during our first visit to Austria, just as my mother told us she herself had done when she was the same age. Then there was her account of her confirmation at St Stephan's Cathedral and the family party afterwards . . . that, too, melted into fantasy before this clear evidence. Mucki had attended my own First Communion. She had heard the same stories and believed them.

'I – I never knew that she was Anglican,' Mucki murmured. 'I had no idea that she converted. The war came, those were strange times, people did strange things. The family was Jewish to begin with, until the turn of the century – of course, no one spoke of that. I can't explain it.' She folded up the papers and handed them to me. 'This belongs to your mother – take it to her in Australia.'

I could only gaze at Mucki in confusion. 'Mucki, explain to me a whole childhood of fabrication. What else did my mother make up? Why did she create the false story of her Catholic family life in such detail? How could it have been so important? It seemed to mean so much to her. Dawn and I made our First Communion in 1953 – the war was long since over, yet she was still making up tales!'

Gently Mucki touched my arm. 'Even ten years is not so long. The terrible things that happened in the war can never be healed, even in a million years.'

Phyllis McDuff

•◆•

I am left wondering who my mother really was. Was she Anglican, Catholic or Jewish? Was she erratic and irresponsible, or a cool professional operator? What is the true version of her life? I see her stories as artful constructions to screen that life from view. Why would anyone build a screen so carefully? I had witnessed many times over my mother's passionate and haphazard personality, yet somehow she found the discipline to stay inside her fabrications, to keep her lies intact.

•◆•

On my return to Australia I hurry to visit Bettina, who is quite fragile now. Aged and at peace. She is sun-browned from sitting in the garden of the nursing home. Glad that I've returned.

Gently I say to her: 'You married a Catholic. Were you always Catholic?'

'Of course. You remember the little church near Villa Mendl, where you and Dawn made your First Communion? I made my First Communion there too – surely you remember my telling you that. And later you were confirmed in St Stephan's Cathedral, just as I was.'

'Yes, I remember. But – I wondered whether perhaps you had converted to Catholicism when you married Dad.'

'What are you saying? It was not necessary for me to convert.'

'Well, perhaps before you left Europe –'

'Never! What makes you think this way?'

I decided to improvise. 'I asked Mucki. She didn't know whether you had converted or not – she thought your family was

Anglican. After all, Lucie married an Anglican in England before she went to New Zealand.'

'What could you expect? England is full of Anglicans. If she wanted to marry a Catholic she should have stayed in Austria.'

Once again Mother had diverted the conversation: now we were analysing Lucie's marriage rather than producing an explanation for those documents in the waxed envelope.

Yet I persisted. 'You went to Cheltenham. I would have thought the college accepted only Anglican girls in those days.'

'They took me.'

'So you were born Catholic and never converted?'

'Of course.' An exasperated sigh. 'How many times do I have to tell you?'

My courage failed. I could not steel myself to confront her with evidence that she chose to hide. She owed no explanations. The time had come to protect her from painful reminiscences of inquiries by 'authorities'. I did not tell her of the document. Perhaps if I had shown it to her it would have opened the door to another version of her life, the version she had chosen not to share. Yet now it seemed too late to rewind that story and rebuild it into a new reality. I left the documents untouched and unexplained.

•◆•

I saved the topic of Otto Schönthal's death for another visit. Possibly Mother's cool response to Otto's death was reflected in her lack of interest in the drawings; she had given them to me just two months after he died. I felt there must be a connection between the two events. An explanation of one would reveal much about the other. I summoned up all my courage and asked Mother why she and Schönthal had fallen out.

'It was nothing,' she said, meaning 'Nothing I want to talk to you about'. I gave her a long silence to reconsider and gently prompted, 'It must have been quite important to you then?'

'Yes,' she replied. 'He betrayed me.'

'Are you quite sure? Was there convincing evidence? Could you have been mistaken?'

'No, I am not mistaken; he betrayed me.'

'Financially?'

'No, not financially; that would not have mattered.'

I knew that was the truth. My mother had never cared about the parameters of money. It must have been a matter of principle, but what principle? I knew I had stretched the conversation as far as it would go. I had been very careful, slow and quiet and very lucky to get the answers she had given.

13

Searching for solutions

Once more I am flying towards Europe – this time to Heathrow Airport. I am going to see Sheila Gadston, an old friend of Bettina's. They met on a Qantas plane when my mother advised Sheila that it was safe to swallow the black seeds in the passionfruit sauce. I have seized the opportunity to spend a few days with Sheila before I travel north.

We are drinking tea and bringing each other up to date on family gossip as I recover from my long flight. Presently we abandon gossip to plan excursions for the next few days. Sheila says: 'We'll go to Oxford, and I have family coming who would love to meet you. I've told them about you and a bit about the Picasso drawings. Are they still under the bed?'

'No. I've brought a few documents with me. Actually I was hoping to find someone who might give me a lead. My Christies' contact seems to have fallen through. They haven't returned my calls. I might go on to Paris. In the meantime, I'd love to visit Oxford.'

On Sunday we had family dinner with whirling introductions and a blur of names until a voice said 'Malaga' and my brain snapped into focus. Malaga is where Picasso was born and lived for years.

'Phyllis, this is my niece Caroline, who lives in Malaga – they have a Picasso Museum there, you know. Caroline speaks Spanish, so if you need some help . . .'

Then Caroline sat down beside me. We did not talk about Picasso to begin with. We spoke of family and made light banter. Later, as the guests were leaving, Caroline said, 'I'd like to help with your Picasso research. I have the time. I speak the language. I can translate documents you may not understand. Sheila can bring you over to see me in the next few days. You could bring whatever documents you have – do consider it.'

Sheila and I drove to see Caroline, who was staying with her sister in a town close by. We spread the thin Picasso file across the table and I pointed out the links. Caroline was making the connections; she was excited and keen to forage for more information. I left her copies of the images and she undertook to visit the Malaga museum soon after she got home.

I couldn't help wondering at our unlikely meeting and her willingness and competence in all those areas where I needed help. It seemed a very lucky break.

◆

A few months later, at home in Australia, a large brown envelope protruded from the mailbox, gloriously decorated with rows

A Story Dreamt Long Ago

of Spanish stamps.

A long letter from Caroline tells me about her visit to the Picasso Museum at Malaga. The building was in chaos and closed for renovation, but she had persisted and some enthusiastic and apologetic staff had come to her assistance. One gentleman *'was really helpful and very interested in your pictures . . . especially the picture of the girl's head. He recognised it at once . . . I have enclosed the article from* ARTnews *he gave me.'* The enclosed article, dated May 1994, written by William Rubin, posed the question 'Who was Picasso's "Woman in White"?'

'That is for me to paint and for you fellows to figure out,' Picasso himself had replied. The content of the article left no doubt that the 'Woman in White' — a mysterious female figure appearing in a series of Picasso works around 1923 – was the same person depicted in 'THAT Girl's Head'. Line for line the reproduced image of Zervos 295 was almost identical to 'THAT Girl's Head'. The caption identified it as Sara Murphy, the mysterious 'woman in white', with whom Picasso had a flirtation in the summers of 1923 and 1924.

I have confirmed that my identification of Sara is correct. I am jubilant – and now I want to know all I can discover about the mysterious Sara Murphy.

•◆•

The fat book arrived at last wrapped in cardboard. It had been recommended by Brisbane writer and art historian Susanna De Vries, who was intrigued by my research and had kindly given me some tentative directions, while explaining that Picasso was not her field of expertise. Later Susanna telephoned me to say she had heard of a book by American author Amanda Vaill, *Everybody Was So Young*, which deals with the lives of Sara and Gerald Murphy, a golden couple of the 1920s and 1930s who lived in Paris and spent long holidays in the south of France. In his novel *Tender Is the Night*, F. Scott Fitzgerald used the Murphys as models for his characters Dick and Nicole Diver, recreating the ambience of their milieu.

The book has taken weeks to arrive from America; by the time it comes I am tense with anticipation. I carry it across my sun-burned lawn into the house, use the bread knife to cut the string and unfold the wrapping on the kitchen bench. It is a good thick book. I flick the pages and glance at the illustrations, some of which were familiar from my research. Then I settle down to read.

I discover that Pablo Picasso was a frequent visitor to the Murphys' villa. And the book enables me to make an even more vital connection.

As I read I recognise an atmosphere, a pace of life, that seems curiously familiar even though it is outside my own experience. Is it the time, that particular era in history – or is it a certain attitude the characters express, at the same time frivolous and tragic? I cannot stop until I arrive at 1923 – the date on the drawing of 'THAT Girl's Head'. I know the detail I crave will not be offered here but I seek an understanding of the atmosphere that gave rise to the 'Sara' drawing and perhaps a clue to the connection between my mother, Picasso, and Sara Murphy herself. I am delighted to discover details of the growing friendship between the Murphys and Pablo Picasso and his current wife, Olga, as they spend holidays together at Antibes.

A Story Dreamt Long Ago

Then one line leaps out at me: '*They [the Murphys] also became fascinated with a visitor to the Hôtel du Cap, the Romanian-British diplomat Sir Charles Mendl.*' My mother's maiden name. This means that Sir Charles would most likely have met Picasso when he visited the Murphys during the summer of 1923.

•◆•

I have found out quite recently that the Mendl family came originally from Eastern Europe, though my mother claims to know nothing of this. My grandfather, Fritz Mendl, held wheat estates in Hungary and Romania. I have found the old title documents but haven't bothered to read them too carefully. As a result of World War I, access to those estates had been closed off in 1917. I feel that the Mendl thread linking Fritz and Sir Charles has too many coincidental fibres to be ignored. The same name, the family origins in Eastern Europe, the identical history of grain estates and grain trading over many generations. At the end of the 1800s both families carefully educated the new generation as speakers of English with strong English connections. This must be a genuine family connection . . .

One of the illustrations in the book shows Sir Charles with his wife, Elsie de Wolfe, a famous American society hostess. Sir Charles and Lady Mendl had homes in Washington and Paris where they entertained the cream of world society and the arts. Elsie de Wolfe was initially an actress. She later 'invented' the profession of interior designer with enormous success in Washington, New York, London and in Paris where they lived during the 1920s. She was a close friend of the society photographer Cecil

Beaton and enjoyed long photographic sessions that captured her in her most stunning costumes complete with exquisite jewellery. In one of her Beaton photographs I am astonished to recognise a brooch on her lapel: it is the same piece I have seen my mother wear on a chain around her neck, an Art Deco design in gold with rubies and pearls. It was handed down to Bettina from her mother. There is a photograph that shows my mother wearing it. I use a magnifying glass to compare the two images. Unless both Mendl women bought identical copies it is indeed the same piece. I now know that my mother's mother, Emily Mendl of Vienna, and Elsie de Wolfe, wife of Sir Charles Mendl, almost certainly had been connected.

•❖•

On my next visit to Bettina I approach her gently, in the hope of establishing a link with this English branch of the family. She is very frail but totally alert.

'Mum, remember when you first went to Cheltenham? How was that arranged?'

'Arranged? My father decided it would be a good idea for me to go there.'

This is a new version. Never before has she said this was her father's decision. She has always told us how she met some English girls on summer holidays in Austria, and made up her mind to go off to Cheltenham with them, without the slightest opposition from her parents. This never rang quite true, bearing in mind that she was the cherished youngest daughter, and taking into account the tensions following World War I and the cruel political oppositions.

A Story Dreamt Long Ago

On the other hand, a determined decision of Fritz Mendl's, based on his systematic plan to Anglicise the family following its conversion from Judaism to Christianity in 1904, seemed quite congruent. It was also something that would place him close to Charles Mendl, the Romanian–British diplomat. Although I have not been able to discover the precise family relationship between Grandfather Fritz and Charles Mendl, the more fragments of information I find the more I recognise that they had similar backgrounds, business interests and tastes. During the mid-1920s, young Fritz had lived in Paris where he painted and studied art. Sir Charles was an associate and collector of modern art, at a time when Pablo Picasso was a key influence and a leading figure on the social scene. Fritz Mendl senior had provided English governesses for all his children. He was determined they should speak English fluently. When in 1925, he made arrangements to educate Bettina at Cheltenham, it would have made sense that he should contact Charles Mendl.

I am fully aware that Bettina may clam up tight if she has the least suspicion that I am approaching her connections or experiences in World War II. I tread carefully.

'A school as prestigious as Cheltenham Ladies College can't have been easy to get into. There would have been a waiting list – in those days I believe parents booked their children's places at birth.'

'Yes,' she agrees, 'normally it was quite difficult, but nothing stood in the way of my father.'

'You must have provided some impressive references and an influential sponsor.'

She nods. 'I had to go and meet her – the lady who formally endorsed my introduction to Cheltenham.'

'Who was that?' I ask, wanting her to tell me and not be frightened off into a flippant response or a claim of not being able to remember. She is so adept at escaping an awkward moment with a comment to lure her inquisitor away from the scent and leave her past safely buried – 'Oh, some old biddy with a weird hat and a squawking parrot,' I half-expect her to say now.

But this time she doesn't shy away. 'It was carefully arranged,' she says. 'My father had the right connections and my mother took me to meet the mother of our first President, Michael Hainisch. They were actually quite good friends. Marianne Hainisch was the founder of the Austrian Women's Movements. Like my mother, she was a pioneer in education. She demanded modern secondary education for females and negotiated women's access to university degrees. She was my official sponsor. There was never any question of whether or not I would be accepted.'

I know about the school my grandmother Emily Mendl established in the garden of the Villa Mendl, and that Emily admired Marianne Hainisch's work. But now I want to discover the truths behind my mother's education.

'Oh,' I said, 'so there wasn't a diplomatic connection?'

'Diplomatic?' She hesitates. 'I suppose you could say it was arranged through diplomatic connections. Why do you ask?'

'I always thought it strange that you were sent to England. Perhaps France would have been a more logical choice, if it was simply intended to broaden your language ability and cultural background. Cheltenham seems a rather strange choice.'

'I suppose my father had his reasons.' And gently the subject was laid down. Inconclusively.

I have failed entirely to establish the connection with Sir Charles Mendl. My mother was quite prepared for me. After days of waiting in order to disarm her, when I finally ask her if she remembers him, she says quite firmly and quickly: 'No, there was no Sir Charles.' She takes no time to reflect. She doesn't ask 'When and where would that have been?'. Her clear hard 'no' tells me this particular memory is unsafe and therefore does not exist. I double back. I say quite casually: 'He was married to a very interesting American woman, Elsie de Wolfe. I thought you might have known her.'

'No,' she says, 'I didn't know her.' Again, she doesn't ask 'What name did you say?' or 'Where did they live?'. The denial is too prompt.

'They lived in Paris and in Washington,' I went on. 'You were often in America, in Washington, I thought you might have bumped into them.'

But my mother turns away, uninterested.

•◆•

I go to the State Library of Queensland in search of Sir Charles. Initially, I am intrigued by the citation for his knighthood in 1924 of 'unspecified services to the Crown'. I hope to make comparisons with Fritz Mendl's experience when he refused a title and was given the miniature pendant of the Golden Fleece by Kaiser Franz Joseph.

I follow the skeleton references to Sir Charles's career in *Who Was Who*. I check the family connections in *Debrett*'s and recognise familiar patterns in education, lifestyle and Christian names. *The Concise Dictionary of National Biography* confirms '1914 served as interpreter with 25th Infantry brigade; invalided out, 1915; worked in Intelligence in Paris for the Admiralty'. I come to the realisation that the intelligence work he did must have been impressive to earn a knighthood in a mere nine years. Inspired by curiosity I discuss this with a military-history researcher. He confirms that this citation indicates distinguished service in the field of intelligence and, more importantly, a continued role. 'You don't just retire,' he stressed. The service would include the period of growing European tension between the two world wars, World War II and the reconstruction period after 1945. In fact, the researcher explained that Sir Charles would probably have been a key player in intelligence until his death in 1958.

Sir Charles would have been in a crucial position to orchestrate Bettina's escape from Switzerland in 1938. But did he have a motive beyond the vague family connection? By then, her anti-Nazi activities throughout the 1930s would have been well known. Perhaps she had become too difficult to protect.

My growing collection of brief comments on Sir Charles fleshed out a picture of a charming, witty diplomat with an international web of connections. By 1946 he had moved from Paris to Los Angeles with his American wife, Elsie De Wolfe, whose career began in theatre and who had maintained her passionate attachment to those old friendships. I discover in a book by Alfred Allen Lewis, titled *Ladies and Not-So-Gentle Women*, that the Mendls lived in Beverly Hills, delighting in the company of 'a group of actors imported to California for roles in the highly successful Thirties American films devoted to the glories of the British Empire... They showed their valor by playing stiff-upper-lip types in early Forties propaganda films... Sir Charles was welcomed among them as their new chief of protocol'.

To my delight I find Sir Charles's interest in film goes further. I discover he played the role of Commodore in Alfred Hitchcock's 1946 spy thriller *Notorious*. A cameo of his own life perhaps? Surely in that milieu he must have known Hedy Lamarr, the beneficiary of Bettina's early fascination with 'the flicks'. I question whether all of these connecting threads can really be coincidental.

In 1982, Bettina's old fiancé, Anton Chlumecky, had visited Australia. He stayed with me and openly discussed his pre-war anti-Nazi activities and, ultimately, his own role in British Intelligence. He revealed the difficulty of remaining 'in character' throughout assignment. With quiet humour he explained that when circumstances changed you could not raise your hand for help, reveal your true allegiance and go safely back to base. Anton, an Austrian, had been captured and imprisoned as an enemy in England. He told me how a senior intelligence officer had been part of an official inspection tour of the prison. By chance, in a fleeting eye-to-eye contact, he had recognised Anton and, without the least acknowledgment, apparently orchestrated his prompt release and appointment to new duties.

All this had been a revelation to me. Through all the years, Bettina had never hinted at it. Anton carefully stopped short of making any comment on Bettina's activities or on her silence.

Isolated scraps of information now seem to form a whole. I struggle to remain objective, wanting to seize on this convenient explanation for Bettina's inconsistencies. I form the hypothesis that in the early 1930s, Sir Charles recruited both my mother and her brother Otto to work for British Intelligence. They would have been perfect candidates. After all, Otto Mendl was a daredevil aeronautical engineer. I deduce that it may have been under Sir Charles's instructions that he overtly joined the Nazi party, lived in Berlin and worked for the Luftwaffe. My mother, distraught at his apparent political alliances, remained unaware of the reasons underpinning his behaviour. Driven by her own loyalties, she tragically withdrew from contact with him, hence her refusal to give him money for fuel in Cairo at their last meeting. By 1937 she had cut all ties.

As for my mother's own possible recruitment, she lived in Vienna – the centre of international intrigue. She was passionately opposed to the Nazi regime; she had a superb education and status that allowed her entry into any milieu she chose. She told me that as a child, she spoke her native German as well as English from babyhood, French by compulsion, and Hungarian and Russian quite fluently. I had heard her speaking all of these languages without hesitiation. She had personal wealth to resource any travel; after 1931 as an orphan she was answerable to no one. Beyond all of this, her unchallenged character trait was that she had 'guts'.

This would have made her a valued intelligence operative and justified arranging her escape in 1938. My conclusions also seem to offer some explanation for her 'secret' entry to Australia and her deep fear that even there she would be pursued, interned, possibly forcibly 'repatriated'. Perhaps she had good grounds to believe that in those years there really was a price on her head. As she had not expected to come to Australia she would not have had a network of contacts here. She would have had no idea whom she could trust to protect her. If my hypothesis was correct, in Australia she had more value as a potential exchange candidate to secure the survival of a valued current agent. She could be easily and legitimately interned – and sacrificed. Responding to intuition, or hysteria, she decided not to trust officialdom but to rely on Joe McDuff.

Who Was Who records Charles Mendl's death: 14 February 1958. This means that there would have been opportunity for him to have post-war contact with my mother – perhaps to convey to her Picasso drawings he had acquired, using Otto Schönthal as a go-between.

Bettina had been back to Europe many times before Sir Charles had died. There would have been ample opportunity for her to reconnect with him – if he had been her contact. The Picassos had appeared on the farmhouse wall at Keepit Dam in the late 1950s. Sir Charles might have bequeathed them to Bettina, having himself acquired them directly from Picasso. Sir Charles was another of Sara Murphy's many admirers; Picasso's drawing of her would have held special appeal for him.

At this point I realise that if I am to find out more about Sir Charles Mendl, my best hope is to consult the archive of his papers held in the Public Records Office in London. I have read the memoirs of Dame Stella Rimington, the recently retired head of MI5, and am shocked by the familiarity of some of the episodes she recounts. The superficial normality of day-to-day behaviour masking carefully controlled undercurrents that swirl out of control causing last-minute changes in family arrangements, an unexplained intensity over a particular road route, brief delay, invitation of a new acquaintance, the inflexible law we lived by of 'do not question!'.

However, Dame Rimington's description of the beginnings and development of MI5 makes no mention of Charles Mendl. I write asking for her assistance and receive the reply that unfortunately she cannot help me in my research into Sir Charles Mendl. Considering the circumstances of his knighthood, this leaves me puzzled as his role could not have been insignificant considering the citation. Later I am advised that Britain's Public Records Office has yet to release classified documents relating to the period.

My hypothesis would account for the many mysterious episodes throughout our lives. It would explain my mother's sometimes passionate preoccupation with forces we did not understand – her near-hysteria over some detail, her unplanned trips, her secrecy, denials and sudden connections to strange people. It would explain so many aspects of her personality.

It would also explain the messages about my mother's brother Otto we had received in 1992, when I took her back to Austria for one last visit. Those messages had seemed so spy-novel fanciful that I had put them from my mind.

My mind went back to our trip to Berlin in 1953. At the time it seemed to have no purpose and no plan. I considered the possibility that my mother had been gathering the last shreds of information about Otto and arranging his 'death' to meet legal requirements, so that his family could inherit. This would give him cover in whatever life he'd gone to.

It seemed that even in death the Old Vienna Network had

protected Otto's secret. I finally grasped the reason for the two distinctly different messages my mother had received from Martin in Vienna in 1992. The strategy was clever. All those present at the first meeting could swear they heard Martin relay the details of 'the message from the East' – that Otto had died in the war. Who would ever know there was another version?

Over the years I had gathered many letters and documents not just from my mother but from our extended family in Austria, New Zealand and America. I had read and re-read them many times, and compared them to the stories that I had heard from my mother and many other relatives. I was beginning to be able to form a clear picture of at least some of her experiences.

Now that I have a better understanding of European history I realise that the two great wars did not come suddenly as unexpected tidal waves submerging countries and their populations, then, just as suddenly, withdrawing. This had been my Australian childhood version in response to dramatic moments: 'War was declared', 'Troops embarked', 'The war is over'. All neatly sanitised. I now understand the complex patterns, the economic background, the motives and growing pressures on the Jewish people.

I am sure that by 1937 my mother was actively involved in getting Jewish citizens out of Germany and Austria. Responding to the politics of the 1930s, I can now put childhood memories in context. I recall conversations around dinner tables during family visits to Sydney, when Dawn and I were small children who half-understood the German language. Other guests, with names such as Raubitscheck and Sachs, let fall half-sentences, implications that my mother had played an active part in such activities, often risking her life. Babies concealed in washing baskets, extra bodies in funeral caskets, crossing borders, obtaining false identity papers . . . I recall laughter at the dinner table at the description of scenes of Bettina tightly rolling banknotes to pack into the handlebars of a pushbike – and then the difficulty of getting the money out again. Now I know that this could not be part of Bettina's 'real' life and the dates were wrong. This was not part of her own escape; these escapades were on behalf of someone else. And now I recognise the Jewish names.

There was no doubt that my mother's overt anti-Nazi activities made her a prime target for reprisal. The fragments of information I knew of her escape had come from her own stories fleshed out by personal memories of Dick's, my cousin, and with some comments from Aunt Lucie, Dick's mother. All this fell into context when Mucki gave me a box of yellowed tissue letters from Roman Abt. They advised Bettina what she must do and ended with the comment that despite the desperate circumstances she should not be too concerned: he could not believe that the temporary madness would result in war. At the time Bettina did not receive the letters; they were sent to Villa Mendl in the hope they would be forwarded. They remained in a box in the attic until 1952 when they were found and filed by Tante Maria – then Bettina refused to read them.

I knew she had been pursued across the border into Switzerland by the Nazi secret police, who had insisted she return to Vienna to make public pro-Nazi statements to endorse the validity of Kristallnacht, that November anti-Jewish rampage of 1938 following the Anschluss. It was to induce my mother's cooperation that two officers confronted her in Zurich with the claim that they had kidnapped Dick Stonnell, her New Zealand nephew, Lucie's child, who had come to Vienna to commence studies at an elite private high school. The Nazi officers claimed to have taken him from his 'safe haven' in Hungary where my mother had sent him in the care of the faithful Maria von Kozaryn while she herself tried to arrange documents for their escape. When the Nazi secret police confronted her in Zurich she hedged, agreed to return to Vienna, and asked for time to make her public support more convincing. They, uncertain of their ground in Switzerland and confident of her desperation to protect Dick, allowed her to go free.

This gave her the few hours she needed to contact Roman Abt, an influential Swiss lawyer, a friend of her father's who had been monitoring her escape. Abt advised her that he knew of the Nazi kidnap plan; however, he had pre-empted it himself by snatching Dick and moving him secretly to a new hiding place. Dick was safe and Bettina could no longer be coerced. Abt gave her the address of a safe house, a beautician's shop, where he would send for her once he had arranged the documents to get her across the border.

Within the next few days, Roman Abt tutored ten-year-old Dick in a speech he was to make to the British High Commission: 'I am a British subject, born in New Zealand, in the custody of my aunt, Bettina Mendl. I have the right to the necessary documents to enable her to accompany me safely to my parents in New Zealand.' Family mythology records that Dick, squaring his shoulders, added: 'And if you don't do that I'll tell my king!' The strategy was successful and was the means by which my mother ultimately arrived safely in New Zealand in 1938.

I began to understand that these collective experiences were the reason she had gone so far to the outback in 1941. She mistrusted the flimsy British protection she had received in Switzerland and she had first-hand knowledge of the brutality and determination of the Nazi secret police. In 1941 its Austrian head, Otto Wächter, was living in her home, in Villa Mendl. It would be most convenient to dispose of her.

•◆•

As I start peeling potatoes for the evening meal, I suddenly recall how my mother used to protest whenever I tackled this chore. 'Don't peel them with a knife!' she would say. I'd hold my breath and brace myself for another onslaught in this potato war between us. There would be silence for a few moments. Then my mother would burst out: 'Why peel them at all? Just eat them as they are.' More silence, until finally she would ask: 'Don't you have a peeler?' I would reluctantly carry out a ceremonial rummage in the kitchen drawer. 'I can't find it,' I'd mutter, gritting my teeth.

At this point she would concede defeat, half-turn away and whisper: 'Such a shame! So much is wasted.'

I was left flinching at the pain in her voice, the evidence of past hunger, the unbearable torment of my extravagant peeling method. Yet I could never retreat from my brutally wasteful habit. My mother's silence locked me out of the hungers of her life.

These days I peel potatoes without her criticism, yet I am haunted still by the memory of it and of my unbending arrogance. And today I reflect on the history behind her criticism.

A Story Dreamt Long Ago

Why was it that she could not bear to watch a potato being peeled wastefully? It seemed part of a secret, hidden past that threw its shadow over us from time to time. A shadow which sometimes frightened me, as though it were a vague genetic memory.

I muse on the years of my mother's growing up, disentangling the threads of family, politics, her life which seemed so privileged before the war, and then the impact of that war. For the first time I really confront the potato evidence, asking myself what sort of experience would leave this scar, how long would it have lasted. I flinch from acknowledging how difficult her circumstances had been despite her wealth and social status. There must have been many times when she was hungry in Australia – in the early days of her struggle, walking from railway stations to outback jobs, walking 'off' and covering her tracks. Once, as she handed me half an apple we were sharing, she told me how she'd sat on an outback railway station desperately trying to resist eating the second half of an apple she'd been given. She had consumed the first half in one bite. I considered her time as a child at the tuberculosis sanatorium, isolated from her family, when the special health foods her father paid for, oranges and milk, dried fruits and nuts, were distributed among the other less 'fortunate' children. My mother never told her parents how little she survived on by sheer strength of will. On this matter she was totally forgiving, murmuring only: 'They needed it as much as I did. I don't blame the matron. What was she to do with so many dying children? I didn't want to get her into trouble. My father would have been furious. But –' a sigh, a rare moment's self-indulgence, 'I was very small.'

14

The curtain closes

My mother has been low. I've sat beside her, pacing her shallow breath – pacing but not hoping for the next . . . letting go. She has lived past her ninetieth year and enjoyed the celebrations. Now she is ready to move on. I have told my boys to get their dark suits ready, to iron their good white shirts.

'We'll be needing six good men to hoist the coffin.' That's what I said before I left home. Then I went out and bought the Strauss CD with the 'Blue Danube Waltz' to accompany my mother's leaving. But Bettina didn't go.

We called the priest – twice.

The first time he performed the sacred rites while the nuns whispered *Hail Mary* and other familiar incantations, floating on the scent of roses. Tradition was observed.

In my diary I wrote:

A Story Dreamt Long Ago

24th November, 1999

Tamworth again.
Bettina will be going soon.
Strange how with prolonged proximity Death loses all morbidity.
Rather, one feels as when a welcome friend arrives, a little overdue,
sipping tea to fill the endless space between the ticking of the clock.
Over-sensitive to the familiar sounds,
the crunch of gravel on the drive,
the opening door.
The footsteps that, this time, go past,
the room where one awaits a welcome friend.

Ten days later I sat beside my mother once again. She slept and whispered, smiled occasionally and finally struggled to enunciate a word I could not grasp. One syllable, repeated, with growing anxiety. At first I thought I understood a whispered *'Please'*.

'Please what, Mum?' I prompted her. 'I can't think what it is you'd like me to do.'

My mother repeated it while I bent to listen. Finally I converted 'please' to 'breeze' and pushed aside the curtain to open the window wide, knowing how she loved the garden and thinking that she might like to feel the breeze. I smiled at her and she seemed to smile back at me. Complicity.

The whispering began again. *'Peeess . . .'*

'Do you want to see the priest? I'm sorry, Mum, I didn't

understand. I have to tell you that your special friend is sick and cannot come. He is in hospital. He visited a few days ago. Do you want to see another priest?'

'*Peeess,*' and a firmer smile.

The nuns went off to find another priest, returning to assure me he would shortly be on his way.

This priest did not wear his vestments but arrived in civvies, ill-prepared, a gentle, tall, thin man in a pullover. My mother would not talk to him because he wasn't 'real'. Before the rebuff I had anticipated trouble. She wanted vestments, incense, candles and he could not oblige. He retreated in defeat – and I apologised. He left clutching the Holy Water; it was not needed now that his blessing was rejected.

It seemed an inappropriate moment to point out the family's ancient Jewish heritage. I kept my silence, except to ring Lizzie, my Sydney cousin, one of those with whom we'd had to break all ties so many years ago. She promised to visit the Tabernacle, to find out what should be done and to perform the ritual for Bettina. She would pass St Mary's Cathedral on the way and she would also light a candle.

Meanwhile the nuns went off in search of Holy Water with which to bless the patient. One of them whispered to me with her lovely Irish voice: 'To be sure I've got plenty of the water, the bottle is the trouble. I'm having the divil of a time finding a bottle.'

She found a whisky bottle, a very small one. Over the Johnny Walker Label she had applied a substitute of blue-lined notepaper, on which was handwritten *Holy Water*. I have vowed to keep it forever.

A Story Dreamt Long Ago

Through the nights I slept in a chair and in the mornings changed places with Dawn.

The crisis passed so I took a bus home to Brisbane.

2nd December, 1999
Bettina – gone.
I am at Stradbroke Island with my family. Phone call in the afternoon.
We walk along the beach to say goodbye.
A brilliant sunset fading,
twilight,
a lone star.

Dawn's son Joe had been close by.

Months earlier, Bettina and I had watched a sunset stretch across the valley below the western windows. She'd sighed and said reflectively, 'I don't think we die all at once, I think we die a little at a time. Slowly. I feel that sometimes I'm here and sometimes I am there.'

Somehow the concept was familiar to me and I agreed with her. The mood seemed to invite my question: 'Mum, you never said where you wanted to go or what you wanted done. Would you like to be in Barraba with Joe?' This was close to Tarpoly where the four of us had spent the early post-war years together.

There was a silence while she considered what I'd asked.

'I did love Joe – such a long time ago. Barraba?' She stopped short of saying 'No, not there'.

'Here? In Tamworth?'

'No, not here.'

And then I understood what she longed for and would not ask.

'Do you want to go home, to the garden in Vienna, to the poplar tree that was planted the morning you were born?'

I was rewarded with a clear bright smile. Her black eyes danced as she said firmly, 'It is where I belong.'

At last she had decided.

'I'll take you back, but you must make a promise. Without the promise I can't ask permission to take you there. There are others in the villa now, other Mendls – your sister-in-law Mimi, with whom you fought so bitterly. Promise there will be no more fighting. No more family politics. Let there be peace and understanding and generosity. There are other Mendl children playing in the garden who deserve a loving atmosphere. Will you make that promise so that I can take you home?'

She smiled contentedly. 'Yes, you're right. I do promise, I won't fight with anyone. Nothing matters any more; it never really mattered.'

I have written to my cousins, I've explained about the promise, they have happily agreed: whenever we are ready I will take her ashes back – Bettina will be welcomed home.

15

Adieu

In the months following my mother's death Dawn and I gathered together her last personal belongings. We sorted through clothing. There were the beloved bits and pieces that she had relinquished as unsuitable but had asked us not to throw away. She needed to know that somewhere the last remaining designer outfits were conveniently waiting should she need them. The crocodile case that had once stored her most precious things, including 'THAT Girl's Head' – empty, scuffed, scarred and shabby but *alive* – was on a pile in a corner of a storage room with other long-abandoned evidence of her past. Perhaps more than anything else this was the sign that told me she had gone.

There also seemed to be a vast amount of paper. Despite my energetic sorting there were boxes of letters and my mother's own attempts at writing: scraps of poems, fragments of an abandoned memoir, business diaries. There were her sketches and half-finished notes to grandchildren, there were cards sent to her marking so many happy occasions, there were the death notices of friends who had gone on ahead.

All this was dumped in cartons and consigned to me to sort and store. I was the elder sister. It was my job, and anyway, I was one of the executors of the will. Thus I eventually received my mother's jewellery to catalogue and value.

Although I'd always known that it existed and from time to time called at the bank to pick up a piece for Bettina to wear to a special occasion, it had been thirty years since I had seen the whole collection. Now I viewed it from a different perspective. Rather than seeing a lot of pretty glitter I saw the workmanship, the fine enamel artwork. I saw the history of the long, slow journey of the Mendl family from far eastern Europe in the 1600s – the painted panel of the Madonna of the eastern Orthodox church, 'not with a halo but crowned as queen of heaven' one expert now whispered to me, reverently. I ponder the many distant influences that formed my family. I'm intoxicated by the exotic cocktail of our history, I'm giddy, I'm confused. What strange responses are triggered by these connections in my brain and in my blood?

I photograph and research the evidence each generation had left in the tiny residual collection. There is a ruby-and-enamel pendant engraved with a family crest, dated 1770. I long to know its story. Who commissioned it and why? What occasion was to be celebrated by this lost ancestor of mine? I would love to know something of his life. I consider the recipient while my mind forms images of ceremonies, of pleasure, hope, satisfaction in a work well done and lovingly acknowledged.

A Story Dreamt Long Ago

Among the treasures I find the miniature Order of the Golden Fleece given to Grandfather Fritz from the Emperor Franz Joseph – one fragment of information when I need so much more. The tiny golden lambskin lies in my palm telling me something of my history in a language I have to learn to understand. To read these messages I'll have to learn the codes of jeweller's marks, to understand the science of metals, to follow the trade routes of gems.

There is evidence of connection to the British Crown in the bracelet surrounding the charming miniature of the young Queen Victoria, bearing the inscription *'From Victoria R May 1849'*.

There are Fritz Mendl's pocket watches which have been handed down for generations. Jewellery historians offer dates: 1760s, early 1800s. A white enamel cross awarded to my mother for bravery in the 1930s, when she rescued an Ankerbrot manager held hostage by disaffected workers. I failed to note the details of this story when she told it to me – now I hold the cross and mourn the loss of information.

•◆•

Prompted by this reverie, nagged by the family ghosts, once again I consider the Picassos. It is time to take them out and work on the more recent end of family mythology. Through the University of Queensland I have found my way to respected authorities on Picasso's work. They have offered to view the drawings and to advise me how I should proceed. But until now I've avoided the decision to make the trip to England and to take the drawings with me. Now I sense an urgency. I need to bring the mystery to some conclusion. I have dabbled long enough and there will never be sufficient time to analyse each piece of paper. Some must be set aside and only the main threads of information dealt with. I finally decide to make another trip to Europe in September 2002, confirm arrangements with the experts and with trepidation book my flights.

The first thing I do in London is to find a big red bus, sit on the top deck and ride around and around. This is a form of greeting to London, which I don't know well and it is a way to get my bearings while still weary from the trip. I happily turn into a tourist, climb to the top of St Paul's Cathedral, meander through Hyde Park and rest eating ice cream by the Serpentine.

I feel the tension build as the day of the meeting with the Picasso authorities draws closer. I have always understood they will offer advice on how I might proceed with my research as distinct from commenting on the authenticity of the drawings. They may be able to cast some light on the links between Picasso, Sara and Gerald Murphy, Sir Charles Mendl and Bettina. They might also know who wrote *Col Alfred Flechtheim, London 1943* on the back of the Sara Murphy drawing – and why. Despite all my futile inquiries over the years it is hard to avoid feeling the excitement of some pending conclusion to the project.

I already know that authentication introduces its own problems. The *Syndicat Français des Experts Professionnels en Oeuvres d'Art et de Collection* has already advised that the process is expensive, as are the valuation, insurance, storage and security costs. If the drawings ever were authenticated I would be forced to sell them to meet all these expenses.

A Story Dreamt Long Ago

At last the hour has come. I have driven into London with an old Australian friend. She has been here a long time and navigates easily. The street is wide, remarkably free of traffic, the houses on each side are tall, traditional, porticoed buildings. The smell is 'Essence of London' – traffic fumes, dry leaves on a cold wind. We stand outside the tall door, then, inside we speak about the history of the sketches and the family while we check my assumptions and conclusions until it is time to see the drawings. I unzip the folder and draw them out, one by one. First the Sara Murphy piece. It is passed around, picked up, turned over and held to the light. There is a heavy silence in the room. Somewhere in my papers I have a very rough image of Zervos V5 No 295, which was also included in the New York exhibition from which I had first recognised Sara Murphy. I rummage for it to use as a comparison while the discussion flows – comments on the lines, dates, paper.

We work our way to the two 'Man with the Lamb' drawings, again checking dates, making comparisons with similar drawings in the growing pile of reference books. Once again I hear the explanation: 'You do understand that the opinions expressed here cannot authenticate. That is the preserve of the Picasso family. The result is the formal acceptance or rejection of the work. I understand that you are interested in the history of the drawings and I do not think that we can add to what you have discovered. I suggest you might show the drawings to other people familiar with this work.'

On the way home I reflect on the advice and comments from the meeting. I agree; it would be best to take the drawings home. For the moment they are safe, they are nothing more than pieces of paper. I wonder whether my decisions echo some long-ago conclusions of Bettina's. Is that why she left me this dilemma?

•—•

Having found it impossible to gain access to the Charles Mendl files at the Public Records Office — they still have not been released for public viewing — I focus on the frivolous social aspects of my adventure. I spend my energies in hot-air ballooning, sailing in the mystical autumn atmosphere on the lochs of Northern Scotland, walking the glens and heather-covered hills by day while, in the evenings, I discuss my mother's schooldays at Cheltenham with some of her old associates, who offered me no clues concerning Charles Mendl. I am freezing cold but happy. I fall in love with the compact, tiny spaces where things are made to fit: houses, car parks, ornaments on shelves, even though I could not endure it permanently.

Sated with novelty, with history, with adventure, with delicious food and intriguing conversations I fly to Vienna, where I revisit my mother's friends who have survived the five years since I was last here. Maria Newald, the mother of Peter, my partner in my debutante season, is ninety-five years old. She is tall, elegant, witty with laughing black eyes. We re-cap on her advice to me of more than forty years ago to avoid wearing a strapless dress to the ball. Now she goes on to tell me about another of her experiences at the Opera Ball, after her marriage. Wearing a glorious concoction of rose-pink brocade, trailing an impressive train (held up by a loop over one finger as she danced) she made her way up a staircase to recover from a particularly vigorous waltz. She was pregnant at the time, feeling 'a bit squashed up', and just a little giddy. To make the right impression she let her train flow down the stair, and as she moved up the steps someone behind her stepped on it. The resultant jerk popped the stitching in the low-cut centre front of the dress – from which her breasts popped out. With regal poise she flicked her ostrich feather fan wide open. Clutching it demurely to her chest she graciously proceeded to her 'box' and sent for help with an emergency reconstruction of the gown.

When we had finished laughing she reflected, 'A lady must be able to cope with these little inconveniences; after all, my husband held a prominent position!'

As I took her hand to leave she asked me to send a photo of Bettina and whispered, 'Don't forget me.'

How could I forget the grace, the humour, and the iron-clad determination of each member of the diminishing circle of my mother's friends?

I have come for afternoon tea in the Villa Mendl, to catch up with my cousins and be introduced to the new additions to the family. Once again the old house has been renovated – in fact, work is still in progress. The family is now using a different section of the house that I have not entered for close on fifty years. This time we move towards the ballroom where, in 1953, Dawn and I paraded up and down enacting the coronation of Elizabeth II. The room seems smaller now, though still worthy of coronation ceremonies. It has been refurbished and to my delight, almost magically, the curtains are the same rich gold as the old curtains I remember. How could this generation have known – or did the walls speak out demanding that the light be filtered through gold cloth to spread the same warm aura? The view out to the Master's garden matches my memory. Standing beside a five-year-old cousin, I press my nose against the glass and ask whether he rides a bike. He nods and then I ask whether he learnt along that garden track, wobbling over bumps, threatened by approaching tree trunks. 'Yes,' he answers, his huge eyes expressing his surprise at how this stranger knows about such things. 'Me too,' I say. 'I was a bit older than you but it was my first bike.' And then with studied nonchalance I added, 'Up till then I only had a horse to ride.' The eyes grew even wider.

I could have told this child stories about his Great-great-grandfather Fritz who once sat exactly where we stood to look out across the terrace to the garden, where the pathway had been widened to make space for his wheelchair. In the last year of his life, pushed by a nurse and accompanied by my mother, Fritz had savoured the long walks through this sanctuary.

The conversation ebbs and flows as the adults bring each other up to date on recent family activities. There has been a stream of colonial visitors since my last visit and the Vienna Mendls have travelled a great deal. They have now met up with many of their distant links.

Inevitably the conversation turned to my family research and the cross-referencing of irregularities that remain beyond explanation. Thomas points out that we know nothing of the artworks that were taken from the villa during Nazi occupation. The letter written by Maria von Kozaryn in 1946 states that she was prevented from making an inventory, but Thomas prods me on. He describes the progress that has been made in the five years since my last visit. A great volume of data has been collected, artists' catalogues and sale lists, private letters, evidence from court cases, museum and gallery archives have all added to the pool of information. Computers have helped analyse material. Thomas insists there must be an inventory, if not created by a member of the household in 1938 then a listing devised from associated evidence. He suggests I visit the art-research section of the *Israelitischen Kultusgemeinde,* the Council for Israeli Culture, where they may be able to help me. He speaks calmly but his request is passionate.

In 1938 Thomas's grandfather Otto had long since left Vienna for Berlin. Thus we believe that any property in the villa would have belonged to my mother. As the executor of her estate, I should make one more effort to discover the inventory. I am reluctant to make a fuss over what I see as ancient history. Thomas insists. 'Now is the time. In another five years all the reparations will have been made based on current evidence. The world will have moved on.'

As I say goodnight I know that I cannot resist his pleading or his logic. It is a small thing to look up the address of the art section, to state that I have very little information, to offer names and birth dates and to leave a contact address.

I have two more days in Vienna. Next morning I set out with my tattered tourist map along the narrow cobbled streets. I stride confidently; Vienna has become familiar to me now. I pass the plague monument on the Graben and enter the narrow Naglergasse with its quaint shops. I hurry past the Ankerbrot shop, supposedly the first one my grandfather opened in 1891. This first shop is still functioning vigorously. The windows offer a tempting display of breads and pastries. Throughout the week I've gone in to sample its wares.

Phyllis McDuff

I am obliged to cross the street whenever the pavements become too narrow to follow. From time to time I burst out into wider spaces surrounded by traditional townhouses five floors high. At street level their entrances, built wide enough for carriages, are fitted with elaborate doors, arched and carved, reinforced with delicate lacework of wrought iron that closes off the access. Windows look down into these squares like so many quietly watchful eyes. There is an aura of observation. No bold signage names residents or offices. Discreet brass plaques identify the organisations which occupy the premises; sometimes blurred, handwritten names beside the intercom indicate the residents.

Despite my careful navigation I am not sure whether I've arrived at the right office. I press the intercom and find it difficult to muster the words to pose my query while I stand in the street with the cold November wind whirling my words away. I hear the soft click of the door-catch opening to an electronic impulse. I push the antique structure gently and it swings wide. In front of me is an airy space with a cloudy marble floor and a single desk. Behind the desk, giving the impression of a painted mural, is a very beautiful receptionist. I make my way towards her while I formulate my queries into German words, although I know instinctively that here, most languages will be understood. It is an international place.

'I am the granddaughter of Fritz Mendl, who lived at Wallmodengasse 11. I live in Australia. I have only one more day in Vienna. My family has suggested I should register with you in an attempt to find an inventory of art assets that were removed from the house in 1938.'

A Story Dreamt Long Ago

I had been told that Jewish citizens were forced by the Nazi administration to complete these inventories. The inventories were carefully filed and later presented to the owners of the property for signature. This constituted the official and 'legitimate' transfer of the asset to the Third Reich – often under the most brutal circumstances. 'Certainly, we can help you,' the receptionist replies. 'If I may take a few details I will make the appropriate connections.' Within minutes she has noted essential names, birthdates, addresses, and with this skeletal information picked up her phone to fix an appointment the next morning with a researcher.

The next day I am introduced to a researcher who suggests I check the information she has gathered while she reads it through. I am amazed at the detail she presents. To my surprise both my mother and her brother Otto are noted as residents of Villa Mendl at the time of the Anschluss. Otto is identified as a pilot. She quickly cross-references information from her computer screen with volumes of property titles and books of electoral information from 1938. She noted the progressive deaths of Emily Mendl, Fritz Mendl, his son Fritz, and my mother's inheritance of their estates. 'Ahh,' she sighs in a tone of satisfaction, 'there *is* an inventory, I have the file number. Bettina lodged it in 1938.'

'But she wasn't here,' I protest. 'She was in New Zealand. Surely she would have known that she had made out that inventory. Surely she would have acted on it immediately after the war. There's even a letter from Maria von Kozaryn complaining that she had no opportunity to make out an inventory on Bettina's behalf.' I am baffled by this new conflicting evidence.

Baffled but not really surprised. I am curious to see whether the documents are in my mother's distinctive handwriting. I cannot imagine my mother following Nazi orders to compile an inventory of her property for their use. Maria von Kozaryn's letter does not indicate that any previous inventory was compiled. I cannot believe it happened without her knowledge nor can I believe that she completed it without Maria's help. I can see my mother weeping, raging, swearing – but never sitting compliantly at her desk compiling lists of property to surrender to the Third Reich. Or was this another example of that mysterious capacity for discipline when everything depended on a cool nerve? A capacity to conceal.

'There is also an inventory of personal art assets at that address made out by Otto Mendl,' the researcher goes on. 'The file numbers indicate that they were both personally completed. The problem now is that if these were particularly valuable items the files may have been emptied out. At the end of the war, as the Nazi forces were retreating they tried to obscure evidence. When we go to the files we could find that there is nothing beween the covers. The workload here is enormous and we must proceed systematically. We cannot begin researching that for a few months.' I shall have to wait.

At this point the senior researcher joins us asking what we have discovered and requests any additional information that may exist only in oral family mythology. I offer what I have, then seize the opportunity to ask whether anything might be known about the three Picasso drawings and explain my efforts to have them authenticated.

He adds something to my knowedge of the authentication

process. 'You do realise that if the drawings are authenticated you lose copyright – that is, the right to reproduce the images.'

My perplexed expression indicates that he needs to explain. 'Picasso's heirs automatically own the copyright until fifty years after his death, until 2023. If you can publish the images you may get some response, trigger some memory, create a match with someone else's research. It would be a shame to forfeit that. You can always make an application for authentication to the Picasso Administration when you have exhausted all other possibilities for an explanation. I don't believe you've done that yet.' Now his speech picks up momentum. 'Just at the moment we are having such success with tracing artwork that changed hands during the war. Information is flowing in each day. Simple things like the eventual release of Charles Mendl's files may throw light on the source of those three drawings.'

His words reinforce my decision to take the drawings home and wait.

He smiles and takes his leave, striding away down a long corridor, radiating a sense of purpose and adventure, more like the Lone Ranger than my concept of a quietly studious art researcher.

The meeting has been relatively brief and it is still quite early on the morning of my last day in Vienna when I find myself in the street again. I wonder if there is something else I should do to bring my inquiries to conclusion. From experience I know that in the months to come I may regret not having posed this question or that, not having checked some detail. This is my fourth visit since my journey here with my mother in 1992. I have a sense that I shall not come back again, at least not for a long time. I shall not come back here to dig about and try to expose secrets. If I come again it will be for the future, not the past. Thomas is right – the world is moving on. I have overdosed on mystery and long for simplicity. I can shut the past away by closing the last heavy, carved, arched door that swung so silently, eerily obedient to electronic impulse.

I reflect on the results of this most recent trip. I would have wished things to be different. I had a dream in which the doors of the Public Records Office flew wide open inviting me along red-carpeted passages to rooms with tables displaying neatly labelled files arranged in order of most interest to me. In these imaginary files the documents were notated and passages marked with colour-coded inks to serve my needs. The inscrutable Sir Charles had noted each contact with my mother, his purposes and plans, the outcomes and connections for every operation. I knew and understood and proved all my hypotheses. This was a dream. In reality the doors were shut. Had they opened, what new layers of confusion would be offered? How would I interpret encrypted messages, and what new insights would I need to read the facts in context? I marvel at my obstinate expectations.

I had always known that even in business matters my mother operated on a policy of 'no documentation'. It was unreasonable to expect Charles Mendl to have looser standards when lives and history depended on secrecy.

I had also harboured dreams about my drawings. Despite pragmatic attitudes in my waking moments there had been visions of Picasso experts with eyes a-pop as I drew the drawings from their covers, voice a-croak, flustered and excited, the butler passing smelling salts on a silver tray as they recognised the images relating to a long-lost, sought-after estate. In this hallucination I heard stories of theft, of famous forgers, romantic liaisons, illegitimate heirs . . . These things had never come to pass.

I longed for fiction to rescue me from the grey conclusions I was left with. I had set out in search of truth. While its body had eluded me I felt I had made contact with its soul.

As I followed the cobblestone alleyways I remembered pushing my mother's wheelchair, at the beginning of the search in 1992. I had bent to let air out of the tyres to reduce the shuddering motion over this inconsiderate surface. I remember her laughter. Was she watching my lurching efforts to discover her? It seemed impossible to believe she wasn't there as I rounded corners into streets so familiar to her, bursting into the slap of the cold wind.

Now I was a child again. I could feel the firm pull of my mother's hand as we hurried somewhere – always hurried. I catch the animal whiff of her long fur coat as it swings to her stride – I see a glimpse of her boot as she steps onto the kerb one step ahead of me. My mother led and drove, prompted and lured. She was a restless force, a curious blend of European aristocratic privilege and Australian outback deprivation and austerity. Or a meld of European desperation and betrayal and reckless Australian colonial enterprise. All her projects, wherever they took place, were driven by total commitment and fierce determination.

Yet when I had asked her to make peace with the ghosts in the garden of Villa Mendl she had understood. She had agreed.

She had promised. She'd said, 'It doesn't matter any more. It never really mattered.' I believe her and I trust her. It is time to stop searching. Bettina is here.

I am heading towards the exquisite Café Centrale for a ceremonial farewell brunch. It was here we'd had our childhood celebrations with my mother – white linen, old silver, hot chocolate, whipped cream. We'd sit in a circle of friends with her gathering our orders for the best treats – Bettina waving her magic wand . . .

•◆•

The next day I am on my way home to Australia, somewhere suspended in the sky between two worlds – between waking and sleeping. Somewhere in the dark, having lost all sense of time, I say 'thank you' to my mother. Thank you for the joy ride and the passion. Thank you for laying out the treasure hunt. Thank you for the clues and clever deceptions. Thank you for secrets and for revelations. Thank you for hiding the things I need not know.

Acknowledgments

Many are the thanks I owe:
to Lynne and Geoff McDonald for their enduring support;
to the staff of the State Library of Queensland for their creative assistance;
to the University of Queensland information technology help desk for their calm solutions;
to Arts Queensland for their generous grant;
to writing mentor Barbara Ker Wilson for her great wisdom and to my beloved family for their certitude.

Without all these, these pages would have stayed inside my head.